A Feminist Introduction to Romanticism

B

THE NIC-NAC;

OR,

LITERARY CABINET:

CONTAINING AN AMUSING ASSEMBLAGE OF

TALES, ANECDOTES, POETRY, BIOGRAPHY, EPIGRAMS,
ENIGMAS, ODDITIES, RECEIPTS, WONDERS OF NATURE
AND ART, THE SPIRIT OF THE PERIODICAL
PRESS, AND GLEANINGS FROM FOREIGN
JOURNALS; TOGETHER WITH
A COMPREHENSIVE

HISTORY OF THE ENGLISH STAGE.

With Numerous Engravings.

VOL. I.

LONDON:
PRINTED AND PUBLISHED BY T. WALLIS, CAMDEN TOWN.
1823.

Title page of *The Nic-Nac; or, Literary Cabinet* (1823)

A Feminist Introduction to Romanticism

Elizabeth A. Fay

BLACKWELL
Publishers

First published 1998

2 4 6 8 10 9 7 5 3 1

Blackwell Publishers Inc.
350 Main Street
Malden, Massachusetts 02148
USA

Blackwell Publishers Ltd
108 Cowley Road
Oxford OX4 1JF
UK

Library of Congress Cataloging-in-Publication Data

Fay, Elizabeth A., 1957–
    A feminist introduction to romanticism / Elizabeth A. Fay.
      p.   cm.
    Includes bibliographical references and index.
    ISBN 0-631-19894-6 (acid-free paper). – ISBN 0-631-19895-4 (pbk.: acid-free paper)
    1. English literature – Women authors – History and criticism.
    2. Feminism and literature – Great Britain – History – 19th century.
    3. Feminism and literature – Great Britain – History – 18th century.
    4. Women and literature – Great Britain – History – 19th century.
    5. Women and literature – Great Britain – History – 18th century.
    6. English literature – 19th century – History and criticism.
    7. English literature – 18th century – History and criticism.
    8. Romanticism – Great Britain.   I. Title.
PR468.F46F39 1998
820.9'145'082 – dc21   98-5902
                                                           CIP

British Library Cataloguing in Publication Data

A CIP catalogue record for this book is available from the British Library.

Typeset in 10 on 12$^1/_2$ pt Sabon
by Best-set Typesetter Ltd, Hong Kong
Printed in Great Britain by MPG Books Ltd, Bodmin, Cornwall

This book is printed on acid-free paper

Contents

Contents

Illustrations

Women Writers Discussed

Jane Austen (1775–1817)
Joanna Baillie (1762–1851)
Anna Laetitia Barbauld (1743–1825)
Frances Burney (1752–1840)
Elizabeth Carter (1717–1806)
Hannah Cowley (1743–1809)
Charlotte Dacre (?1771/2–1825)
Mary Hays (1760–1843)
Felicia Hemans (1793–1835)
Elizabeth Inchbald (1753–1821)
Maria Jane Jewsbury (1800–1833)
Catherine Macaulay Graham (1731–1791)
Elizabeth Montagu (1720–1800)
Hannah More (1745–1833)
Ann Radcliffe (1764–1823)
Clara Reeve (1729–1807)
Mary Robinson (1758–1800)
Sarah Scott (1723–1795)
Anna Seward (1742–1809)
Mary Shelley (1797–1851)
Charlotte Smith (1749–1806)
Jane Taylor (1783–1824)
Helen Maria Williams (1762–1827)
Mary Wollstonecraft (1759–1797)
Dorothy Wordsworth (1771–1855) .

Chapter 1

A Feminist Approach to Romantic Studies and the Case of Austen

Figure 1   The Right Honorable Catherine Maria, Countess of Charleville, engraving by Thomson from a painting by Hamilton. Published by Edward Bull, 26 Holles Street, London

Yet were I grossly destitute of all
Those human sentiments which make this earth
So dear, if I should fail with grateful voice
To speak of you, ye mountains and ye lakes,
And sounding cataracts, ye mists and winds
That dwell among the hills where I was born.
If in my youth I have been pure in heart,
If, mingling with the world, I am content
With my own modest pleasures, and have lived
With God and Nature communing, removed
From little enmities and low desires,
The gift is yours . . .

William Wordsworth, Prelude, 1805, II, 437–48

You – Gentlemen! by dint of long seclusion
  From better company, have kept your own
At Keswick, and, through still continued fusion
  Of one another's minds, at last have grown
To deem as a most logical conclusion,
  That Poesy has wreaths for you alone:
There is a narrowness in such a notion,
Which makes me wish you'd change your lakes for ocean.

. . . You have your salary: was't for that you wrought?
  And Wordsworth has his place in the Excise.
You're shabby fellows – true – but poets still,
And duly seated on the immortal hill.

Lord Byron, Don Juan, Dedication, v–vi

Before they were separated by the conclusion of the play, she had the
unexpected happiness of an invitation to accompany her uncle and aunt in
a tour of pleasure which they proposed taking in the summer.
  "We have not quite determined how far it shall carry us," said Mrs
Gardiner, "but perhaps to the Lakes."
  No scheme could have been more agreeable to Elizabeth, and her accep-
tance of the invitation was most ready and grateful. "My dear, dear aunt,"
she rapturously cried, "what delight! what felicity! You give me fresh life
and vigour . . . What are men to rocks and mountains? Oh! what hours of
transport we shall spend!"

Jane Austen, Pride and Prejudice, ch. 27

The excerpts above are from three extraordinary literary productions
of the age of British Romanticism, and show very different but representative responses to the Romantic themes of nature and art. The

excerpts by William Wordsworth and George Gordon, Lord Byron are well-known opposing expressions of the Romantic spirit, but by saying the third expression, by Jane Austen, is also representative, I have said something quite unusual for Romantic studies. Until recently, the literary tradition has viewed the Romantic period as an intense burst of great poetry by a small, select group of artists: William Wordsworth, Samuel T. Coleridge, Lord Byron, Percy Bysshe Shelley, and John Keats, with William Blake, Robert Southey, and Sir Walter Scott moving in and out of this primary group according to how critics change their evaluations of them. At present, literary scholars are vigorously re-examining who was writing during the period beside the great Romantics, but prior to the work done by feminist critics on Romantic literature we had even forgotten that women were writing poetry at this time. Moreover, the privileged status accorded to the work of these poets meant that novels of the period by both men and women were thought unimportant and unrepresentative until the Victorian Age. To see women poets and novelists like Austen as indeed representative of their era, however, is increasingly the argument feminist criticism makes.

Until recently, scholars have side-stepped the issue raised by Austen's critique of Romantic attitudes toward nature in the excerpt above by claiming her mocking treatment of such topical subjects as sublime landscapes and nature poetry to be simply un-Romantic. Neither poetic itself, nor sympathetic to the great Romantic themes of nature and art, such an attitude has placed Austen outside the accepted limits of Romanticism. Critical tradition has viewed Romanticism as the product of two ways of looking at the world: a *sincere*, and a darkly *ironic* one. Romantic sincerity, according to Wordsworth, produces poetry that "is an acknowledgment of the beauty of the universe, an acknowledgment the more sincere, because not formal, but . . . a task light and easy to him who looks at the world in the spirit of love" (1802 Preface to *Lyrical Ballads*). Romantic irony is the opposite, a dark and often chaotic vision that structures the poem, often includes satiric attacks on others motivated by party politics, and through both its irony and satire targets social corruption. (For distinctions between Romantic irony and standard irony, see Mellor, 1980.) Austen's passage provides a third perspective by critiquing both dark irony and sincerity through a verbal play that is corrective rather than despairing or vituperative, and self-aware rather than wrapped in an inner vision. "Critique" in this sense is different from the literary criticism offered by the great male poets of the period such as Coleridge or prose writers such as William Hazlitt: it forgoes party politics in order to assess more fundamental human values and beliefs; it gently ridicules human folly in order to teach self-awareness; it bases its criticism on an essential optimism that rewards goodness and finds selfishness the greatest evil. All of these traits reflect the way critique is oriented toward a common good, to a community that must support each individual within it, not exploit others for the good of the self. The term "critique," therefore, refers to an assessment of the social and (in its largest sense) political effects; it is meant to sway a general readership on widespread issues, and is for this reason quite unlike the more pointed methods of attack used by satirists for particular events, persons, or party politics.

When Wordsworth addresses aspects of nature, as he does in the excerpt from *The Prelude* I have selected, he is setting himself apart from other men and other poets in order to focus that part of himself that is visionary, and to connect his own internal nature to outer nature. When Byron attacks Wordsworth above, it is a satiric attack on this internal vision which, for Byron, conflicts with the political hypocrisy he sees in Wordsworth and his fellow poets. He intended to use this satire as a prologue to the dark irony of *Don Juan* in order to set the stage for the folly of Juan's innocence as a sincerity gone wrong, but his irony was so dark here that his publisher actually suppressed it for fear of libel when publishing the poem, an indication of the more politically dangerous aspects of Romantic irony. As the crisis of Austen's *Pride and Prejudice* (1813) shows, her critique reads both positions – Wordsworth's internal vision and Byron's ironic pessimism – as inappropriate and even dangerous to women's situation. The attention to such danger is the real difference between Austen's view and Byron's political attack or Wordsworth's assertion of man's insufficient vision. Critique of dominant positions that ignore the vulnerability of marginalized persons in society is usually offered only by writers who have themselves been marginal to their culture, such as a woman writer or a working-class male writer, because such a writer is prevented by education and connections from having a more direct or permanent effect with their publications. Critique as a literary form offered women a way to accommodate themselves to Romanticism while differing from the main perspectives that were defining the times. Although women also tried their hand at more mainstream forms, just as the male Romantics did not confine themselves to the extremes of sincerity and irony alone, the most important works by women of the Romantic period take the form of critique.

This book is concerned with critique when used by women to participate in British Romanticism while also identifying its flaws and seeking to correct its course. Feminist theory assumes social critique to be the mainstay of feminist writing, and social correction the mainstay of women's thought and art. To trace the literary form of critique through women's literature, then, is to follow a fundamental precept of feminist criticism. We will examine the writings of women who are concerned with one or both of these imperatives – social critique and social correction – during the period from the late eighteenth century to the early nineteenth century, known as the Romantic period. This is a period which saw: the French Revolution and the resulting political interest in rights, including rights for women; the madness of George III and the Regency and accession of George IV; the rise of circulating libraries and ladies' magazines; the huge interest in botany, astronomy, and other natural sciences; the rise of literary anthologies, public museums, and leisure shopping as forms of collection and consumption; and the increasing popularity of travel and of travel literature. In short, this is the earliest period recognizable to the modern reader in its attitudes, interests, and tastes.

Women held active roles in several of the defining events and activities just listed, and it was in conjunction with some of these that women writers exercised critique. But another characteristic of the Romantic period less familiar to modern readers had even greater interest for Romantics and for women writers in particular: emotion. In the Enlightenment of the previous period, the "Age of Reason," reason was held to be the only true path to knowledge of the natural world and the human subject. However, by the end of the eighteenth century, emotion was thought to be a more pure response to nature and to other people than reason and proper behavior alone. The emotions, more often called the "passions" or "affections," not only opened up knowledge of nature and of others, but also showed the depth of one's soul, and gave a better insight into the individual's personality than could be offered by outward appearances and behavior. The emphasis on emotions thus opened up the inner as well as the outer world in a way that made it important to begin to understand the relationships between self and other, man and nature, imagination and materials. Emotions also provided the basis for a beginning science of psychology, on the one hand, and for a new and very modern individualism on the other. Moreover, they provided a gauge for interpreting an individual's taste through his or her emotional response to a literary work or to nature. The emotions, then, offered women writers a way to portray women's psychological and social experience, and to assess the effects of gender on the individual's relation to society.

5

In Austen's *Sense and Sensibility* (1811), Marianne uses emotional response to determine which of her suitors she will choose for their superior taste. Taste indicates qualities of character valued by Romanticism, including a sensitivity to women's ability also to be Romantic. Perhaps one of Austen's private jokes is that Marianne chooses wrongly because she has based her judgment on literary representations of emotion written by men, and not from real-life emotion or from critiques by women. She therefore chooses someone who acts in imitation of literary emotional sensitivity, Willoughby, rather than the man who is really the more sensitive and refined of the two, the truly Romantic Brandon. Emotion, then, is also important because it allows women writers to critique society because of the way in which social norms can make women vulnerable to bad choices in love and marriage when they misinterpret how men use emotion. In an even more fundamental way, women found they had to confront emotions in their writing because as women they were expected to have a stronger affinity for the emotional states, and to be more sensitive to those states considered to be feminine such as maternal affections and sexual love.

In addition to their need to respond to a variety of social issues, and to cultural markers like those emotions associated with the feminine, women writers also needed to respond to sincerity and dark irony because these two poles of Romantic attitude represent artistic and ethical positions taken by the dominant male voices of the age. Women writers, then, needed to have a complex relation to Romanticism, one which allowed them to absorb and yet dissent from its main precepts. Our difficulty is that these main precepts and dominant positions have also traditionally been used by critics to understand the art of the High Romantics, so that we now value these positions over those that women writers tended to use. Both the sincere and ironic positions are always presented as moral and philosophically based responses to some problem such as man's debt to nature or man's inner growth. But what women writers often picked up was that these two positions are also emotional responses to a problem. The emotions or "affections" were considered crucial to the artistic impulse, but also to politics, and to the revolutionary spirit, and it was important for serious women writers to understand the political and artistic importance of emotional exploration.

Women had one useful tool of sentiment to help them in this, "sympathy," which had come to be considered the emotional balance between sincerity and irony. Sympathy was the visible outward sign of one's awareness of others and of the community; it was a necessary emotional gift for anyone of refined temperament or sentiment, and was crucial to the "Man of Feeling," the sensitive person of strong sentiments and a responsive sensibility. The Enlightenment "Man of Reason," such as Samuel Johnson, had believed that emotions could outweigh moral judgment and lead to social decay. However, the Romantic emphasis on emotions is not a rejection of Enlightenment reason, only a strong alternative to it, since sincerity and irony can be rational as well as emotional responses to the artistic endeavor. Between the poles of sincerity and irony, Romantic texts exhibit a range of affections made possible by sympathy, the most important for women writers being sensibility.

In the 1780s a cultural phenomenon known as the "Cult of Sensibility" made sensibility fashionable, propelled by a literature that incorporated its feminine aesthetic. What makes sensibility interesting for feminist analysis is that it anticipates the more masculine-oriented high point of Romanticism in many respects. Women were influential as producers and consumers of this literature, and in the 1780s and 1790s the poetry and novels of Anna Seward, Hannah More, Helen Maria Williams, Mary Robinson, Elizabeth Inchbald, and Charlotte Smith appeared, all based on or using aspects of sensibility. While women found sensibility enriching, it also provided imaginative ground for the High Romantics, especially Coleridge, Wordsworth, Shelley, and Keats, because it used sympathy to direct subjective experience outward to an appreciation of natural objects. A philosophically based emotional attitude, sensibility provided a way for the artist to imagine human feeling through personal experience.

The same interest in the emotions that precipitated the Cult of Sensibility was responsible for the High Romantics' intense pursuit of the sublime, an emotionally transcendent and mystical experience associated with the highest levels of artistic and visionary consciousness. Interest in the emotions was also responsible for the slightly later development of melodrama as a dramatic form, and of sentimentality in the novels and poetry of the 1820s and 1830s. The history of this experimentation with the emotions shows that Romantic emotions, which have been critically ignored in the past in order to understand the workings of the Romantic mind, allows us to reconsider the place of women in Romanticism. In the excerpts above, for instance, a witty view of the Romantic mood in Austen's passage points to a very different reading of the passage by Wordsworth as not just sincere, but sincere in a way that suppresses any underlying sensibility in order to project the imagination toward the creative and visionary act. Elizabeth Bennet's rapture is meant as a joke on the use of such repressive sincerity, not only between herself and her aunt, but between narrator and reader. We understand, as does Mrs Gardiner, that Elizabeth's "rapturous cry" only pretends to signal sublime "transport" because the two women are not in the proper natural and emotional setting for this transport to take place (they are at the theater) and the rapture is not, Romantically speaking, proper. This mismatch of emotion to place is the joke, but it also calls into question whether such a sincerity is the proper emotion for the Wordsworthian poet, for a greater sensibility might not have allowed him to substitute love of rocks for love of women. In transporting herself emotionally over the rocks of her frustration, Elizabeth pretends to overleap the problem of men and their attitudes toward love by a simple substitution: "What are men to rocks and mountains? Oh! what hours of transport we shall spend!" Her words mock men's tendency to prefer grander objects to women's love.

Spoken in relation to the theater, the indoors and the city, Elizabeth's words are absurdly situated for the kind of emotion Wordsworth's speaker is describing in the passage from Book II of *The Prelude* above. Although that speaker is not invoking or describing sublime transport, he is with intense sincerity making love to rocks. This emotional relation to nature is one that not only feeds the artistic spirit, but teaches the human soul how to love spiritually (rather than sexually). In addressing the objects of nature specifically ("ye mountains and ye lakes / And sounding cataracts, ye mists and winds"), Wordsworth (see Wu, 1998: 322) acknowledges their own status and being in a way that redresses Elizabeth's careless use of the natural sublime and a sensible love for nature to background her emotional joking ("what delight! what felicity! You give me fresh life and vigour"), but Austen's point is still worth taking. If for Wordsworth's speaker it is the rocks which give fresh life, for Elizabeth it is Mrs Gardiner and the sympathetic female community she represents who will heal her spiritually and emotionally. If men ignore women's needs, Austen implies, women can still have recourse to nature without their guide.

Byron's stanzas stand in contrast to Austen's gentler criticism of Wordsworthian sincerity, offering a deeply hostile view of the Lake School of poets and their poetic project (Keswick being the center of Southey's, Coleridge's, and Wordsworth's "seclusion" in the Lake District). Byron is critical but without the corrective humor Austen offers. His speaker finds the Lake poets without merit, insincere, and narrow-minded. They are "duly seated" on the hill (not high peak) of poetry, but have exchanged their own beliefs about society and nature for money ("You have your salary: was't for that you wrought?"). Instead of being able to love rocks, they sit on them; instead of being able to transcend nature to achieve the sublime (best represented for Byron by the ocean), they can only comprehend their own small world of lakes.

Elizabeth's humor does not mediate so much as address both poets' positions. Austen's critique is, of course, not of these specific passages or even poems – the first two cantos of *Don Juan* were not published until 1819, and Wordsworth's masterpiece was published posthumously in 1850 – but of the very characteristic positions both poems evince of these two poets. Her suspicion of Byron is aroused by the dark hostility and ironic chaos of his Turkish tales, her suspicion of Wordsworth by his lyric poems that both explore the relation of man to nature, and also elevate man as a transcendent being. Nevertheless, we can see her objections more clearly in the anachronistic comparison I have set up in the excerpts. For instance, Elizabeth's joke clearly understands and twists the subtleties Wordsworth is distinguishing, yet she is also critiquing the aggression Byron's speaker employs to demolish his rivals in a man's world ("What are men to rocks and mountains?"). Austen's text complements each of the others in just the way many men's and women's texts pair off more contemporaneously, by provoking the essential issues raised by the other writers. It is helpful to understand Austen's approach as another version of Romanticism, one that many women writers chose to employ as a way of taking part in the Romantic movement.

Standard Definitions and Revisions

"Romanticism" is usually understood in two different ways, which can cause some initial confusion. As a historical period, Romanticism refers to the three decades or so (usually defined as either 1789 or 1798 to 1832) that Britain was in transition between the old world order and the new. In the eighteenth century, the aristocracy still dominated the cultural imagination, but during the Romantic period, the capitalist and technological world we know today was gaining for the first time a recognizable foothold in the popular imagination and in economic reality. However, this historical definition has usually been so strictly set down that it has tended to refer to the years of 1798 through the 1820s because that was when those writers we now consider canonical, the "High Romantics" (Blake, Wordsworth, Coleridge, Byron, Shelley, and Keats), were producing their greatest works. Because we have valorized these particular writers, the literary traits they share, and their political activism, many women writing at the same time as these men, or writing before 1798, have not until now even been thought of as part of the Romantic period.

Confusingly, a contrasting definition of "romanticism" (with a lower-case "r") is used in literature or art history, and even everyday conversations about art and culture, to describe a characteristic trait embodying certain attitudes toward art, emotions, and creativity. But this second definition very specifically identifies such a trait with the historical male Romantic artists, so when we speak of an artist with romantic qualities, we usually mean he is very like Byron, and so on. This sense of the term is not helpful, then, in thinking about women writers who were often critical of High Romantic attitudes; the first term also provides difficulties for thinking about women writers during this period because very often women were writing Romantic texts before and after the strict boundaries of the historical period. Whenever women writers anticipated the movement that would become Romanticism, or reflected back on it after its height, they have until now been said not to be Romantic purely by date. (One exception would be Emily Brontë, who is often treated as a late Romantic writer.) With the recent scrutiny of such definitions to see if they include all who were writing Romantic texts in or near the historical period, we have now begun to think of the Romantic period as more extensive – perhaps from 1750 until 1850, well into Queen Victoria's reign.

Given a more inclusive dating, we can now begin looking for how both men and women writers respond to the Romantic as an "aesthetic" (those attitudes toward art, emotions, and creativity) defined by the artistic term "romanticism," and most often breaking down into sincerity, irony, or critique. The Romantic aesthetic shared by writers during this period involves a group of traits, the most important being a great confidence in the ability of the human *imagination* to create connections between the inner mind and the outer world of nature. This ability also makes it possible for the mortal human mind or soul to connect with the mysterious and the divine. England was only beginning to recover from its distrust of orthodox religion at the beginning of the Romantic period, although by the end of the period the Church had made an almost full recovery. During the early years, then, poetic transcendence offered an important alternative to the distrusted mysticism of Christianity. The belief in the imagination required a very real belief in *inspiration* or the spontaneous quality of artistic production. Artistic inspiration, which brings into play the imagination in its most grand acts of creation, must be real and sincerely felt, but the artwork itself when finished can only be great if it gives the sense of having just been inspired and immediately penned. Inspiration comes from some divine, cosmic, or natural force; for the Romantics, it allowed the artist to declare that his art originated in a superior inspirational gift and, through his genius, can reach out to touch men across all the physical and social gulfs that stand between them. Women have a far more difficult time claiming Romantic inspiration because, according to literary tradition, inspiration comes from the female muse to the male poet. However, several women poets were able to claim that nature inspired them, or that they could receive their inspiration while in a state of extreme sensibility.

Closely related to the question of inspiration is the notion of *individualism*. The Romantic artist discovered in himself a new conception of the self as not just part of society but standing in relation to society. This meant a higher awareness of others as well as the self as individuals, and a choice whether to reject the social or not. Several of the major Romantic writers either lived apart from the high society of London, or went into exile in Europe. The alienation associated with the division of the self from the larger group became a defining trait of the best-known Romantic figures such as Lord Byron. But writers such as Jane Austen, Anna Seward, and William and Dorothy Wordsworth also preferred to live in small hamlets or towns with little intercourse with London, the literary capital of their world. Nevertheless, this sense of individualism led to the artist's sense of a responsibility to assess society and to achieve something for society's progress through art. The idea of a responsibility to assess society, particularly during the turmoil leading to the French Revolution, was driven by *radical questioning*, often also thought of as "transgression," either of limits or of laws. This is the questioning of traditional institutions such as organized religion (the Anglican Church in particular), marriage ("free love," the sincere sexual relation outside marriage, was promoted among some), and, ultimately (as in France), the monarchy. The poet could pose questions of social institutions like those being posed even more radically in France because he saw himself as separated from society even when he had a powerful public voice. It is this questioning position that women writers turned into their own critical perspective on society. But while the male radicalized poet used his posture of isolation in order to have a voice in politics, women writers used their marginal position to criticize the entire organization of society, its priorities, and its values.

The male radicalized poet usually used *introspection* as a mark either of ironic reflection or his sincerity in questioning institutions, himself, or the force and responsibility of art. Sincerity is often associated with the

11

identification of the poet with the speaker – the "I" of the poem, as in Wordsworth's and Keats's odes – whereas irony and critique tend to use personas or characters in the third person to distance the criticism. Introspective interest in the self, whether sincere or ironic, achieves its fullest expression in autobiography as an exploration of the artist as a self-conscious individual. For instance, the full title of Wordsworth's epic work is *The Prelude, or, Growth of a Poet's Mind: An Autobiographical Poem.* Byron's *Childe Harold* (1812–18) is an autobiographical epic that also explores the growth of the poet's imaginative abilities from an introspective standpoint. *Childe Harold* combines sincerity and irony in a manner that shows irony to be the flip side of sincerity, with the ironic attitude as the philosophically and organically necessary counterpart or mirror to the morally sincere man. By contrast, when Jane Austen uses verbal irony to make fun of a particular Romantic attitude in the epigraph above, she is not employing an irony that is the inverse of sincerity, but only presenting a corrective mirror to it. But *Pride and Prejudice* is at least partly autobiographical, and there, too, the protagonist reflects on the individual's relation to society as she learns what role her imagination must play within this relation.

These, then, are the major characteristics we might look for in traditional Romantic writing: *imagination* as a mark of the creative, *inspiration* as indicated by spontaneity, *individualism* as a new definition of the self, *radical questioning* as an act of intervention, and *introspection* as a mark of self-consciousness. This characterization of the Romantic aesthetic derives from what is now commonly termed "High Romanticism," which occupies the most central years of the Romantic period (1798–1816) during which time the greater part of the literary texts exhibiting these traits were published. The High Romantic aesthetic is most famously present in works like William Blake's *The Marriage of Heaven and Hell*, William Wordsworth's 1805 *Prelude* (written but not published during this period), Samuel Taylor Coleridge's "Dejection: An Ode," Lord Byron's *Childe Harold's Pilgrimage*, Percy Bysshe Shelley's *Prometheus Unbound*, and John Keats's "Ode to a Nightingale."

These six poets of what we now call High Romanticism did not think of themselves as "Romantic" or even as working in a common vein. Because of the selective process literary criticism imposes on literary history, these poets have come over time to represent the essence of the Romantic period for us. Moreover, even though we have identified five essential characterizing traits, there are also other elements common to the canonical texts and identified by twentieth-century scholarship as Romantic: a particular literary mode (poetry), the emphasis on a particular genre (the ode), a focus on a particular topic (nature), and the exploration of an important imaginative state (the sublime). These elements become one of the ways in which we define the authors of these texts as not just major, but canonical: the literary masters of the period. We therefore need to look for these elements outside the canonical works, since the current argument in Romantic studies is over a redefinition of what should be considered canonical, relative to where else these elements can be found, and of the way we determine mastery.

In standard descriptions of High Romanticism, the masterful literary text is usually a poem. This is, in part, because those texts most expressive of the Romantic spirit, and the alienated, radical, and introspective individual, were poems. Moreover, they tend to be poems of the elevated poetic genres: odes, hymns, epics. These genres are traditionally the best vehicles for poetic experiments with the sublime, and the sublime holds a dominant position in the imagination of the period. At the end of the eighteenth century, the sublime was still considered something belonging to the realm of landscape painting, a way to depict Nature at her most terrific and awe-inspiring, but people came to transfer the value of the sublime into other elevated moments of their time. They saw the achievements of the French Revolution as sublime, for instance, but also Wellington's defeat of Napoleon. In literature, Blake used the sublime in his poetry to create huge images of the spirit of revolution and transformation. Like Blake, Shelley used mythological figures to give shape to sublime forces in order to present the individual's struggle with corrupt and harmful institutions.

The sublime, however, was still mostly associated with the presence of Nature, conceived as feminine and maternal, beneficent as well as destructive. The rural landscape and the wild tract are distinguished from the female aspect of the natural as Nature (the use of the upper case always indicates this identity). The High Romantics are often thought of as nature poets precisely because each of them took on the question of the natural as a female presence, and used at least some of their poetry to work through the inspirational relation between Nature as the female muse and themselves as the male poet, as well as to use Nature as an access to the masculine sublime. The sublime was also invoked in order to describe more personal, creative, and transcendent experiences, such as Wordsworth's moments of sublime revelation in *The Prelude*. The writer's intimacy with the sublime and his recognition of its quality becomes his mark of mastery, and it is this quality of marked mastery that becomes more significant for a gender analysis than the meditative knowledge the sublime inspires.

13

Because the sublime has had such a masculine tradition in Western culture, particularly as a mark of the highest artistic achievement, male Romantics take the sublime as proof of their visionary gift. Therefore, women often refrained from trying their hand at the sublime, as the excerpt from Austen's *Pride and Prejudice* suggests; it was also usual for a woman writer claiming to have experienced the sublime to be mocked by her male contemporaries, another reason why women are not represented in the High Romantic canon. Women were generally held to be biologically unfit for the sublime even when some did practice it, because men writers continued to portray women as incapable of real thought or imagination, and particularly incapable of vision. Byron's "The Blues: A Literary Eclogue" (1823) is a good example of a satiric attack on literary women who attempted the sublime:

> Oh! . . . sympathise! – I
> Now feel such a rapture, I'm ready to fly,
> I feel so elastic – "*so buoyant – so buoyant!*"
>
> . . .
>
> my Lady Bluebottle, check not
> This gentle emotion, so seldom our lot
> Upon earth. Give it way; 'tis an impulse which lifts
> Our spirits from earth – the sublimist of gifts.
> (Byron, *Poetical Works*, ll. 129–31, 133–6)

Byron's own note to "*buoyant*" in this passage, "Fact from life, with the *words*," uses a word from real life to emphasize what he sees as the educated woman's real inability to understand the philosophical and inspirational significance of the sublime experience. Yet, the sublime, as the High Romantics distinguished it, was not too far off from the silly emotion Lady Bluebottle thinks she is feeling. Certainly it involves transcendence (but of spirit, not body) and an elasticity of self very close to the "impulse which lifts / Our spirits from earth." But the sublime is specifically a male achievement gained *through* women as female objects or through female Nature, and so is closed off to women writers. Yet some women did achieve sublimity in their work. A fine example is Anna Laetitia Barbauld's early version of the greater Romantic lyric, "A Summer Evening's Meditation" (1773). This is a work employing the traits later refined by Coleridge into his "conversation poems," such as "This Lime-tree Bower my Prison" (1797) and "Frost at Midnight" (1798). (For a description of the greater Romantic lyric, see Abrams, 1970.)

Barbauld's ode (Wu, 1998: 19–22) begins with an Enlightenment-style enthusiasm for scientific knowledge of nature. She makes this knowledge more alluring by blending it with hints at mythic figures, something Shelley and Keats will exploit much more fully in works such as *Prometheus Unbound* and the *Hyperion* poems. But Barbauld's figures exert a pressure of femaleness on this cosmos, a force provoking what William McCarthy (1995: 116) calls a "gynetopia" in the poem. Barbauld's speaker pushes her meditative thought outward until she achieves a sublime merging with the natural force she recognizes as the creative spark:

> This dead of midnight is the noon of thought,
> And wisdom mounts her zenith with the stars.
> At this still hour the self-collected soul
> Turns inward, and beholds a stranger there
> Of high descent, and more than mortal rank:
> An embryo God, a spark of fire divine
> ... Seized in thought,
> On fancy's wild and roving wing I sail ... (ll. 51–6, 71–2)

In bringing the recognition inward into introspection, Barbauld completes the sublime moment Byron holds to be impossible for women to achieve. In sailing on fancy's wing while deep in thought, her speaker takes a position regarding creativity's dependence on both thought and imagination similar to that in Keats's "Ode to a Nightingale": "For I will fly to thee / . . . on the viewless wings of Poesy," Keats writes 45 years later, but for his less optimistic speaker, "The fancy cannot cheat so well / As she is famed to do." What Keats indicates is that fancy does not have the power of the more sublime-oriented imagination, but Barbauld is making no such distinction between the creative faculties of the mind. For her, women as well as men, fancy as well as imagination, can access the sublime power that Nature makes available to human nature. Unlike Keats's ode, Barbauld's poem indicates her assurance that the poetic mind has something to hold up against death and loss, and that women have as much capacity for this endeavor as men.

The Historical Period

The traits of the High Romantic character, and of the literary elements associated with it (the poetic genre, the sublime, and nature), portray British Romanticism in its aesthetic or artistic sense. But in terms of a historical portrait (an important part of our reconsideration of what is masterful and what is Romantic), we continue to struggle with the problem of historical boundaries. Just when does Romanticism in its larger sense (beyond High Romanticism) take shape and begin to affect literary and imaginative production in Britain? Should we set the boundaries at literary dates, like the publication of Wordsworth and Coleridge's *Lyrical Ballads* in 1798, as has most often been the case in Romantic studies? Or should we set the boundaries at political dates, such as the onset of the French Revolution in 1789? The latter, a highly accepted alternative, gives us a date nine years earlier, almost a whole decade in which we could use the word "Romantic" before the 1798 dating. This is a decade in which William Blake, Mary Wollstonecraft, William Godwin, Anna Barbauld, James Hogg, Mary Robinson, William Wordsworth, and S. T. Coleridge were producing texts containing Romantic traits, and for which it certainly makes sense, therefore, to use the term "Romantic." If we extend the period back another decade, to the 1780s, we find texts by writers like Anna Seward, Helen Maria Williams, Erasmus Darwin, and William Cowper that exhibit some of these traits, while they foreground other traits, such as sensibility, that under an expanded definition of Romanticism should also be considered Romantic. Likewise, if we end the period in 1832 with the first Reform Bill, as is traditionally done, then how should we consider the remaining years until Victoria ascends the throne in 1837? Are they Romantic or are they something else? These are actually not new questions: Romantic scholars have always debated when the period may legitimately be said to have begun. Since the boundaries have been so long in question, the new revisions of period boundaries (as far as 1750 to 1850) are actually logical extensions of old questions. To understand why the boundaries of Romanticism are themselves in flux, consider a modern comparison.

Today we are on the verge of a transformation from a print culture to a computer-based culture. Both of these cultural modes in the late twentieth century use print and, increasingly, telemedia and computer technologies. But the extent to which they are dependent on hardcopy (print) and softcopy (screen displays) determines which mode we are closer to. The same transformation from one cultural mode to another was also at work during the Romantic period, making it as much a period of transition as our own age is, and as difficult to pin down precise dates for when the shift occurred. For the Romantic period, the shift was from a traditional agrarian culture to an industrial one. Both modes used the technologies of traditional farming methods, but the innovations of what

16

would become known as the Industrial Revolution were increasingly apparent in everyday life. As the period edged closer to the Victorian Age, technical innovation began to dominate more traditional ways of life, candlelight giving way to gas lighting, factories taking over production from cottage industries (especially in the textile industry where weaving frames could produce cloth much faster than could hand looms at home), and even railways beginning to compete with the horse and carriage for public modes of transport. James Watt had invented his steam engine by 1784, and although it made little difference to the average person until several decades later, inventors were also improving other aspects of transportation, such as better suspension design for horse-drawn coaches and carriages to ensure smoother rides. This increase in the ease of transportation and the speed of the production of goods contributed to the increased pace of life that marks the modern era.

Yet even if the Romantic priod could be characterized by its technological advances, there would still be no decisive dating because no one innovation changed life as it was known until later. The full force of the Industrial Revolution, in fact, was not felt outside manufacturing concerns until the latter part of the Romantic era. Innovations in the design of carriages affected a large section of the population, but few experienced until much later the rail transport that was opened to the public in 1809. What *was* felt was the enormous affluence such innovation gradually brought the merchant class and upper middle class during this period. In addition, the wealthy improved their assets through the increased colonial and foreign trade resulting from the French Revolution and its aftermath. These classes were protected from the troubles afflicting their European neighbors through their monopoly on the trade markets, and the protection the superior British navy offered their merchant ships (a fact affecting the plot of Austen's last published novel, *Persuasion*, 1818). Although there was some fear, and on the part of radicals some hope, that rebellion among the poorer classes would well up much as it had in France, England had already empowered its parliament and beheaded a monarch, Charles I, in 1649. Historians believe that because the impossible had already happened in England, and because the populace essentially loved George III despite his bouts of insanity, revolt was contained. Even later, when famine finally did hit Britain with horribly inadequate harvests, and the new factory machines or "frames" deprived workers of jobs and food for their families, the rebels (the "framebreakers" or Luddites) were largely feared rather than supported by the general populace. Had the working-class discontent of the 1810s and 1820s been supported and even promoted by the middle classes, as it was in the French Revolution, British history might have been very different, but this latter part of the Romantic period was reactionary rather than radical, shutting down on individual rights rather than opening up the possibility of rights for the working classes and for women. However much Britain had first hoped for, and then feared, an invasion of French revolutionary fervor across the Channel, it and its wealth remained safe from the Reign of Terror experienced on the Continent. This wealth, combined with fear for its loss, made the period as conservative and reactionary at its end as it was experimental and radical at its beginning. Such conservatism also makes the last years of the Romantic period difficult to distinguish from the early conservative years of the Victorian period. Much of our difficulty, then, is due to the last decades of this period being transitional ones. However, the entire Romantic period is a transition from an old world order into a modern one, and as such it encompasses the blurred edges of both worlds, making the period almost resistant to definition by particular years.

Politically, the period also divides frustratingly into a set of non-defining monarchical reigns: the later reign of George III, the Regency and then short reign of George IV, and the short reign of William IV. George III had to contend during his reign first with the American and then the French revolutions. As important as these political events were, their influence on British life was primarily felt in the area of trade, the changes and shifts in imports and exports, and therefore also in fashion. Everyday life, from dress and furniture styles to the subjects of conversation and the choice of reading material, was affected. As we will see in chapter 2, these influences caused people to turn their everyday thoughts to the experience and consequence of revolution even though it never reached English shores, and to wonder about the ways in which revolution turns the domestic into the public, and the reverse.

The Regency is actually one of the few defining moments of the period, during which art and culture flourished. It occurred when the future George IV ruled as Regent for his father during George III's illness, a period from 1811 until his own coronation in 1820. An extravagant man, the Regent's influence could be seen in the dress, debauchery, theater, and high style of the period. The Regency began the year before Napoleon's fateful march into Russia, and proved to be a high cultural moment with England aware of its own national strength and proud of its power, particularly after Napoleon's final defeat at the Battle of Waterloo in 1815. Paradoxically, this was also a period of retrenchment and reaction, and the art produced during the Regency, unlike the more experimental works of the 1790s and 1800s, tends to be marked by this doubled sense of identity, both self-confident in the new sense of nation, and deeply anxious and conservative. William IV, whose reign covers the final years of the Romantic period (1830–1837), proved a more subdued king than either of the Georges, but he also had to deal with pressing political conflicts. The most intense for him was the Reform Act of 1832, a parliamentary reform bill to reallocate representation so that a minority of landowners could no longer have an unfair political advantage over heavily populated industrialized boroughs. The process of electoral reform would continue through the Victorian Age, but its initiation during the late Romantic period shows that revolution as the French knew it, as the reform of the people's rights, came late to Britain. The Romantic period, then, is not an age of political revolution, but rather an age of revolutionary thought and art; instead of accomplishing real political change, it ushered in a new social and cultural direction, and affected the formulations of the succeeding Victorian and modern worlds.

It is the revolutionary thinking we must follow, then, in unraveling the significance of the period, its historical extent, and its art; and there we find the emotions as well, particularly as they appear in the political work of Blake, Coleridge, Wollstonecraft, Shelley, and others. Political revolution is a sublime goal for the Romantics when the affections compel us to see it as part of mankind's innate reach toward dignity. The artist's role, according to the High Romantics, is to help others appreciate revolution's grandeur by representing an introspective questioning of the social and cosmic forces that produce revolutionary force, and through this individual self-revelation to call on the sympathy of readers by appealing to their sensibility. This coalescence of Romantic traits in the promotion of political causes has been one of the most significant ways in which scholars have identified writers as "Romantic," and especially as High Romantic.

If the affections are part of both the cause and the effects of revolutionary acts, then tracing them provides another way to redefine the period to include women writers. Byron and Wordsworth enjoyed reputations for promoting liberation politics or for having a relation to the political sublime, and come down to us today in this context, but many women were also hugely successful in their writing about politics and liberalism, and their writing was recognized as touching on the sublime aspects either of revolution or its counterpart, nationalism. Helen Maria Williams, Charlotte Smith, Anna Seward, Mary Wollstonecraft, and

Felicia Hemans are only a few of these: why they have not come down to us in the same way, why we have to rediscover both their relation to Romanticism and to revolution, is part of our own twentieth-century politics. Feminist criticism must place these women back into the context of what has already been determined as the center of what we hold Romanticism to be. Perhaps more importantly, feminist scholars also strive to understand how that center was an end result but not the entirety of all the cultural and artistic developments producing High Romanticism, and to see how these other parts of the context are also Romantic and highly significant. Feminism leads scholars to expand the field to include all who contribute importantly to it, which is a goal in opposition to earlier scholarly practices that confined the field in order to determine just a few geniuses. The real impediment to the feminist goal of inclusion is the loss of information, letters and journals, manuscripts, and even published texts by or about these other writers. Even so, some determinate material facts about each individual writer serve as a useful beginning to work with, and these facts begin to give us an overview, providing an important context for each writer. This context, which we can begin to build up in successive chapters, is based on what we already know about the period, and it is worth running over a quick summary of that knowledge here.

Romanticism was a reaction against the social evils caused by unregulated industrialization and an over-privileged aristocracy, in combination with an outmoded legal and penal system, and an under-representative government. Coleridge was to write in his notebook at the end of the period that England's ills were directly traceable to "the misery of our all-sucking all-whirling Money-Eddy . . . But this is the worst sort of Slavery: for herein true Freedom consists, that the outward is determined by the inward, as the alone self-determinating Principle" (July 19, 1826). But in the 1780s this money-eddy had been instead a whirlwind of intellectual energy devoted to the political. In the ferment circulating among clubs, Freemason lodges, salons, and coffee-houses, a critical energy began to be articulated both politically and aesthetically. It gave rise to the French Revolution and to numerous other uprisings, but it also gave rise to highly political and emotional literature and art.

When politics interacts with theories about art, debates can arise distracting our attention from the main focus; one such debate between the classical and the modern initiated Romanticism. This seemingly non-political debate had developed in the Enlightenment between scholars furiously arguing for the higher value of classical over contemporary literature, or the reverse. In the Romantic period this led to revivals of classicism, medievalism, and Gothic architecture, and to the development of archeology. The turn to the past integrated well with the influences of cultures infiltrated by British trade, such as China (the style derived from Chinese culture was known as "chinoiserie"), Japan, and the Middle East (whose influence was known as "orientalism"), or by the influence of ancient exotic cultures such as Egypt. At the same time, Enlightenment culture had fostered a need in the increasingly powerful middle classes for outlets outside the royal court in which to develop intellectual and artistic debates. Elite salons were organized by women such as Bluestocking Elizabeth Montagu and Hester Thrale (later Piozzi), a member of Samuel Johnson's circle; their counterparts were the exclusively male or male-dominated coffee-house clubs, political clubs, Freemason lodges, and scientific societies. Their more formal and institutional counterparts were the academies, such as the Royal Academy of Arts, co-founded by a group including Joshua Reynolds, the American Benjamin West, and the Swiss-born Angelica Kauffmann.

Kauffmann provides a good example of how we can match an overview of history with the personal and specific. One very material fact was her position as the only founder of the Royal Academy who, because a woman, did not become a president of it. A prominent artist, Kauffmann specialized in the moralistic history paintings valued by both Reynolds and West, but she replaced contemporary costumes and settings with Roman versions, and Roman warriors with mothers. She created in her paintings a female version of neoclassicism that became associated with the Bluestockings (a group of prominent women intellectuals), and then with a sensibility strongly contrasting with the cold political messages of French revolutionary art such as Jacques Louis David's more stoic neoclassicism. The very terms of the major Bluestocking intellectual debate of the period were, in fact, sensibility, sentiment and classical stoicism, and Kauffmann's feminist choice of maternal love to oppose the patriarchal harshness of stoicism was a device favored by Romantic women writers in the decades after her. The way she used emotions as recognizable identifiers allowed her to interpret events according to her own views and her perspective as a woman, and influenced women writers who came after her. Nevertheless, society in general did not appreciate this achievement, and Kauffmann earned her income instead from quickly executed society paintings, interior decorative panels (painted especially for homes designed by Robert Adam), and designs. In fact, her contemporary reputation rested on her commercial productions in her own day, and she was viewed as a kind of commercial artist rather than a fine artist, a value judgment quite typical for women writers and artists of the period. (See Greer, 1979, and Roworth, 1992, for more information on Kauffmann's dilemma as a woman artist.)

Artists like Kauffmann and intellectuals such as the Bluestockings were not the only women prominent in the making of Romantic culture. More than five hundred women writers, poets, playwrights, and intellectuals were publishing in the late eighteenth and early nineteenth centuries (see Curran, 1988). Besides earning enough by writing novels and poetry to support their families, these women were active on the stage, writing and acting in both female and male roles (Elizabeth Inchbald, Mary Robinson, Dora Jordan), they worked on periodicals and reviews (Mary Wollstonecraft, Helen Maria Williams), developed a new literary genre of children's literature (Charlotte Smith, Anna Laetitia Barbauld, Mary Lamb), and were very active in the new Cult of Sensibility that was to have such an effect on High Romanticism (Anna Seward, Mary Tighe, Hannah More, Hannah Cowley). Many of these women were involved in starting schools for girls or in other educational initiatives, including Mary Wollstonecraft, Hannah More, Maria Edgeworth, Anna Laetitia Barbauld, and Mary Robinson. At the same time, educational opportunities were increasing to at least rudimentary levels for much of the formerly illiterate population, and "peasant poets" such as John Clare, Robert Burns, James Hogg, and Ann Yearsley began to be an increasing phenomenon. Peasant poets excited considerable interest as examples of native or "original genius," a Romantic concept based on Rousseau's notion of the "noble savage" combined with myths and history spread earlier by Macpherson, Chatterton, and Beattie. Even if we begin with the most basic account of the Romantic period, as I have done, we can quickly see that a standard collection of High Romantic works would not begin to represent the wealth of writing and art produced during this period.

Feminist Theory and Romantic Studies

While considering how to define Romanticism, we must first pause to ask the prime question any feminist inquiry has to take into account: what do we mean by "critical feminism," and what, in the most general terms, constitutes a feminist approach? A critical feminism positions itself as a categorical query underlying and directing a variety of available feminist approaches. Feminist approaches can be based on psychology, class struggle and historical materialism, social theory, theories about language, and even a mix of these, but they must always direct their attention primarily to gender difference, patriarchy, and sexual politics. This means that a feminist reader looks at what is considered the standard literature and the standard scholarship of a period, and asks what choices have been made here and to what purpose. Critical feminism means that we ask initial questions about gender difference, such as "why are there no women writers in the canon of Romantic literature?", "why do the poems in the canon about women treat the female characters from a male perspective without representing women's experience?", or "why is women's experience not the subject of great Romantic literature?"

One of the most radical of the early feminist works of our own time was Kate Millett's *Sexual Politics* (1970). Millett analyzes the politics of sexual difference as represented in literature in the starkest terms, and her book acted as a lever to stimulate academic and popular consciousness of sexual difference. But Millett was not alone. Ellen Moers began working on her *Literary Women: the Great Writers* (1976) in the same year Betty Friedan's *The Feminine Mystique* (1963) appeared ("which turned out to be the start of the political organization of feminists in America," Moers notes in her Preface), and the same year Sylvia Plath offered herself as a feminist icon by publishing her autobiographical novel *The Bell Jar* and committing suicide. Moers was writing her book when other women intellectuals, such as Tillie Olsen and Germaine Greer, were actively changing common perceptions about women's history and experience. Moers's book likewise shifts the way in which women writers are perceived by presenting as "the Great Writers" those incontestably great women writers who had been relegated to the second tier of literary genius: George Sand, Emily Brontë, Germaine de Staël, Jane Austen, Emily Dickinson, Harriet Beecher Stowe, Willa Cather.

Elaine Showalter's forceful *A Literature of their Own* (1977) and Sandra M. Gilbert's and Susan Gubar's hugely important *The Madwoman in the Attic* (1979) were the next publications to strongly influence the direction of what rapidly became known as "Anglo-American" feminist criticism. Gilbert and Gubar (1979: xii) were particularly interested in the recovery of a female tradition: "For in the process of researching our book we realized that, like many other feminists, we were trying to recover not only a major (and neglected) female literature but a whole (neglected) female history." Elaine Showalter was similarly interested in a women's literary tradition, but she provided a more theoretical matrix for this tradition by making the distinction between "feminine," "feminist," and "female." She also complicates this matrix by further distinguishing the "female tradition," the female aesthetic, and androgyny as indicators of the growth of women's imaginative achievement. Patricia Meyer Spacks adds a narratological approach in *The Female Imagination* (1975) by identifying plotted interpretive alternatives in women's narratives. These alternatives are "subterranean challenges" to patriarchal beliefs and social realities. Spacks's work aligns itself with that of Carolyn Heilbrun and Catherine Stimpson, who were exploring similar ground. Gilbert and Gubar (1979) expand on the idea among all these critics that women's texts were marked by absences of various kinds: of gaps in the narrative resulting from women's shared feeling of the inability to make public certain things about women's experience, or to use public (or male) language to represent this experience adequately.

This brings us to the question of biography and feminists' critical methods. How feminist scholars use the intricate relations between surveys of literary history, critical biographies, and autobiographical interpretation is based on women writers' *and* feminist critics' beliefs about women's place in the public and the private world. In order to research what women may have really thought, as opposed to what they allowed themselves to say in public, feminist scholars have looked into the private as much as possible. But this method is also used by most scholars doing non-feminist research; what makes feminist inquiry different is the way in which it interprets findings about the private, called a "methodology of identity." This method (not to be confused with the recent coinage "identity politics") is clearly the product of the women's movement of 1975, but it has interesting uses for us still today. A methodology of identity is a recuperative strategy attempting to understand who the woman being studied was despite large gaps in material information, gaps looking very much like the silences explored by Gilbert and Gubar (1979) but that might include texts a woman wrote but did not publish, snatches of information on texts now lost to us, information on how women lived their lives during this period, and details of the particular woman's life experience. Whatever may be known, there is always more work to do in this area because the interpretation of data and the reconstruction of a life is always subject to the scholar's own views or to a lack of some information yet to be uncovered.

In Britain, literary criticism in the Anglo-American feminist critical mold worked both with the socio-historical research and personal politics of feminist scholars and with the Marxist literary scholarship encouraged particularly by the influential work of Raymond Williams. Works such as Penny Boumelha's *Thomas Hardy and Women: Sexual Ideology and Narrative Form* (1982) and Margaret Kirkham's

24

Jane Austen, Feminism and Fiction (1983) are attempts to integrate different and sometimes contradictory political perspectives, while the more overarching questions of Cora Kaplan's *Sea Changes: Essays on Culture and Feminism* (1986; written between 1976 and 1985) provide a larger context for these agendas. Predating these publications, although often not yet translated into English, were the philosophical writings of French women intellectuals such as Hélène Cixous, Luce Irigaray, Julia Kristeva, Sarah Kofman, and Claudine Herrmann. Their work, highly theoretical and based in the philosophical and psychoanalytic traditions, is now used routinely by feminist literary critics, even though most of the French writings are not literary criticism. Initially, however, there was a wide schism between the Anglo-American and the French schools of feminist thought; Toril Moi helpfully analyzed this divide in *Sexual/Textual Politics* (1985), a book whose title echoes Millett's (1970) work.

Today, feminist criticism is often treated as a blend of Anglo-American and French feminist thought that assumes the domestic and creative life of a writer (female *and* male) to be essentially entwined and inseparable. Since interest in women's lives has historically been a hallmark of women scholars' research, it was an easy step to move back enough to theorize about particular lives, and about the social, economic, and historical background of these lives. Scholars first separated out a woman's culture from the mainstream patriarchal culture, gaining a new knowledge about that culture as well as about women's place in it and beyond it. Scholars are now more interested in piecing back together what has been learned in order to reconceive the entire picture. An interesting aspect of this methodology of identity is its valuing of women's lives, even though, historically, biographies by and about women have remained academically highly suspect. For instance, Boswell's life of Johnson is considered an innovative masterpiece, while Anna Seward's lengthy and critically astute biography of Erasmus Darwin is not remembered. Other women used the double standard to their benefit, as Amelia Opie did with her novel *Adeline Mowbray* (1804), whose heroine and plot were based on Mary Wollstonecraft and her life, and as Elizabeth Gaskell did with her novelistic biography of Charlotte Brontë (1857), in which Brontë appears as the realistic heroine of her own story. Feminists have not yet addressed this interesting question, but, clearly, simply valuing women's lives and their literary relation to them cannot fully answer unless we use it to show how identity reveals something about individual and social forces that can inform our understanding of the period or the larger body of literature.

Depending on how we want to engage these ideas, those biographies by women scholars written during the first half of this century can be worth a revisit, especially since they are often the most recent work we have on women writers newly recovered from oblivion. Florence May Anna Hilbish, for instance, produced a prodigious volume of critical analysis, *Charlotte Smith, Poet and Novelist (1749–1806)* (1941). Although she is less helpful for present-day analyses in her classification of the types of novels Smith wrote ("novels of purpose," "novels of manner," "novels of sentiment," "novels of suspense"), and in the division of Smith's womanly life from her writerly life, the sheer weight of Hilbish's material makes her case. In six hundred pages, Smith emerges as a major figure of her time, and Hilbish's contribution to the knowledge of women writers who earned a living through professional careers is enormous. Yet Smith was little studied and valued even after Hilbish's research became available, because no re-evaluation of the Romantic period was taking place at the same time, and so there was no way to understand this information in terms of Romanticism itself. Things are at a different pass today, and Smith scholarship is flourishing.

Other women scholars similarly engaged in what was considered minor research on women writers included R. Glynn Grylls, whose *Mary Shelley* was published in 1938, and whose *Claire Claremont – Mother of Byron's Allegra* appeared the next year; Helen Ashton, whose biography of L.E.L. appeared as *Letty Landon* (1951); and Margaret Ashmun, who wrote *The Singing Swan: an Account of Anna Seward and her Acquaintance with Dr Johnson, Boswell, and Others of their Time* (1931). Ashton's book shows us the typical fate of such scholarly labor: it was accompanied by a preface by Frederick A. Pottle which focuses on the male authors of "The Age of Johnson," and establishes Seward's relation to Johnson as minor by devoting more space to him than to her, the subject of the biography. "It is amazing," he writes, "that one small society should have included Johnson, Goldsmith, Reynolds, Garrick, Percy Boswell, Malone, Steevens, Sheridan, Burke, Fox, Adam Smith, and Gibbon." It may amaze some of us today that his catalog could have excluded the likes of Hester Thrale, Anna Seward, the artist Frances Reynolds (sister to Joshua), the artist Angelica Kauffman, Sarah Siddons (the most famous actress of her age), the Ladies of Llangollen (Eleanor Butler and Sarah Ponsonby, famous literary recluses), Mary Robinson (who was Sheridan's protégé on the stage), Fanny Burney (protégé to both Johnson and Thrale), and Maria Edgeworth (an important novelist and educationalist).

Yet the significance of these biographies for us today must not be underestimated. In the decades before and after the turn of this century, a few women and men Romantic scholars had devoted precious research time and resources to a handful of such subjects: Hilbish's work on Charlotte Smith, Grylls on Mary Shelley, Goldwin Smith (1890) on Austen, Ashmun on Anna Seward, and James Clifford (1941) on Hester Thrale. But for the readers of these works, and sometimes for their researchers, women writers were either curiosities or helpful (or recalcitrant) insights into the major writers of the Romantic canon. By the time the "new criticism" had begun to be replaced in US institutions with rhetorically based schools of thought such as those of Wayne Booth or Kenneth Burke, and with concerns over reader reception, students had not been taught about these marginal women writers except *as* marginalia for a long time. The biographies helped keep information alive that would otherwise have been buried too deep to recover.

As with these biographies, some of the most important work done in Romantic studies for stimulating feminist criticism has been done by scholars who have not always been feminist, but whose work is highly productive for feminist thought. For instance, Marilyn Butler's 1975 study of Austen, *Jane Austen and the War of Ideas,* laid out new ways to understand a woman writer. Unlike the biographers, her work resists exploring biography and identity in order not to elevate Austen the domestic woman over Austen the novelist. Butler chose instead to recontextualize, historicize, and politicize Austen's work. In doing so, she uses a Marxist approach to test the literary canon; Austen is not held up as an icon of mysterious female genius, but is understood programmatically from her influences, her contemporary environment, and her class politics as the novels reveal them. Although Butler's demystifying and politicized treatment of Austen was attacked by feminists, the groundwork she laid (especially as it is substantiated in a new introduction added in 1987) continues to provide necessary historical background for feminist reconceptions of the Romantic period. In particular, her work has aided new definitions of the Romantic period by delineating sentimentalism as a "radical inheritance," and has provided a chronology of the sentimental phenomenon: before the 1790s sentimentalism was radical and progressive; during the 1790s it became a reactionary template for political response to the horror of the French Revolution; and after the 1790s "the sentimentalists came to be read as moral relativists who threatened to undermine established religion and society" (Butler, 1987: 8). In this assertion, Butler precedes recent new work on sensibility and sentimentalism and its importance to a larger view of Romanticism. Certainly, Butler's Austen book is significant if only for her assertion that sentimentalism could be radical and important because it opens the way to also talk about sensibility – and any other emotion-driven experiment of the time – as a form of the Romantic, and as a politically important phenomenon.

Feminist scholarly interest in private lives and emotions as part of the public culture surrounding them had a useful correlation in the interests of cultural materialism, the theory developed out of the kind of Marxist basis Butler uses in her study of Austen. Cultural materialism is grounded in the value of material objects as they themselves had value within the society producing them. In recent feminist scholarship, feminist theory combined with materialist analysis has produced a variety of approaches integrating the feminist interest in the history of private lives with the cultural context of those lives. Books examining canonical works of High Romanticism, such as Mary Jacobus's *Romanticism, Writing, and Sexual Difference* (1989), use feminist psychoanalytic theory to re-route how we have traditionally read *The Prelude*, for instance, to situate Wordsworth's autobiographical epic within more cultural and historical limits. A work reading the biography of a male canonical poet as a text that interprets itself, such as Barbara Charlesworth Gelpi's *Shelley's Goddess: Maternity, Language, Subjectivity* (1992), combines biographical studies, psychoanalytic analysis, and cultural materialism. Works doing the same for women writers recently recovered for study, such as Susan Levin's *Dorothy Wordsworth and Romanticism* (1987), and for women writers who have not been forgotten but who have been side-lined, such as Claudia Johnson's *Jane Austen: Women, Politics, and the Novel* (1988), use a variety of approaches to recontextualize these women's writings.

Works attempting to sort out the differences between men's and women's aesthetic traditions, such as Anne K. Mellor's *Romanticism and Gender* (1993), or works focusing on a genre specifically associated with women, such as Kate Ellis's *The Contested Castle: Gothic Novels and the Subversion of Domestic Ideology* (1989), use a mix of approaches to redefine and re-historicize the role we allow women writers to play in Romanticism. While remaining feminist, these works employ different approaches, and can do so in order to achieve similar ends because they use one of the principal concepts common to nearly all feminist approaches: that the biologically sexed individual is also socially gendered. Individuals must learn to be masculine and feminine, according to this concept, and it is this, rather than biological sex, that explains how an individual relates to her or his society and culture. By differentiating between sex and gender, we can explain how a person's response to social expectations may be in conflict with her or his biological drives. We can also explain the conflict these societal expectations can cause for anyone whose creativity, genius, or strong personality is restrained or forcibly curbed by them. Feminists can use this concept to examine women writers' thematic and stylistic choices, as well as any indications in men's writings of a coercion to play a particular role themselves, to depict male and female characters in particular ways, or to have a sympathetic understanding of women's lives. Mixed feminist approaches, such as those mentioned above, can apply a key aspect of this concept to a gender critique of social or political forces, or in relation to particular authors and their work.

Finally, current feminist research is very concerned with cultural information and the various ways in which we can interpret this sort of data to reflect on the historical relations between men and women. One ongoing inquiry in feminist scholarship that has been reinvigorated by this recent concern with cultural studies focuses on why certain material objects or particular interests are so often assigned to the feminine. Dress and fashion, for instance, have always been associated with women's beauty and desirability to men, and through this connection have led to an association with their supposed self-centered acquisitiveness and materialism. With the increase in trade and industrialism that characterizes the Romantic period, middle-class women as well as upper-class women became identified with the acquisition of material goods and with consumerism itself (see Campbell, 1990). This is evident from a variety of mercantile innovations, such as the production of speciality china and new household pottery items designed by Wedgwood, the development of shops catering for female needs in cities and towns (which in turn led to the development of the female pastime of leisure shopping, the particular enjoyment of the younger Bennet girls in *Pride and Prejudice*), and the publication of women's fashion magazines with the latest designs and fabric styles. Several of these innovations were linked by their promotion of each other; for instance, Rudolph Ackermann's magazine for women illustrated the interior of Wedgwood's London shop, seemingly filled to the ceiling with affordable fine china, as well as his own London store interior. Ackermann also began including swatches of the newest fabric as soon as they were available in his issues, while the monthly issues of the *La Belle Assemblée; or Bell's Court and Fashionable Magazine* were always sure to have several fine drawings of ladies wearing the latest fashion.

Through such means, women became highly identified with consumerism, even though men inherited, controlled, and accumulated money itself. This identification is what interests feminist scholars, particularly as manifested in objects that are identified with the feminine or with the female body. For instance, fabric as a literal acquisition of material goods becomes a fascinating marker of cultural development during this period, with the equation between material and materialism producing the associative link between consumerism and women's bodies, industrialism (commercial production), and "natural" female beauty. Women provide the link between man-made artifice and nature that reassures society about industrialism's possible negatives. In an odd twist of social logic, women's beauty, which turns young women into objects for consumption in what we would call today the "marriage market," naturalizes the greatly increased production of goods. The connection of material or fabric, so important to a young woman's ability to attract an eligible man's attention, seems so obvious and "natural" an association that it hides the illogical connection of materialism to the female body. The new consumerism seemingly inverts the very old association of the female body as a literal producer in childbearing, a connection that then allows the male to be aligned with cultural production and the intellectual transcendence of nature. The inversion of this old association reduces the woman's role as producer so that she suddenly appears as a consumer only. Women Romantics, as we will see, attempted to controvert this reduction of women's productive powers by highlighting the female role as producers of children, but such attempts reflect the tension women clearly felt from these patterns of cultural identification. (For important discussions of the gendering of culture and nature, see de Beauvoir, 1952; Ortner, 1974.)

Another connection that hides behind the natural one is that between the "female" currents of fashion and cultural fads such as the changing interest in Grecian style, Oriental style, Parisian fashion, and so on. These fads, which were also reflected in architectural and furniture designs, were not just idle enthusiasms, but indicated changes in "male" activities such as trade patterns, national political interests, and intellectual currents. Thus feminist inquiry can use the gendering of material interests to locate important cultural changes. Although this technique will not be pursued in any depth in this book, since this is only one facet of the various feminist critical approaches demonstrated here, I have included two fashion illustrations from *La Belle Assemblée* magazine (see figures 2 and 5). These illustrations, and the fashionable portraits of Elizabeth Montagu and Sarah Siddons (figures 4 and 6) point, if only superficially, to the connections between fashion and literary activity in women's magazines and the representation of fashion in literature by or about women. By this inclusion, I hope to provide one more line of inquiry for student researches, in addition to those suggested in the various chapters.

This book, then, engages gender critique as well as the other feminist principles discussed above to examine some key issues of a period currently undergoing substantial redefinition; it also demonstrates how different approaches can be used together to clarify women's roles in literary production, and points to other possible directions for research such as a feminist use of cultural studies. We will apply these principles and approaches to a Romanticism that has been redefined as a larger, more inclusive period containing many more writers than has previously been thought. When a gender critique is applied to the study of these writers, both traditional and newly included, we develop a clearer idea of the social, economic, and political forces at work in this period. It is a period characterized not only by traditional Romantic attributes of the mystical poetic sublime and the pastoral nostalgia for nature, but also by social sentiment (especially in sympathy), by political criticism or social critique, and by sensibility. Because sensibility is related to the sublime in its affinity for Nature as a female entity, and in its introspective and psychologized attitude toward personal feelings and memories, it belongs with the sublime as an emotional marker of Romantic literary texts. Sensibility, then, as well as the sublime, will characterize our period; novels and prose as well as poetry will describe it; and the question of high art versus popular art will be complicated by what contributions women and men writers made to the period through the variety of their art forms and the ways in which they responded to the social, economic, or political tensions of their time.

The chapters that follow investigate from a feminist perspective texts produced by women writers important to their times, as well as several texts by male writers. The examination of male texts through a feminist lens is, of course, as much the project of feminist criticism as is the study of female texts. Further, when the definition of the period is undergoing revision, it is especially important to place men's and women's texts in contextual relation to each other in order to more fully understand the nature of their endeavors, and the culture they respond to and critique. While I only begin this process here, readers should continue their own contextual reading of men's to women's texts and vice versa. Many of the works discussed in this book have been available for a long time; some are only recently available in the several newly published anthologies. Still others will be reissued in the near future as more presses recognize the need to make retrieved women's texts available for students and scholars. It is my hope that readers will begin to recognize the moves and gestures of feminist criticism in the following chapters so that even the discussion of a text not easily located can be taken and applied to another text by the same author, or to a similar text by a different author. In this sense, the following chapters provide selective discussions that can then be more broadly applied, rather than explanations to be taken literally or as a complete representation of the period.

Jane Austen: a Case Study

In order to provide the broad strokes of how to engage a feminist critique, I have organized the four succeeding chapters to treat from a literary perspective the issues feminist studies have deemed most important to women's concerns: public versus private life (chapter 2), domestic abuse and female psychology (chapter 3), women's intellectuality (chapter 4), and women's self-perception as objects and subjects (chapter 5). To provoke a way of thinking about these issues, this section begins with a step back to understand how a woman who writes about such things may suffer critical misunderstanding. Jane Austen confronts the divide between public and private when her characters are seduced and abandoned (Colonel Brandon's ward in *Sense and Sensibility*, Lydia in *Pride and Prejudice* who nearly is); she confronts domestic abuse in *Northanger Abbey* (1818) with General Tilney and in *Mansfield Park* (1874); Elizabeth and the Bingley circle discuss women's intellectuality in *Pride and Prejudice*; and all of her heroines must resolve the dilemma of being subjects when they are, for the most part, only wanted as objects. Because Austen highlights these concerns, she has until recently been interpreted as a domestic novelist of limited range whose works shed no light on more important issues such as politics and war. This section will address the vexed relation between the so-termed minor and major issues defined by the literary canon, ones allowing a writer to be acknowledged for her artistic mastery while being disallowed for her subject matter and range. I will trace through some of the changes feminist criticism has made in our understanding of this writer's accomplishments by giving a selective survey of earlier and recent scholarship on Austen, noting the general direction taken by these feminist works as indicative of feminist scholarship in Romantic studies as a whole. Finally, I will propose a reading of *Pride and Prejudice* that foreshadows how subsequent chapters approach texts.

First, some background. Jane Austen was born at Steventon Rectory in rural Hampshire on December 16, 1775, and died in Winchester July 18, 1817. She spent her life in southern England, never traveling to the Midlands or north, or abroad. She was educated for several years with her sister at boarding schools and then at home by her father, the Rev. George Austen, and by two brothers who were both Oxford educated. The family also read together, giving Jane her first audience when she began to write at the age of 12, and they put on private theatricals; the girls possibly also had visiting masters for drawing and music. The Austens were gentry, but were at the lowest end of their class due to their limited income, subsisting on the family's small farm and dairy. Yet Austen knew members of the upper social register, including a distant cousin who adopted her third brother, and one of her own suitors. In addition, she was acquainted with the wider world through her cousin, Eliza, who had married a French officer of Marie Antoinette's regiment in 1781 and had lived in the glamorous world of pre-revolutionary Paris before escaping back to England. From her aunt, Eliza's mother, who had lived in India for 13 years, and from Warren Hastings, a friend of her father's, she also knew about Indian affairs, and she probably knew about the American Revolution from several neighbors at Steventon who had experienced it at first hand. In addition, she had relations who had dealings with Jamaica, and her father was trustee for a plantation in Antigua (see Tucker, 1994: 69–71). Finally, two of her brothers served in the Royal Navy: one served in the East Indies, under Nelson, in the Battle of St Domingo, and in the War of 1812; the other took British troops to Egypt, suppressed the slave trade in the West Indies, and served in Burma. Never traveling widely herself, Austen could exhibit a knowledge of the world in her novels that extended beyond the seeming limitations her life imposed on her.

Austen's early work, unpublished in her lifetime, includes her mocking critique of sensibility *Love and Freindship* [sic], and her exuberant satire, *A History of England*. The publishing history of her six finished novels indicates the difficulties a writer might face who is not working in a popular vein: *Sense and Sensibility* (written and revised 1795–8, published 1811), *Pride and Prejudice* (written 1797, rejected and revised, published 1813), *Northanger Abbey* (written 1798–9, sold in 1803 but not published, published posthumously in 1818), *Mansfield Park* (published 1814), *Emma* (published 1816), *Persuasion* (published posthumously 1818).

Despite the late recognition of her talent, which began seriously with *Mansfield Park* and was aided by Sir Walter Scott's 1815 review of *Emma* in the *Quarterly Review*, Austen has been ranked as one of the major literary artists for over a century now. Yet, until recently, she was not considered a Romantic writer. Classed sometimes as a late eighteenth-century writer in the tradition of Fanny Burney, or a late Augustan writer as Byron is often considered, Jane Austen has been difficult for scholars to pigeon-hole. Not until recent rethinking about what Romanticism means have we been able to talk convincingly of Austen as Romantic. Once certain questions were asked about this period, we could view Austen's examination of key Romantic issues, such as Britain's trade or inheritance laws, as informed representations following a definably Romantic pattern of social critique.

Our earlier understanding of Austen, already formed in the past century and carried over into ours, has been of a writer whose genius can be recognized but not explained, and which is unrelated to the productions of her contemporaries. In *The Great Tradition* (1948), F. R. Leavis begins with the sentence, "The great English novelists are Jane Austen, George Eliot, Henry James and Joseph Conrad," adding "Since Jane Austen, for special reasons, needs to be studied at considerable length, I confine myself in this book to the last three." Leavis explains his thesis to be based on a definition of the great novelist that depends on "some challenging discriminations": the great writers are those who "change the possibilities of the art for practitioners and readers," and "are significant in terms of the human awareness they promote; awareness of the possibilities of life" (Leavis, 1979: 2). Although he does not discuss Austen's work in depth, Leavis does explain why he includes her as one of the writers critically important to the novel tradition: "Jane Austen, in fact, is the inaugurator of the great tradition of the English novel . . . [because] The great novelists in that tradition are all very much concerned with 'form'" (Leavis, 1979: 7). This noted, Austen's larger importance lies in "her intense moral preoccupation," and her "unusually developed interest in life" (1979: 8–9), traits marking the great novelist. By rooting these traits in Austen, Leavis creates the basic structure for his approach: Austen will be the original author from whom all the other authors will in some way derive and identify themselves. At this point in Leavis's introduction he leaves her, coming back only for the purposes of touchstone as he concentrates on the other three novelists in his study, to whom he adds Dickens as an afterthought. By giving Austen the place of "inaugurator of the great tradition," but then displacing her to a touchstone only, Leavis sets up a critical ambivalence towards her highly characteristic of Austen studies in general. If Leavis includes Austen in his canon, his silence on a definitive reading of her texts betrays the commonly shared anxiety over her place (eighteenth-century or Romantic author?), thematic importance (is she a miniaturist or concerned with the larger world?), and the real importance of form (despite Leavis's claim, is it really as important as concepts like the epic or the irregular ode?).

In his book, *Some Words of Jane Austen* (1973), Stuart Tave undertakes to counter absences such as the one initiating Leavis's discussion. Tave's work was a useful intervention at this point in Austen scholarship because he explains how it is possible for Austen to be the inaugurating author Leavis claims (but does not prove) her to be. But his study also indicates an incipient feminism in his willingness to grant Austen the terms and the authority of genius, and to locate that genius in a limited range. Tave argues that Austen's greatness lies in her ability to inhabit small worlds, whether these are defined by space and time, by lexicon, or by a knowledge of character. Without reference to political or national contexts, Tave builds up from the novels' own language a cultural context for the characters' behavior. He begins his study with a reference to dancing, which plays a large role in several of Austen's novels. Dancing is, as he notes, the act of moving meaningfully in time and space, making use of limit and definition. Austen's writing can be explained by the same dynamic: masterful explorations of time and space for her characters, and the delimiting of herself as an author in order to condense meaning and wisdom. Tave's interpretation of Austen could be said to resemble William Wordsworth's own interpretation of artistic intensity in his sonnet "Nuns Fret not at their Convent's Narrow Room," where he limits poetic space to that of a sonnet in order to increase the depth and force of his meaning. Curiously, Wordsworth and Tave both view this artistic phenomenon, mastery achieved through confinement, as feminine and powerful.

For Tave, such masterful limitations are not only feminine, they are dynamically active, thus transforming a heroine into a heroic figure; indeed, he understands Austen's female heroes as being in contrast to the passive heroines of romance. The Austen heroine must be actively in command of the set of limitations she is given, and her task is to meet the challenge posed for her by the particular moment of the novel. Importantly, this crisis will force her to know the hero as the man she desires but may not be able to marry, and thus to know herself. In Tave's view, each novel plots the protagonist's mortification; her survival, after believing she has lost the hero's interest, marks her growth into a deserving

35

heroine. The woman who, having made peace with a loss resulting from her own errors and blindness, grows in self-knowledge, becomes the woman who can deserve marriage with the right man. Moreover, the hero can only be the right man if he, too, gains in self-knowledge, and both characters must fulfill this heroic quest. In *Pride and Prejudice*, Darcy and Elizabeth finally earn the right to marry because each has mortified the other out of her and his pride and prejudice. Tave's analysis, using the material made available in the texts to build a cultural context, presents a comprehensive picture of the gender relations in the novels without depending on psychological interpretations of Austen's life circumstances to do so. Nevertheless, the larger contextual picture of how Romantic Austen's approach may be is missing, and Austen's place in Romanticism is never a proposition or even a question for Tave's study.

By contrast, early feminist scholarship on Austen did focus on extra-textual contexts, but did so in a fragmented and unsystematic manner that allowed critics to point out interesting recurrences in Austen's texts without allowing them to hypothesize how these themes or material aspects showed Austen to be available to a feminist analysis or to have a Romantic identity. Such research tended to focus on Austen's seemingly obsessive interest in women's relation to money, inheritance, and economic circulation as representatively feminine, such as Ellen Moers carried out in the 1970s, or on Austen's repeated depictions of women's restricted circles of contact and communication, such as Nina Auerbach parlayed into a larger study of nineteenth-century women writers in *Communities of Women* (1978). Because no systematic theory had yet been developed to understand writers who were not, like Charlotte Brontë and Virginia Woolf, self-defined feminists, descriptive analyses of material context could only begin to build larger bodies of knowledge based on the general and ahistorical interests that women writers have shared across several centuries: the family, the sexual and economic vulnerability of a young heroine, love, maternity, poverty in old age. Writers like Austen could only be seen as additional evidence for these stereotypical concerns when viewed from the purely contextual perspective. This contrasts sharply with the research of Leavis and Tave, both of whom see Austen as original and uninterested in larger or popular literary trends. Both approaches, one of which ties Austen to general gender stereotypes and the other of which deliberately severs such ties, cannot see Austen's relation to her own literary period either in its broadest intellectual and imaginative concerns or in its political agitation for human rights. Austen could not be properly understood either as a

Romantic or as having an interest in women's rights as individuals until a theoretical feminist perspective had been developed.

However, before looking at works that employ such a perspective, we need first to consider a work very important to our discussion that followed the contextual line of thought without being feminist, both in its insistence on contextualizing Austen's work with contemporary novels, and in its resistance to biography: Butler's *Jane Austen and the War of Ideas* (1975). This study would be important if only for the shocking juxtaposition in its title of Austen with the words "war" and "ideas" – two terms not usually associated with Austen. Butler's is a debunking work, designed to take the mystery out of an author who has been so regularly placed on a pedestal. Butler also views Austen as more conservative than she is now considered, commenting that *Pride and Prejudice* is *not* a critique or satire ("The fact is that [the novel] does not read like a satire at all. Generations of readers have received its love-story as archetypally romantic, and they have been right to do so," 1987 edn: 201). Butler also views Austen's social constructions in her fictional world as antithetical to the radical constructions proposed by Mary Wollstonecraft and other jacobinical or pro-French revolutionary novelists. In viewing Austen as a member of the conservative reactionary camp, Butler denies her the feminist status later critics often give her, but provides the terms that a sophisticated feminist analysis needs to make its case.

A subsequent work taking a strong feminist stance toward Austen was Margaret Kirkham's *Jane Austen, Feminism and Fiction* (1983). Kirkham follows Butler's lead in contextualizing Austen's work, but shows how Austen can be associated with a political position. Kirkham uses biography judiciously to show that Austen is not a solitary genius, but a woman whose life was influenced by those radicalizing feminists whose work preceded hers, such as Mary Astell, Catherine Macaulay, and Mary Wollstonecraft. The moralizing strain Butler identifies as reactionary, Kirkham sees as "indicative of [Austen's] sympathy with the rational feminism of the Enlightenment" (1983: xii). For Kirkham, Austen's "insistence upon Reason as the supreme guide to conduct" is the vehicle for her feminism and her critique of Romanticism, not the key to our ability to evaluate her.

Both Butler and Kirkham refuse to situate Austen solely within the obvious constraints she herself imposes of dowry, income, and investment, or within the stereotyped discourse of love and emotional attachment. A whole other school of Austen scholarship, while also interested in material contexts, accepts these constraints as the key to a feminist

37

reading of her work, beginning with Ellen Moers (*Literary Women*, 1976) and Judith Lowder Newton (*Women, Power and Subversion*, 1981), and continuing through feminist Marxist analyses of Austen's obsession with the niceties of class and rank and social histories of the same. Many of the essays in a recent pedagogic volume, *Approaches to Teaching Austen's "Pride and Prejudice"* (Folsom, 1993), such as those by Copeland, Smith, and Brown, address these issues, while more recently the volume *Jane Austen and the Discourses of Feminism* (Looser, 1995) includes essays taking a cultural approach with an interest in material history. Despite the variety of work represented here, there is a sense in all these essays that Austen has predetermined any criticism of her by publishing novels so carefully constructed about such seemingly unimportant themes that there are no loose ends to seize on. Such a sense of frustration, however, often comes of not analyzing the text according to a strongly defined feminist approach. Many approaches are now possible, but the critic must clearly choose, and must ground her or his approach in the set of shared feminist precepts that we have already discussed.

One interesting way in which a developing literary theory of feminism has directed scholarly attention has been the ongoing concern in Austen criticism with her biography in non-psychologized, culturally contextualized ways, in order to illuminate how her novels reflect her interests, the major events of her life, and the world she lived in and recorded. As the history of feminist criticism suggests, women's biographies, as texts themselves and as reflections of the woman writer's life and mind, have been very important to feminist theory. For instance, many of the essays in the *Approaches to Teaching Austen* (Folsom, 1993) invoke Austen's biography in order to explain the structure and plot of the novel. Yet even though we know surprisingly little about how Austen thought about or interpreted some aspects of her life, some scholars continue to be willing to take chances with psychoanalyzing her life and work. When this form of criticism resorts to speculation about what we don't know rather than focusing on what we do, it becomes difficult to see the distinctions between the feminist approach and more standard textual approaches. As useful as biography has proved to be in developing feminist theory, it is important for us to remember that when biography is taken as idiosyncratic rather than reflective of an individual's place in the cultural context, it can block critical attention to the text by directing that attention to itself. It is imperative that feminist critics use biography contextually only and according to feminist precepts, without attempting to interpret a text according to the psychology we impute to the author. In this way, we avoid speculation about an author's love life or unfulfilled ambitions – a popular way to interpret and then dismiss women's art – and we concentrate on the serious literary, historical, and cultural implications of the artwork.

The dilemma of needing a strongly defined feminist approach, while maintaining an effective use of biography, has faced the most recent scholarship on Austen, such as Claudia Johnson's *Jane Austen: Women, Politics, and the Novel* (1988) and Deborah Kaplan's *Jane Austen among Women* (1992). Johnson's work systematically addresses a larger social and cultural framework by explaining how Austen's novelistic attitudes, her avoidance of overtly political or pedantic tones, and her feminine rather than feminist mastery, allowed her to be admired even during the reactionary last half of the Romantic period when women novelists had to restrict their radicalism severely in order to be read. It was not Austen's romance but her novelistic tactics that later allowed Leavis to consider her genius to be of tradition-forming stature. Johnson further- more addresses how we understand Austen; how we, like the editor of the standard edition, R. W. Chapman, insist on "the lady" as her only possible character. While taking issue with Butler's interpretation of Austen's intellectual abilities, Johnson uses the contextual approach ini- tiated by Butler's *War of Ideas*, together with a feminist theoretical overview, to create a much more complex understanding of Austen as a writer.

Deborah Kaplan (1992) narrows and deepens the contextual field for Austen's work by situating her in relation to the female community. Although a scholar runs the risk of marginalizing a woman artist by restricting discussion of her to the context of other women, the opposite occurs when this is done within a theoretical structure forcing a recupera- tion of knowledge about the intricacies of women's lives previously simplified or overlooked. Here a forceful use of biography combined with archival material allows Kaplan to extend her range of reference for the female community that fostered Austen's complex intellectual nature: "My search turned up a number of documents, some of them in county record offices, others still in private hands, many of them not previously consulted for studies of Jane Austen. I found letters, diaries, memoirs, and poems by neighbors living around Austen's Hampshire homes at Steventon and Chawton and around her brother Edward's Kent estate at Godmersham . . ." (1992: 7). The use of biographical material, situated here by the reconstruction of a female community through cultural artifacts, allows Kaplan to investigate the conditions of a woman writer's life without attempting to re-read her psychology through a modern lens.

Using different but equally theoretically informed approaches, Johnson's and Kaplan's books together provide a richer understanding of how Austen could have produced the novels she did, and of how conscious Austen was of the political sphere from which critics have so long believed her domestic novels to be divided. These works, like much recent feminist Romantic scholarship, have grounded themselves in the question of the separation between public and private in turmoil during the Romantic period, with gendered distinctions less constrictive prior to the French Revolution and much greater after the Napoleonic Wars began to threaten Britain's security. Students of the period can benefit from this scholarship without having to do their own difficult archival research for contextual materials, particularly if they take the larger feminist framework of seeking the difference that gender makes, and the importance of discerning disturbances in the representations of the public and private. There is much room for further discovery if students remember the question Butler's work begins to investigate for Austen studies on the radical promise of the sentiments, and if they apply the subsequent question of Austen's authorial relation to sensibility.

Although we have seen that the most promising of recent feminist work on Austen has relied on contextual material and biography, I want to turn to our own exploration of one of Austen's texts by returning to the restricted focus taken by Leavis and Tave. I want to show that, even without contextual aids or a particular feminist approach, we can still produce an informed feminist reading of Austen so long as it is grounded in basic feminist precepts. We can perform this experiment because sophisticated feminist theories have already been developed, and so it will be clearer to us when we have misread and misapplied our precepts. Although this is not the best way to proceed to gain new knowledge, it is a helpful way to begin reading through a feminist lens and for seeing just how basic a feminist interpretation can be.

Following Butler's lead, I will begin with the sentiments, particularly the emotion of sensibility. Because critical consensus has found *Pride and Prejudice* to be one of Austen's most masterful novels, and because of this novel's more subtle treatment of emotion, we will begin there. But Austen herself clearly delineates sensibility in her first published novel, *Sense and Sensibility*, and if we were to do a thorough job of this topic we would want to begin with her first published exploration of the joys and difficulties raised by sensibility in order to apply Austen's own sense of the importance of emotions to her other novels. However, we can do much even with one novel. *Pride and Prejudice* concerns an intelligent and spirited young woman of marriageable age whose father's lack of financial planning, and whose four other sisters, mean that she has little chance of making a good marriage. Elizabeth Bennet appears little concerned with this fate because she enjoys the love and respect of her intelligent but cynical father, and the company of her eldest sister Jane. Her difficulty, rather, is to endure her difficult and stupid mother, and to avoid Mrs Bennet's machinations for matchmaking, such as her clumsy attempts to force Elizabeth to marry her cousin, Mr Collins. Elizabeth is aided in her difficulty by her loving aunt and uncle Gardiner, and it seems that if no opportunity for marriage entered the plot, she would have a happy, if not full, life.

Austen's intention, of course, is to provide a tantalizing opportunity for both a full and a happy life for her heroine by introducing the wealthy Darcy into the first ball attended by the Bennet women in this novel. Jane will fall in love with Darcy's wealthy friend Bingley, Elizabeth will watch Bingley's sister Caroline attempt to attract Darcy, and Elizabeth will consider herself safe from such activities. But her seemingly intelligent distance from such emotional entrapments, her belief that she is not attracted to Darcy or any other man, will not safeguard her from the dangers of sexual attraction or from its humiliations. Elizabeth begins to believe herself attracted to Wickham, who proves to be a libertine and liar, and believes herself repelled by the haughty Darcy, whom she slowly discovers to be both a true gentleman and the man she could truly love. Both these revelations are humiliating discoveries for a woman who had thought herself intelligent enough to know her own heart and to discern readily the character of others. Her final humbling, which will match Darcy's own severe humbling after he had abruptly and arrogantly proposed marriage to Elizabeth the first time, only to have her reject him, comes when her youngest and most embarrassing sister, Lydia, elopes with Wickham without an accompanying marriage. Such an event provides the opportunity to study the cultural context of this novel, since the mores of the time specify that elopement will mark Lydia as a fallen woman because her relation with her lover is sexual only. Without a subsequent marriage, it must lead to her own prostitution when he inevitably deserts her, and her family, now socially degraded, must reject her. Moreover, a daughter's prostitution disgraces her family to such an extent that none of her sisters can then marry. Lydia's act, which Austen portrays as a clear extension of her mother's obsession with getting a husband at any cost, ruins all her sisters' chances for marriage, thus showing in the most logical manner the irrationality of Mrs Bennet's scheming. More importantly, it shows how Elizabeth has already begun to know herself by this point, since she is now fully aware of her developing interest in Darcy and the interruption of it Lydia's ruin causes. When Darcy's rescue of Lydia allows Elizabeth to save face socially while completing her own self-growth, and encourages Darcy to prove he too has come to know himself by proposing a second time, the novel ends. The plot is clearly centered on romantic love, its frustration and eventual fulfillment, but the Romantic themes that concern us are the psychological development of Elizabeth and Darcy as individuals of free will, the tight maneuvering each must manage as they get to know one another within the acceptable boundaries of class distinction, the confinement of social manners, and the issues of family inheritance and sexual indiscretion.

With our synopsis in place, how do we now begin interpreting such a novel from a feminist perspective? A reader examining *Pride and Prejudice* for its gendered roles might question, for instance, the way in which the terms of the title seem to invite one to set up a parallel with the novel's characters. We might ask which character is proud and which prejudiced, and whether these traits were considered particular to either gender in Austen's time. In fact, the puzzle of the title turns out to be a commonplace of criticism on this novel, and it is a useful place to begin a critical reading since there is no one acceptable resolution of the problem. Investigating this thought further, then, the reader might notice Austen's use of parallelism as one of several structuring devices she employs to put a semblance of casual design over her tightly constructed novel. A casual quality helps the novel to appear naturally developed, to appear as a tale of the rural gentry carrying the tone of country life, with an accompanying organicism of form and structure. The organic is an important quality for Romantic texts to exhibit, yet Austen would be equally concerned to avoid any loss of the highly controlled formal structure she favors. Most of the important Romantic writers, particularly Coleridge, Wordsworth, Shelley, and Keats, excel at disguising a highly formal design within a natural or inspired appearance; Austen does not go so far, but she does use the Romantic dualism of inspiration and structure to make her tight plots seem both unselfconscious and organic. By showing that Austen is working within the same vein as the great male Romantics, we have already begun working as feminist critics.

The title itself can seem a light reference to the main characters' personalities, or can appear to indicate a parallelism in the novel's structure by its nouns "pride" and "prejudice." But although we will choose the second interpretation because it helps us follow the structure rather than simply make an impressionistic evaluation, it would be incorrect to portion the nouns of the title out as adjectives (Elizabeth is proud, Darcy is prejudiced, and so on), as scholars have long noted. If we pay strict attention to how the hero and heroine both exhibit these flaws, as well as how pride and prejudice are traits that mark many of the other characters, we can see that these nouns do describe a psychology born of the social milieu of the novel, and that it is one both heroine and hero must outgrow in order to deserve marriage to each other. This is a marriage signifying growth into wisdom that reveals, through the exorcism of such flaws, the possibility of a new social order. Pride and prejudice can be seen as holdovers from the old regime as demonstrated in outrageous excess by Lady Catherine de Bourgh, and as markers of class and rank which help bar social change. But they have also been adopted by the new wealthy middle class, proud and prejudiced about money only, and a threat to the harmony of the new social order Austen envisions. Austen neither approves Lydia Bennet's abandonment of proper judgment when she elopes with Wickham as a kind of revolutionary disregard, nor Charlotte Lucas's rational marriage to Mr Collins as an old regime anachronism. Neither does she approve Mrs Bennet's middle-class emphasis on wealth, the bourgeois Caroline Bingley's attempts to hook Darcy, or the social-climbing Wickham's financial scheming. Her critique of contemporary mores clearly indicates what she believes the proper course to be, and how the protagonists are to achieve it. She also shows how difficult such a course is to follow, given the gendered restrictions society imposes on the individual.

A feminist reading of the novel needs then to move beyond the title to recognize the other kinds of parallels present, particularly those between characters and character roles. The outrageous mother figures, Mrs Bennet and Lady Catherine, are particularly important as they embarrass our two protagonists, Elizabeth and Darcy, and encumber or unwillingly promote their love interest. Although several critics have explored the peculiar construction of the maternal figure in Austen, often represented as absent, dependent, or obstructionist, it is rarely observed that these two particular figures, Mrs Bennet and Lady Catherine, are mirror images of each other. Both preside at courts of their own making, imposing their will on their dependants, and attempting to marry off their dependants according to their own financial designs. In this sense, the important parental relation of the novel is not that between Mr and Mrs Bennet, but the ineffectual behavior of these two mothers to their children. Mrs Bennet's seeming ability to get her girls married has little to do with whether any marriages ever take place, and ends with her evident powerlessness as her youngest daughter elopes. In mirror fashion, we watch as Lady Catherine's seeming power over her relations, especially in her plans for her daughter and Darcy, is revealed as real impotence when Darcy makes Elizabeth his choice.

In this interpretation of the novel, we have at its center two women who together represent a kind of disorder: one from the old regime, the other from the economically unstable middle class, and both depicting ineffectual models of maternity. Once viewed in this way, it then becomes clear that Austen is making a case for a new social order based on self-worth and emotional stability over the present disorder, caused by the abuses of rank and emphasis on financial gain that these two mothers evince. The unmotherly mother symbolizes the larger social issues blocking younger women from going beyond what society dictates for their gender. By criticizing the mother, Austen shows how everyone, including powerful parental figures, contributes to the sexual politics that force women to act or to refrain from acting in particular ways. One example of this is Mrs Bennet's anger with Elizabeth when she refuses Mr Collins's marriage proposal, even though the terms of his suit are humiliating to her pride, while he himself is blind to her intelligence, ignorant of her personality, and lacking in any emotion beyond his own self-love. As Charlotte's experience shows when she does marry Collins, such marital arrangements serve only to confine and repress women further, and verge on domestic abuse.

Mr Bennet, then, is not the powerful man who either withholds his power or intervenes as he sees fit as we first believe him to be, since he, too, is impotent with regard to the elopement and rescue of Lydia. In fact, Mr Bennet, on whom Mrs Bennet leans so selfishly, is the mirror of the impotent man Lady Catherine also leans on so selfishly for support: Mr Collins. The parallel is completed by Mr Collins's eventual inheritance of Mr Bennet's estate as his next male kin, while his clownish servility is an ironic mirror image of Mr Bennet's genteel cynicism. Neither man, like neither woman, can prove the true parental model for a new society based on love and merit, rather than status and wealth. Both men are, like the mothers, a kind of absent figure, unable to achieve change and invested in preventing change from taking place.

Another way to locate structural parallels is to examine those characters having a relationship to the hero and heroine that is other than parental. Like most of Romantic literature, *Pride and Prejudice* absents the parent or removes her or his ability to resolve or intervene in the plot. Early in the period, when enthusiasm for revolution was first viewed as a positive response to a new era, in which the patriarchal politics of the old regime would be replaced with fraternity and equality, authors began substituting powerful parent characters with sibling figures. The capacity to act becomes the provision of the hero and siblings, or characters who become sibling-like through affection. This representation of siblings as central to the plot is an attribute of the literature of sensibility, and is one indication of Austen's use of sensibility in her novels. For example, Wickham was raised with Darcy and remains a brother figure to him, just as Darcy and his good friend Bingley treat each other as brothers. While Lydia and Wickham, as sibling figures to Elizabeth and Darcy, can effect changes in the plot through their elopement and other acts, Mr Collins must be viewed as a parent and not a sibling figure, since his marital threat to Elizabeth becomes parental when he woos only to please Lady Catherine. Siblings represent the only community of importance, as the parallels between the two beloved sisters – Elizabeth's sister Jane and Darcy's sister Georgiana – prove. Elizabeth and Darcy establish their relational matrix between siblings, those unloved as well as loved, through their use of sensibility – their innate emotional sensitivity and empathy – to establish and secure the relation. Thus, siblinghood represents community established on the feminine terms of sensibility rather than the patriarchal terms of class and financial gain. And the great struggles of the novel, the struggles between pride and prejudice that every character must undertake or succumb to, revolve around correct interpretations of sensibility. We see, for instance, how Elizabeth's quick "first" impressions of both Wickham and Darcy, with their incorrect interpretations, result in misjudgments that are dangerous to her own happiness. Austen analyzes the dangers of misapplied sensibility in each of her novels, but here her interest is so strong it formulates her earlier title for the work: "First Impressions." The implications are complex in that Austen shows women vulnerable both to excessive sensibility (as Georgiana is) and to excessive rationality (as Charlotte Lucas is). First impressions can lead women astray in either direction, and the heroine's task is to determine the direction of her future life – to choose the right path – through a mediation of both heart and mind, while developing heroically into the kind of woman who can fruitfully live such a life.

Sensibility, finally, can prove the key to a feminist reading of this novel. Austen's prior novel, *Sense and Sensibility*, retains the emphasis on such dangers in its title. Her heroine must be the victim of sensibility, as the heroine's sister Marianne is in the first novel, but must be possessed of it within a rational framework. Sensibility must combine with heroic action to fit the Austen mold. Such a heroine must actively engage her own self-development without being controlled altogether by reason, and without losing the emotional refinement of her sentiments, as Elizabeth success-fully does. By contrast, Caroline Bingley, Elizabeth's rival for Darcy's affection, is a woman who has no sensibility, and for whom only her material existence and the status of her future matter. Offering another contrast, Lydia Bennet is a woman whose self-indulgence obliterates both sensibility and material logic; her spiritedness is a jacobinical one leading her easily astray. Finally, Elizabeth's beloved elder sister Jane is self-possessed, but while her passive serenity provides a possible model for a good woman, it is not enough for an active heroine. Such passivity is too often attributed to the victim heroines of romances written by men, such as Samuel Richardson's *Clarissa*. Although such passivity is stereotypically "feminine" and is a characteristic often assigned to novel heroines, Austen favors the properly active woman. To illustrate the significant difference between proper and improper action, she eschews the gendering of action and passivity (a standard way to structure oppo-sitions in novels) to show women and men being both active and passive. Mr Bennet, Jane and Georgiana are all extremely passive, with negative consequences for all three (Mr Bennet is unhappy in his marriage, Jane nearly loses Bingley for ever, and Georgiana nearly elopes with Wickham), while Mrs Gardiner's seeming passivity is rather a wise prudence, positively based on moral precepts and moderation. Mr Collins is more truly and destructively passive, in the sense that he does nothing without Lady Catherine's orders. Mrs Bennet, Lady Catherine, Lydia and Caroline Bingley are all conspicuously active, again with negative results. Darcy appears passive, but is actually increasingly active through the novel, motivated by his sense of responsibility for others and his increasing desire to help Elizabeth. Thus his proper activity produces exceptional results. Elizabeth's activity falls somewhere be-tween all of these. It contrasts with the negative examples of her mother and of Lady Catherine, yet her active stance can produce negative rather than positive results if she does not choose her course of action carefully. Her ability to act correctly and productively determines her heroism. Thus, Austen redefines gender stereotypes in ways that redress precon-ceptions inherited by the Romantics about activity as a way to achieve male heroism, and about passivity as the female behavioral ideal. Austen thus critiques Romantic attitudes that she finds to be in contrast to social progress.

One way Austen achieves this is to emphasize the heroine's psychologi-cal development in *Pride and Prejudice* by keeping Darcy's activities from view. These are activities that powerfully affect the plot, but Austen keeps them off stage in order to keep our attention on the active nature of Elizabeth's behavior against the passiveness of Jane's. It is important to understand how Austen is defining activity for her heroine: although Elizabeth is active in the sense of her ability to achieve changes in the plot – as her resistance to both Collins's and Darcy's first marriage proposals shows – we must also understand her active role as an enactment, a development of her character into the heroine she must be by the novel's end. Her ability to change herself is an attempt to do something about the state of the world as well, and her relation to that world. Elizabeth's eventual marriage to Darcy signals the possibility of a new social order built on the loss or impotence of the parental old regime, and grounded in a relation determined by the affections rather than by rank. This enactment is the proper resolution Austen finds for the meeting of sensibility, reason, and action; it is her definition of a proper Romanticism, a proper fit between ideas, desire, and political activity.

By focusing on the parallels that follow from the novel's puzzling title, starting with the sexual politics established between the two central sets of parental characters (Mrs Bennet and Lady Catherine, Mr Bennet and Mr Collins), and by seeing how all four exhibit negative models for behavior, we are then led to analyze the main difference between all the characters as being an opposition between active and passive attitudes and actions. We could then determine how Austen was using such an opposition against gendered stereotypes in order to redefine particular elements of Romanticism that she wanted to critique. This is a somewhat simplified example of how feminist criticism can be applied to a woman writer's text. I did not, for instance, bring Austen's biography into my analysis of the text, and I left all culturally and historically relevant information aside except for the import of elopement. Nevertheless, by applying a few of the central concepts of feminist criticism, we have analyzed the novel according to the depiction of gender relations and sexual politics, the role of the mother, the heroine's character and purpose, and how the novel itself leads us to think about these issues. We have thus gained an insight into Austen's famous novel that leads to a contextual comprehension of what might otherwise be confusing or mystifying elements of the text itself. It is an insight that shows Austen to be Romantic, and yet also critical of certain elements of Romanticism.

Throughout the chapters that follow I will apply the set of feminist concepts introduced in this chapter, but will further complicate the analyses with a variety of approaches chosen according to the critical task in hand, and vary my procedures as necessary in order to direct the topic under discussion. It will not be possible to deduce one single approach that can be determined "feminist criticism" from these discussions, but it will be possible to taste the variety of approaches available. The critical positioning of the material in the chapters that follow defines a feminist mentality: that to engage in feminist critical debate requires an understanding of the complex relation of women's texts to men's texts within the context of historical and cultural demands on the individual. A feminist approach means watching both the politics of the gender relations and the feminist awareness of the writers under study.

To this end, the focus of study for each chapter – women's literary relation to the public sphere, the Gothic genre as a representation of domestic abuse, women's intellectuality, and the cultural fascination with vision – forces our attention to the material context, but always through gender and subjectivity. Again, this book is not an introduction to a particular branch of feminist criticism but to concepts and approaches constituting a feminist frame of mind. It demonstrates how feminist scholarship resists definitive answers, and instead opens up areas of inquiry and knowledge by engaging stories that can be told in different ways through comparative readings of a variety of texts. And it means these stories are just a few of the ones needing to be reconstructed and written about.

Further Reading

Harold Bloom (ed.), *Romanticism and Consciousness* (1970). A collection of essays that definitively outline the view of Romanticism held before the advent of feminist or poststructuralist thought in Romantic studies. Bloom's "The internalization of quest-romance," Wimsatt's "The structure of Romantic nature imagery," Abrams's "English Romanticism: the spirit of the age," and his "Structure and style in the greater Romantic lyric," remain classics in the field.

Marilyn Butler, *Romantics, Rebels and Reactionaries* (1981). A detailed survey of the historical and political background of the Romantic period that affected the production of the literature in a variety of ways. Chapters 1, 7, and 8 address general questions providing useful background to the period; chapters 2–6 discuss specific authors in relation to cultural forces and historical specifics.

Anne K. Mellor (ed.), *Romanticism and Feminism* (1988). A collection of essays that produced one of the first representative surveys of how feminism can be combined with historical and material critiques of Romanticism.

Anne K. Mellor, *Romanticism and Gender* (1993). An interesting survey of women's texts produced during the Romantic period from an American feminist perspective, which is particularly focused on the social sphere.

Toril Moi, *Sexual/Textual Politics* (1985). Moi's study categorizes feminist theories according to national schools of thought, which shows the philosophical basis for each basic kind (British, American, French). However, the broad strokes of her analysis are generally more helpful for understanding the foundations of feminist thought, while the individual treatments of texts and theories vary in usefulness.

Chapter 2

Women and Politics:
Writing Revolution

Figure 2 "Cossack Spencer Parisian Full Dress," engraving, *La Belle Assemblée; or Bell's Court and Fashionable Magazine* (1807)

You tell me that the court treasons rendered the massacres of the 10th August necessary. None of those imputed treasons are proved. They never wore the semblance of probability – The accusers are the judges. Seborned witnesses and forged papers are easily procured, where no one dares, perhaps even wishes, to detect their fallacy . . . Politics are almost as much the general theme here as with you.
Anna Seward to Helen Maria Williams, January 17, 1793

This chapter is about women and politics, yet Romantic studies has traditionally considered politics to be the preserve of the great male writers of the period. One way to understand this state of affairs and to broach our topic at the same time is to consider the recent critical attention that has been increasingly focused on how women's lives were affected by the division of the social and political world into public and private halves. In broad terms, "the public" is associated with the generally masculine domain of political debate, legislation, and social order; "the private" is associated with the feminine domain of family, home, and hearth. The way women interacted in these two spheres can be illustrated by two extreme examples: the domestic situations of home and love depicted in Austen's novels versus the court situations of Queen Charlotte, wife of George III, or of her French contemporary Queen Marie Antoinette. To a far greater extent than any real woman of the period, Austen's heroines experience life within the privacy of the home; public affairs – politics, business, war – have relevance only in how they affect the men in these heroines' lives. Charlotte and Marie Antoinette represent the opposite possibility as women belonging to the public world of politics, intrigue, court ritual, and gossip columns, a world that made their home life public.

The London Times, for instance, kept daily tabs on the British queen's and princesses' health, attendance at parties and balls, and dress. Charlotte could use this public gaze to advantage because it supported her own efforts to present the royal family as domestic and exemplary, and her efforts were, in part, aimed at making her own appearance in public seem less unusual, more like an icon of the privately feminine. Fanny Burney (1752–1840), whose novels deeply influenced Austen (her first novel, *Evelina*, made her literary reputation when she was 26), served as a lady-in-waiting to Charlotte as a young woman, and her diary records the painful restrictions enforced on Charlotte's retinue. Such care was necessary to ensure the appearance of a domestic purity in the court ladies' behavior, allowing no hint of scandal, and effectively countering through appearance the very real and uncontrollable sexual intrigues that were part of court life. Burney entered the post with her own expectations of public domesticity: "I am *married*, my dearest Susan – I look upon it in that light . . . What then remains but to make the best wife in my power?" (letter to her sister, July 17, 1786). Marie Antoinette was less concerned with the public interpretation of her behavior, with the result that Parisian scandal sheets began manufacturing "news" about her intimate life that created a public image of her as monstrous. She quickly became viewed as a woman whose participation in the public world of government and politics was "reported" to cause sexual perversions in her and a desire to dominate others, including her royal husband (see Hunt, 1992). The manufacture of this scandal resulted from the belief that the power available in the public sphere, which men use to legislate and judiciously control, only feeds women's natural greed for sexual excess and power. In the private sphere, accordingly, men's domestic role as master of the home was supposed to keep women's natural urges under control, a belief Charlotte's carefully circumscribed behavior supports. While men participate in both spheres, Marie Antoinette's alleged behavior shows that women should not.

Here we see the representation of both literary and historical women reduced to the simplest terms. Women did find it possible to complicate their domestic lives with politics if only through reading, and with business, especially through writing. But the concept of this simple division between the private as the appropriate place for women, and the public as the place that makes women monstrous, became increasingly accepted as the representative norm. This view of life stemmed from middle-class ways of thinking, diminishing the aristocratic and royal woman's role in the public world to one of a simply more visible privacy, while eliminating the working- and servant-class woman's role from notice by absorbing it into the workings of the home. When Austen's Mr Collins in *Pride and Prejudice* makes the mistake of thinking that one of the Bennet girls had cooked the dinner they were consuming, Mrs Bennet is mortified that he believes she has no servants. But when Darcy's aristocratic aunt, Lady de Bourgh enters the novel, her power has been so reduced from having any public effect that she can only assert it, like Queen Charlotte, through a strict control of the domestic behavior and conversation that is also the middle-class Mrs Bennet's province.

It is important for us to understand that if such a strict division between public and private for women orders historical and fictional representation, the reality was that both spheres could and did exert pressure on each other, particularly during times of political upheaval such as the French Revolution. France was close enough geographically and through historical connection that its political unrest was of great interest to Britain. Its democratic ideas, at least initially, made citizenship available to everyone regardless of class or gender. Such concepts forcibly collapsed the middle-class view of a public and private divide, since a woman citizen must make her home and family life an active part of political activity. Even those who were content to think only of domestic cares sported with the public sphere through dress fashions. France provided early revolutionary influences, Napoleonic ones, such as Josephine Bonaparte's famous empire waist style, and later ones, such as the "Cossack Spencer Parisian Full Dress" of 1807 depicted in figure 2. But British women who wanted to engage others in thinking and writing about these dramatic changes in social ideas found themselves compelled to move purposefully across the divide between the private and public of their own world. For many, this involved the ordinary activities of reading newspapers and writing letters about reported events, as Anna Seward does in the epigraph to this chapter. For other women, it meant an escalation of such activities into pamphlet writing, which were often written as letters but published in order to influence public opinion. Such political pamphlets, therefore, became part of the public world of political activity in a way that the familiar letter was not.

Nevertheless, it is the letter, or rather the idea of the letter, that provided a vehicle for women's political expression. Because political thought is one of the hallmarks of the male Romantics, it is necessary that we consider women's similar engagement. The main focus of this chapter is to view how, despite the constraints put on their involvement by different forms of representation, women Romantics were indeed involved in politics, and on a larger scale than a traditional definition of politics would allow us to see. The letter is a form of communication that crosses the divide between private and public, between a single reader and an audience of readers; the very informality of letter writing makes it unnecessary for the author to be an authoritative source. Therefore, letters between friends, pamphlets and treatises written in epistle form, letters circulated or actually published, proved to be women's route to politics. Men also used the letter form, as in Joseph Priestley's *Letters to the Right Hon. Edmund Burke* (1791) or William Wordsworth's "A Letter to the Bishop of Landoff" (composed 1793), but usually for direct attacks on another's publication, and certainly much less often than women did. We need to examine how women exploited the letter as a vehicle not just to respond to another's publication but to win a public voice in the first place. We can then gain a better idea of how women thought about politics, what constituted political and even revolutionary

53

writing, and how women put such writing into practice when the early radical years of the Romantic period gave way to a more conservative time.

First, let us turn to some well-known examples of Romantic women writers who used letters to transform their political activity into acceptable literary material. Mary Wollstonecraft and Helen Maria Williams both went to Paris to witness revolutionary activities for themselves. Wollstonecraft gave her political analysis of events two years after returning in her *Historical and Moral View of the French Revolution* (1794). This work is a political analysis that chooses to use the forms of philosophy and history rather than the letter. By contrast, Williams engaged public opinion by immediately transcribing her feelings, sensations, and observations as she witnessed the momentous happenings of her first visit to Paris in 1790, publishing these along with anecdotes of the revolution in her *Letters Written in France in the Summer of 1790*. The very titles of these two works indicate the retrospective and interpretive intention of the first, and the attempt to capture the present moment as travelogue or news reportage in the second. Both of these approaches form events into an appealing historical narrative for readers at home, readers who cannot imagine the large-scale turbulence, disruption of everyday activities, excitement and fear experienced by the French people.

Wollstonecraft's is the more intellectual and politically motivated of the two works, while Williams attempts to hide her radical sympathies in a more emotionally and rhetorically accessible text. Several factors help here, and they are instructive for seeing how women writers could gain an audience and a public voice for such unfeminine subjects as revolution. Williams's first important choice is that of the familiar letter, a form associated with the female voice. Wollstonecraft's choice of political history, on the other hand, is a decisive one of a male form associated with the male voice; the epistle form provides Williams with a ready audience, whereas Wollstonecraft's audience is delimited by her genre choice. Secondly, Williams courts her audience, particularly her male readers, by presenting herself as a sentimental tourist, unauthorized but observant and sensitive to her own emotions and to details of interest. For instance, her correspondence often focuses on subjects dealing with the loss of privacy suffered by victims of the revolution, her sympathy for these victims stemming from her self-representation as a private person. Finally, Williams invokes the literary genre of romance to construct sentimental tales of people's lives. Strung together, letter after letter, these tales combine with the letter writer's own story of her travels

54

to form what Gary Kelly calls "a romance journey," thus making the *Letters* even more an appropriate production for a woman writer (Kelly, 1993: 39).

Taking the stance of the tourist whose travelogue describes events not normally suitable for women's language, and interpreting public events through the romance of private individuals, Williams's letters effectively broker the divide between public and private, allowing her to depict herself as domestically minded and feminine while reporting on political injustice. Wollstonecraft's book, by contrast, is intentionally public. Its political analysis and critique assume the authority associated with the masculine judiciousness of the public sphere. This breach of the private–public divide left Wollstonecraft vulnerable to misinterpretations of her person, adding to her already controversial reputation. Eventually Williams, too, succumbed to the dangers of a public voice despite the seeming privacy of the letter form; unable to maintain the fiction of a sentimentalist, she, like Wollstonecraft, became vulnerable to the equation of her private life with her public or published appearance. Thus, when women Romantics' interest in politics pushed them beyond the privacy of their own circles, they faced the same charge of transgression that Marie Antoinette experienced. Although women's sense of urgency about the political did not diminish under this threat, their willingness to speak out publicly, except through literary works that obscured their real political intent, did decline once early Romantic figures such as Wollstonecraft, Williams, Mary Hays, and others were disparaged.

One of the main interests of this chapter will be to compare Williams and Wollstonecraft before they lost their ability to persuade readers politically, and to contrast them with Anna Seward. Because she was a poet who refused to publish on politics, her effective use of letters to engage politics in the private sphere is instructive. First I need to introduce each of these writers before proceeding with the body of the discussion. All three writers were active in the earliest years of the Romantic period, all were interested in politics and the public sphere, and all enthusiastically supported the early phase of the French Revolution because of the possibilities its reforms held out to women.

Helen Maria Williams was born in London in 1762 (died Paris 1827), but was brought up by her Scots mother in Wales after her father's death. In 1781 her mother moved the family to London. With the help of her mentor, Dr Andrew Kippis, Williams met Samuel Johnson, Fanny Burney, Elizabeth Montagu, Anna Seward, and Benjamin Franklin, and later members of the London Dissenting and radical circles. In the summer of 1790 her French tutor Madame du Fossé invited Williams and her sister to visit Paris to personally witness the activities of the Girondists, the result of which was the first volume of the *Letters*. She continued this format of public "correspondence" in a series of volumes of *Letters from France* (1790–6) that constructs a sympathetic account of the revolution's republican goals and achievements up to 1795. She established a Paris salon in 1793 where expatriate Jacobin sympathizers met, including Thomas Paine, Mary Wollstonecraft, and Gilbert Imlay, and she became friendly with the Girondist Madame Roland (executed in 1793). She also had a long-term affair with the Unitarian leader John Hurford Stone. And, like Wollstonecraft, she associated the early struggle for rights in the revolution with a concurrent opportunity for women's rights to develop.

Anna Seward (1742–1809), the oldest of the three women and the most domestically oriented, led a privileged life as a poet and intellectual with her father, the Canon of Lichfield. She was famous early for her odes on the explorer Captain Cook and the patriot Major André, and later for her novel in verse *Louisa* (1784), her *Original Sonnets* (1799), and her contributions to *The Gentleman's Magazine*. She was friends with Erasmus Darwin (grandfather of Charles Darwin), the poet William Hayley, and Williams, and knew the arts patron Lady Miller, the intellectuals Lady Eleanor Butler and Sarah Ponsonby, Richard Lovell Edgeworth (father of the Irish novelist Maria Edgeworth), and Samuel Johnson. She convinced Sir Walter Scott to edit her collected poems after her death (*Poetical Works*, 1810), and although he decided against doing the same for her large manuscript of letters (which she had already collected and edited herself), they were published by Archibald Constable in 1811. Seward's letters reveal, even more than her poetry, her extensive circle of friends, her intellectual life, her literary critical abilities, and her sense of herself as a public figure.

Mary Wollstonecraft (1759–1797), the most famous of the three, was also the brightest and most ambitious of these women. Although her first books were an educational tract and a reader for girls, even these early publications revealed her interest in women's condition, and in the political causes of this condition. All of her subsequent political and philosophical works, including the *Vindication of the Rights of Men* (1791), the *Vindication of the Rights of Woman* (1792), and her *Historical and Moral View of the French Revolution* (1794), dwell on the social and political condition of the individual. The last two also engage her thinking about gender politics. Because of Wollstonecraft's outspoken style and impassioned rhetoric, and her affairs with Gilbert Imlay (hinted at in her popular travelogue *Letters Written during a Short Residence in*

Sweden, Norway and Denmark, 1796) and with the philosopher William Godwin (whom she finally married when pregnant with Mary Godwin Shelley), Wollstonecraft's life came to be interpreted after her early death as a version of the inappropriately public life of Marie Antoinette. This public interpretation of her as scandalous and monstrous began with reactions against her radical publications and "masculine" views during her lifetime, but escalated through Godwin's unintentional exposé of her in his *Memoir* (1798).

The combination of political idealism and a public voice was dangerous for Williams too, and for six months in 1793 she was imprisoned in Luxembourg Palace by Robespierre. Because Williams chose to live in France for the rest of her life, to endure its political vicissitudes whatever the cost, and because she made such strategically astute choices as a writer, she becomes a centering figure for this chapter. However, it is not feminist concerns, nor the difficulty of a woman writer's life, but politics – the French Revolution as radicalism on foreign ground – that draws these three women together through the public sphere, utopian idealism, and letters.

Besides her *Letters*, Williams's published correspondence included her edition of the *Political and Confidential Correspondence of Louis XVI* (1803), a forgery she believed to be genuine, and *Letters on the Events which have Passed in France since the Restoration* (1819). Although she wrote one novel and translated another, produced an important travelogue on the influence of French politics on the Swiss, *Tour in Switzerland* (1798), and was originally known for her poetry, it is Williams's letters that make up the largest part of her published works. Mary Wollstonecraft's *Letters Written during a Short Residence in Sweden, Norway and Denmark* (1796) is her most obvious use of the letter form to translate private experience into public discourse, but she also used letters to introduce her most important works. Her first *Vindication* is, in fact, framed as a letter: *A Vindication of the Rights of Men, in a Letter to the Right Hon. Edmund Burke*. But most women writers who thought about publishing letters either wrote private letters with an eye toward later publication, as Anna Seward did to be a retrospect of her own life, or for circulation through their social circles as an unofficial "publication." When Seward wrote her own political pronouncement on revolution, and her response to another by a friend ("To Mr Courtenay, on his pamphlet entitled Philosophical Reflections on the late Revolutions in France"), she did not publish them as pamphlets. Instead, she circulated them as letters among friends and then included them with her manuscript of letters for Constable. Her use of letters was for immediate effect within her own circle, rather than the widespread influence both Williams and Wollstonecraft strove for. If a person were famous enough, a relative or friend would sell or edit their letters after their death, since the reading public was hungry for the personal insights and high-minded meditations such correspondence presumably contained. Thus Williams clearly combines Seward's restricted approach with Wollstonecraft's outspokenness to achieve the best of both: she uses social acceptance of letters as a preferred genre for women's writing in order to create a public voice for herself.

Williams maintains the necessary fiction for letter writing in her first volume of 1790 by entitling it *Letters from France ... to a Friend in England*, this pretense of a specified reader being widely used in novels, poems, and philosophical tracts. But what is less obvious is that she adopts the stuff of letters – relating experiences, explaining social connections, describing scenes, comparing the known to the new – to her reportage of events whose interpretation she has already decided beforehand. That is, Williams turns letter writing into history writing, most notably in the eight volumes of *Letters* where she focuses on the Girondist party's vision of a true republic. But Williams's use of history differs from that of other women writers we will encounter here because she is not overtly committing herself to history as such. Although she is indeed turning events into history, her narrator remains in the immediacy of the present moment, and the present has more to do with news, as in familiar letters and in newspapers. By using a writing style closer to that of newspaper reportage of the day (which was more subjective, more anecdotal, and less concerned with accuracy than we are used to today), Williams conveys more of the real experience, both physical and emotional, than an objective history could. Her letters were also easily transported, and several individual letters were printed in *The Gentleman's Magazine*, an indication of the breadth of her audience and the enjoyment her letters gave.

Moreover, Williams manages to encapsulate the historical moment she commits to writing, almost by virtue of taking on its emotional intensity in her own life. Such an adaptation of the pulse of the times to a writer's own sense of self actually means incorporating a combination of the public with the private, a significant feature of several of the great Romantics' lives, such as those of Wordsworth, Byron, and Shelley. We can understand this feature better if we understand what lies behind Williams's political emotion. Historian Peter Gay (1966) subtitles one of his books on the Enlightenment *The Rise of Modern Paganism*, with "paganism" a term describing the Enlightenment thinkers' ability to combine scientific thought with some belief in a divine power. This more objective mode of thought continued to inform the initial years of the Romantic period, but struggled with the recently embraced and competing subjective belief in the power of emotions. Many thinkers, then, were already trying to combine subjective with objective ways of understanding the world, but the French Revolution pushed this endeavor further. Many saw the revolution as the logical outcome of the discoveries and teachings of the Enlightenment, but it also sought to replace organized religion and crippling superstition with nationalistic fervor (political science empowered by emotional force), thus offering idealists like Williams a new "religion" to embrace. While many in Britain found the revolution to be a false religion after the Terror, some – like Shelley and Byron – continued to believe in its promises; Williams refused to see its negatives and continued to hope for a resulting utopian society. That she felt an almost religious fervor for the republican project is clear from the very start, when she describes the festival she witnessed to celebrate the fall of the Bastille one day after her arrival in Paris:

> The night before . . . the Te Deum was performed at the church of Notre Dame . . . The Overture, which preceded the Te Deum was simple and majestic; the music, highly expressive, had the power of electrifying the hearers: and near the conclusion of the piece, the composer, by artful discords, produced a melancholy emotion; and then, by exciting ideas of trouble and inquietude, prepared the mind for a recitative which affected the audience in a very powerful manner. . . . (Williams, 1790: I, letter i)

Here we see the religiosity of the setting and the impressive aural component being manipulated to affect the audience's senses on a large scale. By politicizing the components of religious ritual, the orchestration of this event transforms an evoked religious fervor into patriotic fervor. Williams captures the sensual effects of such public drama and shows her readers how radical enthusiasm is created. It is an easy step from there to imagine how such feeling can then be translated into an actual transformation, a democratization, of the public sphere. Williams's ability to translate emotion into politics for her readers at home through the eyes of a sentimental tourist gave her letters a persuasiveness that Wollstonecraft's hard logic in her *History* lacks. Her own enthusiasm was not only embodied in her letters, but readers came to identify this enthusiasm and fervor with Williams herself as a private individual as if she were not intentionally revealing herself in a public way through her letters. Williams's deliberate identification of her political enthusiasm with her person was a strategy that aided her literary popularity, but eventually it backfired when her private life and her feminism showed her to be no sentimentalist but an active participant in the political scene.

Important literary figures like Horace Walpole and Hester Piozzi withdrew their support of Williams because of her feminist principles and her personal application of them to marital relations through her affair with Stone. But they were even more direct in their attack on Wollstonecraft who criticized the institution of marriage and who openly lived with two men before finally marrying Godwin. Hannah More (1745–1833), another friend of Walpole's and an influential anti-feminist, agreed with the criticisms of Wollstonecraft. More was a highly popular author whose greatest influence was felt in her *Cheap Repository* tracts (an interesting variation on the letter-pamphlet), begun in 1795 to provide a strong counter to Thomas Paine whose revolutionary views were feared to be disaffecting the lower classes. However, More was not only strongly conservative but also an Evangelical, leading her to take part in the Sunday School movement. This reform movement sought to improve the condition of the poor through literacy, morality, and religion, rather than through increasing their civic and political rights or their working conditions. Evangelicals not only fought the individual-centered theories of the rights of man, but of the rights of woman too. As Warren Roberts (1979) points out, even though More's views on the education of women were not far different from Wollstonecraft's, she feared the instability that feminism threatened to bring to marriage and gender relations. She wrote to Walpole that she absolutely refused to read *Vindication of the Rights of Woman*:

> I have been pestered to read *Rights of Women* [sic], but I am invincibly resolved not to do it . . . there is something fanatic and absurd in the very title . . . So many women are fond of government, I suppose, because they are not fit for it. To be unstable and capricious, I really think, is but too characteristic of our sex; and there is perhaps no animal so indebted to subordination for its good behaviour as woman. (quoted in Roberts, 1979: 185)

It is clear from More's criticism that to speak about politics, as women like Wollstonecraft and Williams publicly did, or as women did privately in their letters to each other, required of these writers a series of transgressions. These transgressions involve the seemingly stable boundaries that define a culture (as in, men go to war, women stay at home) and the interacting and changeable boundaries of social space (sometimes women are required to participate in war). Women writing during the Romantic period were just as influenced as men writers were by the changes taking place in cultural and social boundaries, but they needed to discover ways to negotiate these boundaries that would not endanger their precarious position in the public sphere. Women's difficulties with making themselves public stemmed, as it does even now, from a common perception that women are psychologically and politically conservative because their most basic instincts are oriented toward the preservation of the home, the family, and the future of the child. The transgressions women writers had to commit in order to publish, and the ways they individually chose to mask, justify, or apologize for those transgressions, color our reception of their writing, and have influenced us to perceive their politics as essentially conservative. That is, we read their political thought as so conservative in its essence that it is not actually there, and as non-political because it appears to reside in the domestic sphere of home and family, separated from the legislative and properly political public sphere. Women writers' transgressions, even when politically motivated, are viewed as private ones, the transgressive or deviant move out of the home into public view. It is hard for us to shake ourselves out of this way of thinking, hard for us to imagine that women of the late eighteenth century could be embroiled in the passions that fueled the French Revolution. Even when we cannot ignore that Mary Wollstonecraft wrote books about the rights of the common man and the events of the French Revolution, we focus on her book about the rights of women in their homes as her proper material, her most important work. What considerations about how women thought about politics during this period should we take as a guide, then, and how should we define politics in relation to the issues women defined for themselves as political?

This chapter places women writers in their social context by examining their private and public writing about politics. "Politics," as I am using it here, does not refer to local issues of government, but to the larger issues that seized the imagination during this period. These are the French Revolution during the radical 1790s, and the consequences of the revolution that focused the relation between the state and the family during the reactionary years of the Napoleonic Wars and their aftermath. These were issues of particular interest to women, who were intensely curious about a revolution that sought from the outset to reassign meaning and value to the public and private spheres of life in old regime society. We can discover how women related to the promise and threat of this new division from their responses, whether as a middle-class

liberal concern for the individual (Williams and Seward show this tendency), or as a republican concern for society as a whole (first associated
with radicals like Wollstonecraft and Hays, but later with conservatives
like Felicia Hemans and Jane Austen). Although women's approach to
political matters was impeded by the few ways in which their interest
could be expressed, they did, nevertheless, write extensively about politics. We need to treat such writing as an important aspect of Romantic
women's literary production.

Letters and the Maternal: Political Metaphors

Private letters between individuals provided a convenient form of communication and an approved one for women even when writing about
public matters. As Roger Sales (1994) has noted in writing about Austen,
letters were often used by women to incorporate public news from
the papers into a private medium. While this transaction from public to
private often concerned issues of the private sphere like weddings, scan-
dals, births, and deaths, the method used was not substantially different
when the issues were of revolution and war, especially if, as for Austen,
war meant sending news of her two naval brothers, their whereabouts,
ships, and promotions ("Frank has rec'd his appointment on Board the
Captain John Gore, commanded by the Triton . . ."; "we have just had
another letter from our dear Frank. – It is to you, very short, written from
Larnica in Cyprus . . . He wrote a few days before to you from Alexan-
dria by the Mercury"; "As Charles will equally go to the E. Indies, my
uncle cannot be really uneasy, & my aunt may do what she likes with her
frigates"). Whatever the news, it gained in opinion and interpretation
what it might lose in fact, so that news was often not far from gossip or
rumor. This translation of news into private gossip retains a level of
sincerity very much like the authoritative tone of Austen's novelistic
narrators, whose opinions and gossiping provide the basis for narrative
knowledge (see Spacks, 1985, for an analysis of the social and literary
uses of gossip).

It is also very much like the reportage in newspapers of the day. *The
London Times*, for instance, is striking in how few real facts it provides,
particularly on important subjects. Articles dealing with current events
such as the Parisian revolt or the Napoleonic Wars have to vie for space
with the shipping news and court gossip columns on the one page
relegated to "news." Often the news is sent by a correspondent unused to
making official reports, such as British officers stationed with their troops

in preparation for doing battle with Napoleon, knowing only what they can gather within their limited purview. Other reports are combinations of fact, rumor, and anecdote appearing closer to fictional accounts; or, by contrast, are dense with facts, but lacking in any overview that would put the facts into a usable perspective. Reports of any kind often lack a follow-up story so that the factual appears fragmentary. In this context, gossip provides the fabric that stretches between such fragments to make sense of the whole.

When letters take on the role of knitting together fact and gossip, fragmentary knowledge and an interpretive perspective, they bridge the public and private in a way that can prove powerful for women writers who turn them to a literary use. But letters can also prove dangerous when they are misinterpreted, misdirected, fall into the wrong hands, or are lost. Mary Favret has written about the public and fictional role of letters; she shows the ambiguous status of a document that, once sent, is dissociated from its writer, becoming open to new interpretations and overwritings (see Favret, 1993: ch. 1). She also explores the public uses of a document that we associate with the private and the individual, both in real life and in fictional representation, especially in epistolary fiction. The letter's origin and associations mark it as feminine or as coming from a feminized space:

> Throughout the eighteenth century, the letter's ability to define and confine personal experience had already been subject to a centripetal force which carried the private into the public realm, offering the individual's most intimate self for mass consumption. Epistolary fiction invaded, then shattered, the closed areas of home, family and personal identity. . . . Meanwhile, other fictions of the letter as a "feminine" genre emerged to contest the belief that a letter expressed only private, individual desires. (Favret, 1993: 12–13)

Thus the "feminine" or non-threatening aspect of letters could be used to cloak their real purpose. For instance, the zeal of Correspondence Societies for the promotion of revolution in France and reform at home, as Favret indicates, shows one way in which letters could originate in the social rather than the domestic. Letters coming from the communal rather than the individual could thus intend a public effect even though kept to the privacy of its members. That these letters were perceived by the British government as products of dangerous conspiracies to overthrow king and parliament shows not only how tenuous such gendered fictions were, but also how difficult it was for groups as well as for private individuals to control who reads a letter, and how. Once sent, the letter is in effect "published." It is therefore a woman's easiest and most approved method of writing to others; at the same time, the letter's easy publication makes it less stable, more open to hostile interpretation both of it and its sender. Despite all the difficulties of using the letter to publish, whether that of factual control, lack of interpretive control, or merely the letter's lesser literary status, it remained the most plausible outlet for women writers. And the association between women and letters in real life carries over to fictional heroines, whose plots and narratives are often determined by letters and their reception, thus re-affirming the feminine association of the epistolary form.

One advantage of the feminine letter is that, when employed as a fictional form, the author can use letters to tell the story in the characters' own words. Austen uses this device in her early epistolary works *Love and Friendship*, *Lady Susan*, and in the early versions of *Sense and Sensibility* and *Pride and Prejudice*. Because these narratives contain nothing but letters, no intervening narrator or dialogue, the gossip of the letters is the only way news can be conveyed, and they are the heroine's only avenue for telling her story and making sense of her limited world. This situation is not too far removed from real-life letter writing, which, as Sales (1994) notes, is the activity by which something is made of women's boring and often empty lives. In order to turn nothing into something to tell, and in order to assert control over apparently meaning-less activities, letter writers inventively work with their materials to produce something worth reading. Nevertheless, it is dangerous to read such letters as apolitical. Austen, who masterfully manipulated her infor-mation in her fiction to critique and mock social situations and persons whom she could not control in real life, has until recently been con-sidered an inferior letter writer, capable only of gossip (Sales, 1994: 43). Because she chooses not to discuss her art or political matters at length with her correspondents, her real-life letters do not have the same critical value assigned to the letters of Keats or Byron, yet they nevertheless maintain attacks on social issues affecting women's lives. Like her novels, Austen's letters are concerned with the social experiences that can lead to misery and unnecessary poverty of spirit or restricted experience, or a better social construction of balanced and productive relations. It is our mistake to view her comments as unproductive gossip rather than politi-cal critique; Austen exploits the capacity of letters to disguise critique even in her non-epistolary novels. Other writers agreed with Austen's principles, using epistolary fiction to explore the causal and changeable relation between public and private, as well as imaginative solutions to current social problems.

One such writer, whose epistolary fictions were popular several decades before Austen was writing, was Sarah Scott (1723–1795), the sister
of Bluestocking Elizabeth Montagu and, after a bad marriage and separation, a philanthropist. Her novel *A Description of Millenium Hall*
(1762; see 1995 edn) reflects the same concerns Williams shows in her
initial publishing choice, by announcing its author as "a Gentleman on
his Travels." The novel itself responds to the kind of political thought
that propelled the American and French revolutions by proposing a
utopian society where women can escape the evils of patriarchy. In its
utopian theme, its epistolary form, its depiction of moral and immoral
homes, and its use of a male narrator to disguise the woman writer's
identity, this novel anticipates the way subsequent Romantic women
writers chose to represent the consequences of dividing the public and
private. *Millenium Hall* depicts a female utopia in which all the dire
problems that would soon give rise to the revolution in France are solved
at the local and private level through the charitable projects of a community of women. Scott's novel voices the rational and more public ideas of
the Bluestocking circle, but she also uses the novel in a more personal
way to portray a social alternative to harsh or punitive marriages such as
she herself had suffered. The novel's utopia resolves both the economic
inequities that would lead to ever greater class and wealth differences,
and the legal inequities that allow women to suffer in their husbands'
homes. In other words, she critiques the role of the legal, political, and
economic bodies of the public sphere as they intrude upon the private or
domestic sphere, and then solves the problem by eliminating them from
the picture.

Scott presents her argument in a series of letters by a gentleman,
framing her radical text with an acceptable, but also approving, male
gaze. Because she is proposing a radical society of women only, Scott
cannot use Williams's later solution of a female narrator because her
radical plan demands male authority. To cushion the authority she
imputes to her narrator, she does not allow him to reside with the women
of the hall even though he approves their society as Williams approves
radical Paris. This exclusion is emphasized by the fact that this narrator
is not the novel's only male authority. A young friend accompanies him,
Lamont, who is traveling to finish his education; as the stereotype of the
hero figure, we watch Lamont as he interacts with the ladies, waiting and
hoping for him to fall in love. Instead, he becomes the Romantic figure
who seeks knowledge and wisdom, and this is an education the ladies of
Millenium Hall undertake. As Lamont learns to appreciate the female
vision of the Hall, he becomes the link between the male frame repre-

sented by the gentleman narrator and the female center of the utopian society. In what will become a Romantic convention, the Romantic hero bridges the external social patriarchy and the internal feminine ideal (which can reside in nature, in art, or in an alternative society). Yet Scott's early use of this device is not to transcend a division of public and private, as it will be for later Romantic poets, but to put forward her social plan as if through the authority of the male. Moreover, because the letters, and thus the narrative, are transferred through the male narrator and substantiated by Lamont, this novel is not implicated in gossip as Austen's novels and letters are. The anecdotes related have a sincerity and authority to them unavailable to female narration – they are not news but "fact," authorizing the fiction Scott has devised.

This use of the male figure or template is the general case with women writers who engage political topics. Even radical thinkers like Wollstonecraft do not propose discarding male models, but instead critique and even revise them as potentially stronger methods for effecting change. These conceptual male models include: the idea of the nation (and utopian societies), the maternal (as women's only accepted social role), and revolutionary thinking. Letters, as we will see, play a role in women's intervention in each of these models because they can represent the private experience or the public voice, or both at once. Part of our thinking about letters as a vehicle that crosses the division between public and private has to include thinking about the domestic as a place not just of privacy, but of family. Thinking about family, particularly in terms of women writers and politics, means we need to understand how motherhood was understood, and how it might change in a utopian or revolutionary society. In the middle-class perspective, maternity produces gentlemen and ladies, but in a radical society, maternity is somewhat dangerous because it produces citizens.

British class divisions were supposed to maintain the kind of social norms that the French Revolution attacked. For instance, "gentleman" should refer to male members of the gentry, and thus to those who represent social order and who take part in its maintenance through the public sphere (by engaging in political debate, running for office, acting as magistrate). But the intermarriage between the increasingly wealthy middle class and the sometimes newly impoverished gentry and lower ranks of the aristocracy meant that "gentleman" could refer to a whole range of the male population that could see itself as representing the ranks responsible for social and political order. Their ladies were responsible in turn for bringing up new generations of gentlemen. In contrast, in revolutionary states, people are ideally no longer subjects of a kingdom ranked according to their class status, but classless citizens of a nation; that is, citizens are "leveled." In France, where class divisions were kept absolute (unlike the British practice of intermarriage and thus class betterment), the leveling of classes was the only quick way to reform the old class distinctions that were leading to the two extremes of incredible wealth and desperate poverty. The term "citizen" runs across class divisions, meaning that all men participate in politics, social order, and the writing of laws. From the British perspective, the status quo of law and order in such a case would be impossible to maintain, and social order would become subject to political currents more rapidly than is healthy. This is the subject of the exchange between Williams and Seward excerpted in our opening epigraph: "None of those imputed treasons are proved . . . The accusers are the judges. Seborned witnesses and forged papers are easily procured." Seward believes that leveling has got out of hand, giving legal justice little chance. When the French Revolution had degenerated into just this kind of chaos, British writers and politicians began to depict the citizen-state as a kind of plague that could easily be spread across its borders to other nations. But, tellingly, when men used the metaphor it was always the depiction of a female plague, as in the illness of the mother country whose female body represents and incorporates the nation. The connection between political illness and the maternal is a male one. But women writers were quick to see that by claiming the positive relation of motherhood to nation and revolution, they would be able to write about politics in a way that could allow them to cross the private–public divide. Thus they could gain a particular access to political writing without having to resort to the epistolary form. Nevertheless, to embrace this connection was to encounter the many difficulties of its negative associations.

The idea of the "nation" to replace the idea of the "kingdom" is a growing notion in Europe during the late eighteenth century, especially in France. The society composed of male subjects could be turned into a nation of citizens, men with new political responsibility for determining the health and power of their state. Because women produce both subjects and citizens, the maternal as a concept also undergoes scrutiny during this period; in particular, the mother figure was used symbolically by the French to signal a new relation between the citizen and the state. But women writers in Britain came to understand that a political use of the maternal only makes the woman's identity as a mother vulnerable to a symbolic manipulation that can affect real social constraints on how women are represented and on how they may behave, and can make their identity as writers even more difficult.

This difficulty becomes clearer if we look at the conceptual model that organizes the difference between good mothers and bad mothers. If the mother is herself a lady and not a citizen, she can give birth to a son who has all the political privilege she does not. For men writers, this model does not pose a problem because the mother is equated with other fertile, nurturing, and inspiring female entities such as Nature. Because becoming a poet has long been understood as a form of birth, then the idea that the maternal thing (Nature) can produce an entitled person (man) seems an accurate one. But for women writers, the idea that a mother without rights can produce an entitled subject also means that she will not be able to educate or really control him; and it means that her female children can only be future mothers, without rights and without privilege. It is then difficult to conceive how a mother giving birth to a future mother could thereby be producing a poet or writer. It is also difficult to understand how the mother can actually produce the son who has the right to the public and to publication she does not. For writers like Mary Shelley the idea is literally monstrous, as she demonstrates with her creature made out of male parts and fitted together by a male scientist/creator in *Frankenstein.* For the same reasons, the idea of Nature as a mothering and birthing metaphor for poetic inspiration is horrifying to women writers. "Monstrous" is the same adjective used to describe women like Marie Antoinette who publicly act in too masculine or authoritative a manner, but here it refers to the inability to make a female (mother)-to-male (poet) model fit a female-to-female reality for creative writers. Thus the women in Shelley's novel – Frankenstein's mother, his wife, his servant, and the female he begins to piece together as an Eve for his male creature – must all die horrible deaths. They are all torn apart (quite literally in the case of the female creature) by the violence of the novel's metaphors for subjectivity and art.

Through the first few decades of the Romantic period women struggled with the difficulties of this concept, and there is some argument that Dorothy Wordsworth did not publish her poetry or write more of it because she could not reconcile the Nature–muse model (see Homans, 1980: ch. 2). However, later in the period both men and women writers began to feel the power of this model waning. Men writers tended to explore the new lack of confidence in a female Nature by traveling in order to experience other cultures, or by locating their inspiration in classical or oriental literature. For women writers, an easier way around this difficulty than travel or classicism could be borrowed from the

68

French idea of a "maternal nation." The appeal of this idea is that it takes the new conception of a country as a nation rather than a kingdom, as a society made up of citizens rather than subjects, and uses it to replace the "mother" part of the troubling Nature–muse model.

This is the tack Wollstonecraft takes when she insists in *The Rights of Woman* that until women are properly educated they will be poor wives and terrible mothers to the detriment of the nation. But the associations Wollstonecraft makes here between maternity and the nation itself are those familiar to the mid-1790s, political associations from which one could logically argue for reform of education, marriage laws, and so on. In the mid-1820s, however, poets like Felicia Hemans are writing of a far different association between maternity and nation, a metaphorical rather than logical representation, in which the nation is the mother. The difference between the earlier French idea of the maternal nation, and the later British idea of it, is that the French depicted their new revolutionary nation as one that nurtured and supported her children-citizens. That is, the new "mother" of the French nation actively provides the environment in which male citizens can work for the good of the society, and she even intrudes into the home to do it. The British depiction is that of a mother as old as Mother Nature, for whom one feels nostalgia rather than inspiration; unlike Nature herself, this mother supports the nation-state, but her children should be loyal to that state because they feel nostalgic loyalty to her. She is a passive figure who does not support or actively inspire, but who represents the hearth and home that are then associated with nation. She becomes a passive inspiration for those whose art also promotes the good of the nation, as Hemans does in poems like "The Homes of England" (1828; Wu, 1997: 574–5).

Whatever strategy women writers used to tackle the difficult relation between maternity – women's "natural" condition – and politics, they found using letter writing in addition to their other writing strategies helpful because its feminine associations made a "natural" outlet for them. If they could not revise the muse–poet model, they could resort to this other model of the natural to work out their opinions and beliefs.

Revolution as a Frame of Mind

The relation between women and revolutionary politics is most discoverable as a relation between mother and nation. Less discernible is women's role in making revolution possible. We need to discover exactly what revolutionary thinking meant to women Romantics in terms of gender and motherhood, and against the larger context of radical politics, before we can assess women's role in political thought.

Gary Kelly argues in *Women, Writing, and Revolution, 1790–1827* (1993: vi) that women writers "initiated the feminization of culture and civil society in the cultural revolution and the Revolution debate." By cultural revolution, Kelly means the process by which the middle classes wrested power away from the court and gentry, reconfiguring society around their professional and investment interests. Aiding them was the growing print system (periodicals, cheaper books, and rising literacy) and the resulting spread of ideas to those not able to attend upper-class discussions (the salons) or middle-class coffee-house debates. As Kelly points out, the shift of power from the upper to the middle classes was in itself revolutionary, and it became important in the print media to mask this shift through images of nature, particularly female nature. Kelly isolates three tropes (or language-created images that are powerful enough to be widely shared and used) that work in this way: "woman," representing middle-class subjectivity; "Nature," in opposition to the old culture that needed to be overturned; and "national culture," as a way to create a feeling of unity about this renovation. But clearly the concept of the "mother" and the "Romantic child" are equally important and effective cultural images. All but one of these images are feminized through their relation to the mother. The only one not so related, "national culture" or the "nation," does undergo a process of feminization by those women writers who take advantage of the print media to express their perturbation or excitement at the events on the Continent. The resulting trope becomes what I call here "maternal nationalism." In these images we see how the Romantic fascination with the interior and with privacy as feminized spaces is reflected outward, transformed into what Kelly calls the "feminization of culture." How women writers think about revolution, then, becomes one way to witness women's willing implication of themselves in the political milieu created and sustained by these powerful tropes.

An exchange of British political pamphlets on revolutionary events led Williams to engage in the political fervor that sent her to Paris, and led Seward, at least initially, to support her. Richard Price, who begins the pamphlet exchange, was a Dissenting minister and co-founder of the Unitarian Society. As a Dissenter, Price was interested in education, governmental representation, and all other issues that were formative in shifting British culture from an aristocratic and monarchic one to a more democratic one. As Price notes in his *Discourse on the Love of our Country*, the worst grievance that he finds with British politics is the lack of representation for those not of the propertied classes. "The inadequateness of our representation . . . is, in truth, our fundamental grievance," but little will be done until, "some great abuse of power again provokes our resentment – or perhaps till the acquisition of a pure and equal representation by other countries (while we are mocked with the shadow) kindles our shame." The "discourse" that lies behind Price's belongs to Jean-Jacques Rousseau, whose First and Second Discourses contrast the natural man with the discontented civilized man; Rousseau's "discourses" led to his 1762 work *The Social Contract*, where he imagines a new relation between citizen and state.

Price's *Discourse* was written in 1789, nearly 30 years after Rousseau's, and shortly after the storming of the Bastille in Paris and the subsequent assault on Versailles. It was written first as a sermon, and it demonstrates Price's continuing support of rights-based revolutions such as that of the American colonies and of France. It also demonstrates the early Jacobin or revolutionary faith in the utopian society that the uprising in France would supposedly make possible. Price was friends with Joseph Priestley (scientist and discoverer of oxygen), Anna Laetitia Barbauld, Benjamin Franklin, and influential with Samuel Rodgers and Helen Maria Williams. The circle to which these radicals and intellectuals belonged included the radical publisher Joseph Johnson and his own circle, which included Mary Wollstonecraft, Henry Fuseli, Thomas Paine, William Godwin, and William Blake. Price's radical group opposed itself intellectually and politically to middle-class culture and ideas. As Dissenters and radicals, men and women without a claim or an interest in a property-based political system of rights and privileges, these activists supported the revolution in France. They urged British support of it because they saw the French effort (at least in its early stages) as a "natural" and uncorrupted effort of a society to spontaneously self-correct. This is the group that engaged in the pamphlet war that followed Price's *Discourse*, caused by *Reflections on the Revolution in France* (1790), Edmund Burke's defense of the monarchical state against Price's attack. Wollstonecraft's *A Vindication of the Rights of Men*, and later *Vindication of the Rights of Woman*, and Thomas Paine's *The Rights of Man* were only some of the resulting attacks on Burke that took up the banner of Price's original sermon.

What is interesting about Price's *Discourse*, when compared to the pamphlets that followed it, is his argument that a worry over individual representation is not a worry about the individual but about the country. He sees political representation as "this essential blessing" without which the country cannot function harmoniously, and it is the country and the populace's "love" for it that will both sustain national identity and, he implies, prevent destructive activity from taking place. The implication is a subtle one, since France's catastrophic 1789 summer activities had obviously impelled Price to write his sermon, and since "love" can be both a sustaining and a reforming emotion. But the phrase "or till some great abuse of power again provokes our resentment" allows his readers to understand that there is a power behind the populace that can turn love into hate, tolerance into change, reform into revolution. However, when Price exhorts "all ye friends of liberty" to "Be encouraged" a few pages later, the vehemence of "love" comes home: "Tremble oh ye oppressors of the world! Take warning all ye supporters of slavish governments and slavish hierarchies!" The "Love of our Country" suddenly has a proprietary ring which emphasizes the capacity of an under-represented people to rise up; hereafter, any discourse on such a love is free to dwell on the people rather than the country, and on the individual rather than the people at large. But also hereafter a discourse of nationalism is plausible, a discourse of the love of national identity (rather than of the kingdom or state) with its own sense of the love for a mother nation based on the individual's relation to that identity.

When Burke attacked Price publicly with his *Reflections*, he was contradicting his own earlier liberal and reformist leanings, his sympathy for the American and Irish struggles against British rule, and his friendship with Paine. Like many of the later Romantics who followed him, Burke discovered his own conservatism when he found the idea of revolutionary change hard to embrace on home ground. Most of British society would eventually come to agree with him after news of the endless deaths under Robespierre and the young Bonaparte. However, Burke's early and very public reactionary statement, a defense of monarchy, made him the prime target for Jacobin attack. In contrast to Price's radical sermonizing, Burke chose a secular and undemocratic posture, that of courtier, for his argument against the cultural revolutionaries.

Burke's most famous use of his courtier strategy is to imagine the vulnerable and threatened Marie Antoinette attacked in her private bedroom by the hysterical mobs who, somewhat less hysterically in real life, had dragged Louis and the Queen from Versailles to Paris just before Price wrote his sermon. Notably, Burke eschews the maternal metaphor for that of the helpless court lady whose vulnerability symbolizes the vulnerable French state in need of rescue by its knightly politicians. Behind Burke's rhetorical flourishes lies public memory of the common women in that mob attack on the French court who helped carry out the betrayal and capture of the one royal woman. Burke emphasizes both the terror and humiliation of Marie Antoinette, and the lack of any true courtier present that could protect her as he imagines he himself would have done. In refusing the maternal metaphor and in transporting himself imaginatively to the place of another court, Burke rhetorically and effectively contains revolutionary feminized hysteria in France, represented by those women in the mob. To do so is to deny female power at any level of the political and the public sphere, an important aspect of Burke's *Reflections*. Burke then transforms mob revolutionary fervor into a male sense of unchivalrous and churlish misbehavior, which allows him to view the revolution in France (and any similar activity that might come to Britain) as the barbaric destruction of a civilization rather than the production of a utopian society.

Mary Wollstonecraft was quick to perceive the problem with exalting one royal woman at the expense of all those common women, and to see that Burke's main thrust was to refuse the political to women at all. She wrote a heated response to Burke, published by her friend Joseph Johnson as *A Vindication of the Rights of Men* (1790). She also understood that her argument would be better received if she put aside the maternal connection (which she later takes up in the *Vindication of the Rights of Woman*) and underscored the tragedy of impoverished millions rather than of women alone:

> Surveying civilized life [in London], and seeing with undazzled eye the polished vices of the rich, their insincerity, want of natural affections, with all the specious train that luxury introduces, I have turned impatiently to the poor to look for man undebauched by riches or power. But alas, what did I see? . . . a broken spirit, worn-out body, and all those gross vices which the example of the rich, rudely copied, could produce . . . What were the outrages of a day [the march on Versailles] to these continual miseries? . . . Man preys on man – and you [Burke] mourn for the idle tapestry that decorated a gothic pile . . . . (Wu, 1998: 142)

Written like a long letter, Wollstonecraft continually addresses Burke in her pamphlet in order to force him to hear her arguments and her voice. But she did not put forward her full critique of Burke's gallantry in the *Rights of Woman* (1792) until she went to Paris and witnessed the participation of women political leaders in revolutionary activities, only to see them later vilified, guillotined, or dismissed. Her full attack on Burke's courtly defense of the French queen as a vulnerable romance heroine appears two years later in her *Historical and Moral View of the French Revolution*. But this attack is presaged by the *Rights of Woman's* criticism of society's demands that women romanticize themselves and deny their maternal responsibility, and of society's tendency to demonize any woman who refuses to do so. Like Wollstonecraft, Anna Seward also sees Burke's chivalry as ill placed, a screening device only that ignores the real plight of men and women. Seward openly refers to it as "Quixotism" in her letters to friends, a term that reveals Burke's self-representation as a falsely romantic and knightly attempt to sway public opinion. In the *Rights of Woman*, Wollstonecraft takes this critique of false romance to its logical extreme, depicting the average English household as a Gothic castle in which marriage becomes an institution of female slavery.

Seward's response to the *Rights of Woman*, which she sent to a male correspondent, rejects the charge against the institution of marriage, but is typical of women readers' general agreement with Wollstonecraft that women's political and legal subordination was directly related to their lack of access to a good education – something both Seward and Wollstonecraft had personally worked hard to achieve for themselves. It is this education that should have allowed women readers to see the flaw in Burke's argument for the French queen, and that allows Seward, like Wollstonecraft, to be skeptical of Burke's rhetoric. She writes to her good friend, Mrs Mompessan (December 10, 1790), "As yet I have seen only the extract from Mr Burke's pamphlet, which the newspaper presented."

> I am afraid the French carry the spirit of freedom too far; – but no powers of wit and eloquence can persuade me to think a government, so barbarously oppressive, ought to have stood – where, if a libertine of rank chose to debauch the wife of a tradesman, and found the husband an obstacle, – or the son of a man in high station marries against his consent, – a *lettre de cachet* could be procured to imprison the obnoxious person for life, amidst the solitary horrors of the Bastille; and perhaps have him chained by the neck to its accursed walls. (Seward, 1811: III, p. 42)

Seward's reference to secret (rather than private) letters as the clue Burke misses in his denunciation of the mob reaction to restrictive government indicates her identification with the feminine privacy of the *family* rather than of the queen who represents that government. The "powers of wit and eloquence" that Burke uses cannot persuade a woman educated to think for herself. The *lettres de cachet* referred to here were the government's secret tool to circumvent normal legal statutes: persons carrying such letters would be themselves beyond any lawful punishment, or they would deliver the letter to another to imprison them without proof of crime. Seward's attention to the reasons why the infamous *lettres de cachet* were so dangerous makes her politics

74

personal. She not only focuses on the injustice of imprisonment for political reasons rather than for crime, and for crime accused but not proved; she also focuses on the indecency of such patriarchal abuse, and implicitly on the use of the familiar letter as a transgressive instrument. She objects to its use as a device that moves in an unnatural direction from public to private, from illumination to imprisonment. Seward is deeply concerned here that prisons, instruments of public punishment, could be used in cases of sexual abuse to destroy family bonds, the very relations letters are meant to sustain. In this, she shares Wollstonecraft's view that civil freedoms are meshed with family bonds, that domestic affections cannot stabilize a nation where they are weakened by patriarchal abuse infiltrating the family unit. But her emphasis is on strengthening family bonds, not (as Wollstonecraft argues in the *Rights of Woman*) on altering the institution of marriage. And, ironically, Seward's interpretation of the use to which the *lettres de cachet* were put derives from Williams's own "letter" on the secrets of the Bastille *in Letters Written in France in the Summer of 1790*, a volume Seward highly admired and recommended to all her friends. "We saw the hooks of those chains by which the prisoners were fastened round the neck to the walls of their cells . . . and to these regions of horror were human creatures dragged at the caprice of despotic power" is a passage from Williams (1790: I, letter iv) that clearly infused Seward's own deprecation of old regime "caprice" and libertinism.

Yet Seward's interest is personal politics and not a literary treatment of the Terror, even though her fame had been established by her early poem on the political and revolutionary Major André. Perhaps part of her lack of interest in a poetic treatment of the revolution is that she is at a distinct disadvantage living in Lichfield instead of in London, while a writer like Wollstonecraft can stay current with the political situation. Because of Wollstonecraft's editorial position with the radical publisher Joseph Johnson, for instance, she is given first crack at Burke's pamphlet to write her *Rights of Men*, while Seward cannot get hold of it and has to rely on correspondents' opinions and extracts from the newspapers. But the split between those women who have some access to the public and women who remain in the private becomes in this instance more than a matter of information; it is also a matter of living the political. Seward writes to a friend, "As to politics, I do not think myself at all qualified to talk about them; to speak with any degree of certainty upon the event of that great, but hazardous experiment, which France is making to render mankind more independent of each other, more virtuous, and consequently more happy" (to Rev. William Fitzthomas, June 5, 1791; Seward, 1811: III,

p. 80). But both Wollstonecraft and Williams go to Paris to experience the tumult and excitement of revolution. Wollstonecraft and Williams also practice a personal revolution while in Paris, participating in the new liberal vogue for "free love" which Seward strongly disapproves of at home. However, Wollstonecraft uses her Parisian stay to witness and analyze revolutionary experience, and to turn philosophy into radical art. Williams uses the drama of revolutionary Paris to stage herself, to create a public figure enhanced by the production of art but that is already itself a consumable art form. Yet Seward also understands the revolution as high drama: her imaginative response of sympathy and sensibility is not only poetic and political, but, as for Williams, theatrical. Indeed, for Britain, the events at the Versailles court and then at Paris after 1787 took on the effect of an immense spectacle, a staged affair that could be understood in dramatic terms.

Joanna Baillie's important treatise of 1798 on the nature of tragedy as a dramatic mode provided both a retrospect for the revolutionary plot of French politics and a way to understand in aesthetic terms what would come to pass. Her use of drama to plot a political frame of mind is particularly helpful for understanding women writers' artistic interest in political events. Even more than the outraged responses of philosophers like Wollstonecraft, the responses of sensibility from poets like Seward and of sentimentality from correspondents like Williams prepared the way for Baillie's reading of the tragic mode. Baillie (1762–1851) was born in Glasgow and moved with her sister and widowed mother to London in 1783. There she began writing, first poetry and then plays. Baillie's reputation was established by her three-volume *Series of Plays in which it is Attempted to Delineate the Stronger Passions of the Mind* (1798–1812), even though only four of these were ever produced, and only one, *De Monfort*, was a stage success. Baillie's main interest is a truly Romantic one – psychodrama. What particularly belongs to tragedy, she notes, is the work of "unveiling the human mind under the dominion of those strong and fixed passions which, seemingly un-provoked by outward circumstances, will from small beginnings brood within the breast till all the better dispositions, all the fair gifts of nature, are borne down before them" (Baillie, 1836: 30–1). In describing a better way to reveal the drama of mind and heart in conflict, she centers this revelation on a description of the individual. Yet in doing so she is also describing an entire people and their response to oppression. Here priv-acy is not imagined as feminine, but as a deeply personal experience which for both her male and female protagonists have a public effect that often negatively impacts a large circle of people. By working against the

76

feminizing and naturalizing tropes, reconfiguring them as human passions that can be dramatically illuminated for all to see and to learn from, Baillie suggests an alternative route to cultural renovation. Her understanding of how the passions work on the mind reflects the importance of imagination and imaginative constructs in the British response to revolutionary politics, but even as she writes against the dominant uses of those tropes her ideas were often taken as representative imaginings. Baillie's work demonstrates how vexed women's relation to the cultural revolution was, principally because the feminizing tropes collapsed the distinction between women's experience and figurative experience: "women" and "woman" too easily seemed the same thing.

Indeed, writers like Baillie, Wollstonecraft, and Williams suffered from their inability to personally garner a critical distance from revolutionary ideas. By contrast, male writers like Wordsworth and Coleridge worked hard to establish just such a distance, using cultural feminization to address political issues, and thus establishing powerful public voices for themselves. But Seward, who maintained a safer relationship to politics, also denied herself a public voice in such matters and thus loses even more than the others. As the efforts of all these writers make clear, the turn inward into subjective, imaginative experience that we think of as properly Romantic was almost necessarily displayed outwardly as an expression of the public sphere, although how well this turn was received publicly depended very much on the author's gender. Furthermore, Baillie realizes, in her choice of drama as her *métier*, the fundamentally dramatic nature of the public–private crossover in letters, pamphlets, and periodical publications by writers like Wollstonecraft, Williams, and Seward.

Revolutionary Writing

Once we begin to think about revolution as a frame of mind, we begin to see that writers who appear to be engaged with only some aspects of Romanticism are really participating much more fully in the staging of Romanticism. In other words, we need to change the way in which we read these authors to see how their writing is revolutionary. Seward and Williams, for example, are not that distanced from the revolutionary writings that we more commonly associate with the early male Romantics. When Williams first went to Paris to witness at first hand the dramatic progress of the revolution, Seward wrote to several of her habitual correspondents that she cheered her going. This enthusiastic response was widespread, extending beyond the Jacobin circles of radicals to members of the middle class like Seward and her wide range of correspondents. Williams and Seward had both written encomiums of noble male subjects very early in their poetic careers, thus gaining public notice for what was actually a political subject, although acceptable enough for young women encouraged to admire male achievement. This shared history, as well an ironic sense of how their gender restricted their ability to discuss politics, continued to inform their correspondence on poetic matters. Only months before the French king agreed to call the Estates-General to assembly, Seward wrote to Williams about her mentor Andrew Kippis, "I have read your glowing poem, in Dr Kippis's Life of Cook, and felt at once thrilled and warmed by its solemn fire . . . though I smile to see how curiously he guards against either you or me growing too vain on the subject of our poems on Cook, – deploring, as he does, that our hero had no *abler* panegyrists" (October 19, 1788; Seward, 1811: II, p. 178).

Despite their awareness of gender prejudice, Williams and Seward did not turn to overt critique as Wollstonecraft did. Their political exchanges retain the same imaginatively poetic sensibility and sincerity that first gained them repute, and they both strove to sustain this identity to assure their feminine appeal with their readers. Part of this appeal is the seemingly non-threatening nature of their politics. Readers eagerly followed Williams's translation of her patriotic fervor into public terms in her "letters," or epistolary reports. These letters would imply in and of themselves that as a woman Williams was not confined to the home (or to the nation). They would also allow her political discourse to be staged in such a way that she herself acted the role of a sentimental heroine, an acceptably feminine political position. (See Favret, 1993: 53–95 for a discussion of Williams's radicalism.) However, this masking of politics with femininity could also backfire. When Seward later came to worry for her friend's safety and to excoriate the French thirst for blood, Williams's drama, as we have already noted in her imprisonment by Robespierre and the rejection of her for her affair with Stone, had taken a turn toward tragedy. Seward, who refused to publish political writings, suffered for her feminine stance in a different way. Her views could not be taken seriously since they were only printed after her death. And, among her circle of friends, her letters on political matters were read as part of her domestic news because she was not more direct and critical, and because she was unwilling to commit herself publicly as did Wollstonecraft.

Against Williams's public and Seward's private ruminations on revolutionary events, Coleridge's "Fears in Solitude. Written April 1798, During the Alarms of an Invasion," composed the same year that Baillie published her dramatic treatise, offers an interesting comparison. Williams's and Seward's exchanges with their readers, public or private, offered a sharp contrast to Coleridge's poem, a deeply personal meditation, written in solitude, that ponders the effects of invasion on both the public and the private. Coleridge, like Baillie, uses psychological insight, but to probe his personal responses to imagining the transferral of the French Revolution onto British soil. Certainly, the fear of invasion remained a very real, even likely, possibility throughout the revolution and Napoleonic Wars, but what is essentially a public or nationalistic fear becomes in Coleridge's hands a mediation between personal memory and public event. This translation of the public to the private, reversing the direction of women Romantics' writing of private to public, is Coleridge's particular genius. Such a translation between the personal and the national is characteristic of early High Romanticism (that is, the full expression of the aesthetic we now associate with the Romantic period, consisting of individualism, the quest for the sublime, the transcendent imagination, and so forth). But it is also a variation on the hallmark of women's writing, and, indeed, Coleridge acknowledges this relation when he considers his genius to be feminine in some of its aspects. It should not be too surprising, then, to find that the highly political "France: An Ode" (Wu, 1998: 465–8) actually begins as a poem of feminine sensibility: "Ye clouds," "Ye ocean waves," "Ye woods," he intones, "How oft, pursuing fancies holy, / My moonlight way o'er flow'ring weeds I wound, / Inspired beyond the guess of folly . . . ." But between the first stanza and the second, the speaker has shifted from a feminine diction of sensibility to a High Romantic one: "With what a joy, my lofty gratulation / Unawed, I sung amid a slavish band . . . / For ne'er, oh Liberty! with partial aim / I dimmed thy light, or damped thy holy flame." From the language of fancy, enchantment, and folly, we move to the language of joy, loftiness, and holy flames. By an almost necessary logic here, stanza III moves into what is essentially a predecessor text for his masterful "Dejection: An Ode": " 'And what,' I said, 'though blasphemy's loud scream / . . . A dance more wild than ever maniac's dream; . . ." In mapping out the revolutionary course, Coleridge simultaneously uses this ode to map out his own poetic development. The political is the personal, and even more, the political is the personal is the artful.

Seward and Williams began their careers by using sensibility in order to project themselves without apparent violation of social order into the public sphere, to create a space in which they could discuss politics.

Coleridge uses sensibility, despite having already published and lectured on politics, in order to establish the feminine private as a state of mind that can be violated by invasion. He then transforms sensibility into a more overt (or High) Romanticism in order to discuss revolution. The equation of sensibility with a publicly female voice causes Williams to be read as sentimentalist, while Coleridge transforms sensibility into a transcendent Romanticism that captures the spirit of revolutionary turmoil more expressly because more universally. His free movement into the public sphere with a public voice, in other words, allows him a move both Williams and Seward are denied: to transcend the private and the individual in order to capture an essence that applies to all.

Coleridge's meditative poetry, whether ruminating on a foreign invasion or imagining the voices of suffering in the wind, as in his famous later "Dejection: An Ode," integrates elements of the letter writing that constitutes much of the women's texts discussed here. Seward's actual letters, Williams's epistolary journalism, even the epistolary novels that were so popular, such as Scott's *Millenium Hall* and Seward's *Louisa*, all attempt to enter into the experiences of turmoil and suffering of those undergoing revolution, and do so as imaginative acts. The private circulation of letters is mirrored by the private and circular acts of meditation Coleridge employs in his odes; both modes address an expected reader in order to anticipate their response, and to incorporate that anticipation either as criticism or agreement. If Coleridge remembers by 1798 that "Unawed, I sung amid a slavish band; / And when to whelm the disenchanted nation, / . . . The monarchs marched in evil day, / And Britain joined the dire array" ("France: An Ode"), Anna Seward was writing in 1791, "Mr Burke is detected in the grossest misrepresentations concerning the state of that country. Time has already, in many respects, given the lie to his gloomy prognostics of its anarchy and ruin"(to Rev. William Fitzthomas, June 5, 1791; Seward, 1811: III, p. 80). Her confident remarks show that educated women were deeply involved in France's revolutionary affairs, but they also reveal how she expects her comments to be part of the general circulation of ideas taking place both in the private and public realms. If Coleridge's poetry uses a discourse of private meditation which he will then publicly publish, Seward's letters use a discourse of public opinion even within private exchange. All of these texts are pushing the boundaries on a deeply serious subject, and they do so by crossing textual limits, by engaging in the use of letters as a malleable form to create a sense of privacy within a public exchange. This use of the private to access the public is the most productive way for women to express their opinions on what they hope will eventuate in a feminine culture of equality. And because letter writing was such a familiar part of the literary tradition by the 1790s, letters were conceived as strong vehicles for storytelling as well as for opinion-making.

Williams, and to a lesser extent Seward, clearly conceived of the letter as a way to use narratives to form opinion. Even though denied the same access to political pronouncement as Coleridge, particularly through their feminine stance, Williams and Seward did use their letters to critically influence readers. Williams's *Letters Written in France* chronicle primarily events in Paris, but the popularity of these volumes is clearly due to more than their journalism and history; each volume's subtitle conspicuously advertises its narratives, called variously "Anecdotes," "Sketches," "Scenes," or for the third and fourth volumes, simply "Important Events." Williams's anecdotes turn real events into tales just as Wordsworth does in his *Lyrical Ballads*, in which he tells poetic tales of rural Lake District inhabitants in order to make a larger point. Williams's tales, so popular that several of them were reprinted separately as chapbooks, grabbed the reader's imagination powerfully because, unlike Wordsworth's ballads, they cloaked terrifying events in pleasurable sentimentality. Where Wordsworth chose to examine how poverty and an unfair class system can painfully affect a dutiful person, as in his "Simon Lee, the Old Huntsman," Williams chose to paint an enthralling love story over the real facts of patriarchal despotism, as in the tale of the du Fossés. This tale, told serially in letters ix–xxii of Williams's 1790 volume, gives the painful events of the old regime a sensual allure that appeals to readers familiar with the conventions of sentimental literature. In the du Fossé narrative, a retelling of events whose protagonists were Williams's real-life friends, Augustin François Thomas du F— is persecuted by his tyrant father, the Baron du F—. Both the son and his mother are treated despotically. When the son falls in love with a middle-class young woman, Monique, the father blocks what he sees as a disadvantageous marriage with a *lettre de cachet*: "though he would have dispensed with any moral qualities in favour of rank, [the Baron] considered obscure birth as a radical stain." Thus far we have the elements of the Gothic: the decadent aristocrat, love between the classes, and the abuse of power. But Williams finds a new twist in the Gothic mode when she structures the tale as a democracy brought about by love: "Yes, the character, the conduct of this amiable person [Monique], have nobly justified her lover's choice. How long might he have vainly sought, in the highest classes of society, a mind so elevated above the common mass! – a mind . . . endowed with the most exquisite sensibility . . ." (vol. I, letter xvi). And, as an antidote to the Gothic, the tale produces what one critic has argued is a feminine democracy, a political state that is for Williams marked by "the most exquisite sensibility" and regulated by true love (see Kelly, 1993: 35–40).

The power of this form of politicized narrative is that it wins over not just the sentimentalist, but even the more thoughtful and educated reader of sensibility like Seward. Her letter to Mrs Mompessan, quoted above, concerning the relation between the *lettres de cachet*, the Bastille, and sexual abuse shows how strongly she is influenced by Williams's *Letters Written in France*. The power of the familiar letter to mitigate the distance between author and reader, subject and author, is enhanced when politicized, allowing the reader to experience at a heightened intensity the excitement or the sentiment of the moment. It can do so not only because enthusiasm for the French cause is high in 1790, but because Williams strategically places this love story after her appeal to the honor and bravery of French women, and to the hidden but effective power of women in general. "The women have certainly had a considerable share in the French revolution: for . . . we often act in human affairs like those secret springs in mechanism, by which, though invisible, great movements are regulated" (vol. I, letter v). The shift from the third person ("The [French] women") with a weaker participation in the action, to the first person with a strong agent ("we act"), signals Williams's literary intention in her tales as well. She wants to make the reader identify so strongly with the French victims and heroines like Monique that the identification is itself active and revolutionary.

Seward operates as an exemplary reader for us here; it is important that she accepts Williams's strategy as legitimate and inspiring, and that she so fully supports Williams throughout the early years of her Parisian life. She enthuses over the *Letters Written in France in the Summer of 1790* and eagerly awaits the subsequent volumes (1792–6), just as she loved Williams's 1790 novel *Julia*, with its liberal politics and enthusiasm for radical thinking. But at this point Williams has yet to experiment with free love, a questionable blending of private with public. And, despite new evidence, Seward as yet remains convinced that the French are involved in a Romantic experiment that engages personal passion as well as patriotic fervor: "If Helen Williams goes again to France, and for so long a time, it is probable she will be lost to her native country. Her graces will fire some patriot heart, with whom she will, in turn, be charmed" (to Miss Weston, July 7, 1791; Seward, 1811: III, p. 89). But Seward has marriage and family life in mind when she writes of being charmed, and not free love. In seeing it as a great love adventure, a meeting of like spirits and high patriotic fervor, Seward turns Williams's politics into a domestic affair, a romance of great sensibility. "The flame of liberty must glow in your bosom with no common fervor, to make you choose to be so near a spectator of the struggles of that yet distracted country," she writes to Williams (July 26, 1792; Seward, 1811: III, p. 147). Seward is not exhibiting feminine illogic in the face of revolutionary politics here, but rather she chooses as for herself the safer course for her friend's public career. Even when she changes her mind about Williams's politics, it is clear that she is not swayed by changing public opinion but rather experiences the vicissitudes of every thinking man and woman in response to media releases during a political crisis. Tom Paine's pamphlet, for instance, is at first wonderful not because she agrees with it, but because it agrees with everything she has been thinking – that is, it takes the pulse of the liberal times. But later she castigates his radical ideas, even holding him accountable for the bloody Terror in France.

Writing in response to Wollstonecraft's *Vindication of the Rights of Men* (1790) as well as Burke's *Reflections*, Paine entered the pamphlet war with his version of *The Rights of Man* (1791–2). What is immediately interesting about the rhetorical strategies of Wollstonecraft, Paine, and Burke is what each writer chooses to depict. Wollstonecraft looks around her at the London streets and sees terrible poverty juxtaposed with exaggerated and unjust privilege; she directs the reader's gaze to the here and now of his or her own life in order to make the realities of Paris more gripping, and the events at Versailles more comprehensible. Paine steps back from the present moment to give the reader a historical overview of Britain's own adjustment of monarchical rights: "The English Parliament of 1688 did a certain thing which, for themselves and their constituents, they had a right to do, and which it appeared right should be done," Yet

> Man has no property in man, neither has any generation a property in the generations which are to follow. The parliament or the people of 1688, or of any other period, had no more right to dispose of the people of the present day . . . When we survey the wretched condition of man under the monarchical and hereditary systems of government . . . it becomes evident that those systems are bad, and that a general revolution in the principle and construction of governments is necessary. (*The Rights of Man*, part I)

Against the immediacy of Wollstonecraft's anger and the historical purview of Paine's rights discourse, Burke's elaborate, figurative descriptions of how he imagines the horrors of Paris and Versailles are melodramatic and staged. But the effect of Paine's schematized rhetoric, in which he gives the reader a larger perspective for the events in France, is to legitimize the revolutionaries, Seward will later largely blame Paine for the Reign of Terror as if he alone directed the heightened passions of that period with his words and his "levelling system." He is "that specious, that mischievous sophist, whose absurd and impossible system of equality seeks to kindle the fatal flame of selfish ambition in every heart" (to Williams, January 17, 1793; Seward, 1811: III, p. 203).

"Instructions, Supposed to be Written in Paris, for the Mob in England" (1799), by Mary Alcock of whom little is now known, capitalizes on this new fear that the pamphlet war would somehow turn the French reform into a transportable revolutionary anarchy: "Of liberty, reform, and rights I sing – / Freedom I mean, without our church or king; / . . . Such is the blessed liberty in vogue" (Wu, 1994: 16–17). If, as is entirely possible, "Alcock" is a pseudonym and not a historical personage, this text nevertheless represents the kind of fear that fed the reaction against France.

After nearly a decade of war, however, the British mood was difficult to pin down. Anna Barbauld wrote to a friend in 1803, "Pray are you an alarmist? One hardly knows whether to be frightened or diverted on seeing people assembled at a dinner-table . . . [saying] with a most smiling and placid countenance, that the French are to land in a fortnight, and that London is to be sacked and plundered for three days, – and then they talk of going to watering-places" (to Mrs Beecroft, July 28, 1803; Aikin, 1825: I, pp. 92–3). Later in the period, after the Battle of Trafalgar (1805) and just before the Peninsular War and the Convention of Cintra (1808), the national mood was tense, reactionary and anxious. It was during this period that Charlotte Smith, in the last year of her life, wrote "Beachy Head" (1807).

Charlotte Smith (1749–1806) was married at 15 to the son of a wealthy West Indian merchant after her father died, but it was an unhappy marriage. Her husband was both extravagant and inept in business, and eventually there were 12 children to support. Smith first turned to writing for publication while sharing her husband's room in debtor's prison. She was immediately successful with her first volume of poetry, *Elegiac Sonnets* (1784); she also published six novels, including *Emmeline; or The Orphans of the Castle* (1788) and *The Old Manor House* (1793); an anti-revolutionary poem, *The Emigrants* (1793); and several children's books, including *Conversations, Introducing Poetry*

(1804). "Beachy Head" (Wu, 1998: 110–31) refers to a landing point on the Channel crossing from France; it therefore represents the most obvious site of invasion if Napoleon were to attempt to take England, as he had taken Portugal and then Spain. But if the poem, a short epic, is geographically about a vulnerable site, its subject is a strong nationalism. Beachy Head represents a geological and botanical history of England, a narrative of its very being. "On thy stupendous summit, rock sublime, / . . . while Fancy should go forth / And represent the strange and awful hour / Of vast concussion" the poem begins (ll. 1–6), much in the same tone drawn from Milton that Williams uses to describe the French Revolution as sublime and disruptive. Situating her narrative on the natural history of the beach summit, Smith can produce a historiography of the nation itself that reminds the British that they were once before conquered by Frenchmen in the Norman Conquest. The short epic, with its several shifts into native song, and its inclusion of individual stories, serves as a visionary dream for the country at large. Smith uses a device here that Keats will later take up in a sonnet that is almost a kernel of this one, "On First Looking into Chapman's Homer" (1817): she positions the speaking "I" on the rock, and uses that vantage point to project her vision of a previous history. "Contemplation here, / High on her throne of rock, aloof may sit / And bid recording Memory unfold / Her scroll voluminous . . . ", she writes (ll. 118–20); while Keats will turn this device itself into the vision: "Or like stout Cortez when with eagle eyes / He stared at the Pacific, and all his men / Looked at each other with a wild surmise – / Silent, upon a peak in Darien" (Wu, 1998: 1013). Keats refers to the charting of new worlds in order to redefine the experience of his own, while Smith charts the layered history of the world she knows. Keats's poem offers another way of defining nation, still necessary even after Napoleon's defeat because political and economic unrest at home has continued the sense of national anxiety that Smith's poem addressed eleven years earlier.

Smith's purpose is a retrospect that also looks forward into the future. Written nearly a decade after Coleridge's "Fears in Solitude," it represents a confidence that Britain can present a strong defense against Napoleon. Curiously, Smith's nationalism does not acknowledge the debate over women's rights or the role women have in sustaining the country. Her reference to a general sense of citizenship but not her personal experience as a woman may be due in part to the conservatism that overtook the rights debate after the excesses of the French Terror. That "Beachy Head" is so readily comparable to men's poems' on citizenship and nationality, but less so to Wollstonecraft's *Rights of*

Woman, is due both to Smith's own more conservative view of women's political role and to the fears Britain began to experience for its own political future by 1806.

But earlier, even non-radical women had looked on the issue favorably. The connection between political optimism and the rights debate, as much a function of national mood as of governmental policy, cannot be over-stressed. Seward, again exemplary, writes to her good friend Thomas Whalley on February 26, 1792:

> Have you read that wonderful book, The Rights of Woman [by Mary Wollstonecraft]. It has, by turns, pleased and displeased, startled and half-convinced me that its author is oftener right than wrong. Though the ideas of absolute equality in the sexes are carried too far, and though they certainly militate against St Paul's maxims concerning that important compact, yet do they expose a train of mischievous mistakes in the education of females; – and on that momentous theme this work affords much better rules than can be found in the sophist Rousseau, or in the plausible Gregory. It applies the spear of Ithuriel to their systems. (Seward, 1811: III, p. 117)

Seward can look favorably on these notions because she, perhaps purposely, sentimentalizes the issues through an equivocation over Wollstonecraft's "ideas of absolute equality in the sexes," and the lack of romance in such a conception. The political situation has not yet led her to equate sexual equality with political vulnerability, and so she can impute sentiment to rights issues without worrying about the safety of future generations. But Seward's interpretation leads us to an interesting point within its optimism. Wollstonecraft's work concerned whether or not the French revolt was justifiable and realizable, but Seward's essentially conservative reading sentimentalizes the issues at the very heart of nationalism: the distinction between a defense of the monarchy and the new rights discourse. The first posits a society's strength in its institutions and in the monarchs who represent those institutions on behalf of the society; the second posits the individual as a society's strength, and argues that, if individuals are institutionally supported, they can represent themselves or can choose their own representatives. For Seward not to interest herself in the difference, and to locate Wollstonecraft's most persuasive point in the need to improve women's education rather in the need for women's rights, indicates that even intelligent and liberal-minded women were unwilling to consider the full implication of revolutionary writing. It is not until the national mood turns pessimistic that

86

the import of this difference will become unavoidable and threatening to women.

Such conservatism coming from women writers like Smith and Seward, who both had great sympathy for the French if not for the later stages of the revolution, reveals a yet deeper issue confronting those engaged in revolutionary writing. A serious problem arises when rights discourse is applied to women's rights, whether in the public mode of voting rights and access to the professions, or in the private mode of marriage laws and education. This is the difficulty in thinking of women in public or "rights" terms at all. In part, this has to do with the nature of rights language, which stresses the strength of the individual through an institutional recognition of the citizen. When this kind of language is applied to women, it demands a political recognition of women as subjects or citizens rather than objects, producing what in the Romantic period was an unimaginable idea fitting no known conceptual model. Furthermore, those most interested in applying rights discourse to women tended to have been educated according to nonconformist or Dissenting traditions, or influenced by political radicalism; these associations would make such writers suspect for middle-class readers, yet women's rights were generally only discussed as a middle-class goal. It is this combination of conceptual difficulties, as much as any social or governmental constraints, that made clearly worked-out challenges to women's condition in society hard to articulate and nearly impossible to sustain.

When Anna Laetitia Barbauld, educated within a Dissenting tradition, sits down to write about women's rights, for instance, her task is complicated by her own sense of herself as marginalized. Barbauld (1743–1825), the daughter of a tutor at the Warrington Academy for Dissenters, was highly educated and revealed her intellectual abilities at an early age. With her brother John Aikin's encouragement, she published *Poems* in 1773, and together they published *Miscellaneous Pieces in Prose* in the same year. The next year she married a graduate of the academy and they opened a boys' school together. Many of her subsequent publications were written for children, but after selling the school she turned to politics, writing *Epistle to William Wilberforce* (1791) against the slave trade, and *Sins of the Government, Sins of the Nation* (1793) against the war with France. After engaging in literary criticism and biographical introductions to *The British Novelists*, which she edited from 1810, she returned to politics with her controversial poem "Eighteen Hundred and Eleven."

Many of Barbauld's works illustrate her awareness of her marginal position, primarily as a Dissenter, but also as a woman writer. Her response to this double lack of authority in her poem "Rights of Woman" (1795) is to use rights discourse to the exclusion of any introspective thought about the effect of rights on the individual. She particularly avoids linking herself with her rhetorical object, woman, in order to prevent an association between that object and the poem's speaker, choosing to make her argument on impersonal grounds instead. This approach contrasts sharply with Coleridge's use of the personal in "France: An Ode" to express his views on a public issue. But Barbauld felt that even Coleridge, and male poets like him, carried the meditative and personal identification with the poetic object too far, which she warns him against in "To Mr Coleridge" (1797); she herself avoids this Romantic impulse. In her "Rights of Woman" she goes even further, distancing herself as far as possible from the oppressed "woman" she exhorts to action, yet whose gains would also be her own ("Yes, injured woman – rise, assert thy right!").

We have seen how a variety of writers approached political writing, and how, for each of these important voices, the act of engaging politics within the context of gender produced what we are calling revolutionary writing. By this definition, whether we consider Coleridge's or Williams's use of the feminine or Barbauld's rejection of personal female experience to express public views, we are witnessing revolutionary writing. By invoking gender, the individual was necessarily positioned against the public whole; by invoking the individual, writers necessarily positioned themselves as anti-establishment. Thus, for women to write about politics at all was revolutionary; for men to consider gender a vehicle for political thought reveals a radical and highly Romantic mind-set. But each of these writers complicates politics with gender differently. Part of the difference lies in how men view women and how women view themselves. Women's social role, so important for how their political writing is received by readers, is divided into that of object (the woman as others see her), mother (her primary social value), and subject (how she experiences herself). This division, not shared by men, causes a sense of split identity that lies beneath every political argument made by women, whether liberal or conservative. We return to Wollstonecraft at this point because she offers the clearest attack on this problem, and because she recognized the inherent dangers of this identity problem in a way that no one else did.

Wollstonecraft's treatment of women's social identity in her *Vindication of the Rights of Woman* (1792) begins with a basic strategy to reconcile both rights and individual discourses, to make it possible for women to assert themselves confidently. Because she combines reason with personal argumentation, her rhetorical strategy causes her train of thought to double back on itself at times, but, as a remedy for women's split sense of identity, the doubling is essential to work through a mediation of political reality and potential. She must convince her female readers of what is possible, convince male readers of the beneficial effects of such change, and critique the current system. Moreover, her approach must analyze the difference between *women* and *woman*, and between *woman* and *mother*. Only by asserting the appropriate way to understand these terms can women understand their proper identity and their rights. It is an overwhelming agenda, and as Seward's response indicates, even liberal readers are not yet ready for it. Nevertheless, the treatise was widely read on both sides of the Atlantic and its influence felt (see Davidson, 1986: 131).

To achieve her purpose, Wollstonecraft takes the middle-class woman as her audience and her object of analysis, but she differentiates her from "ladies," by whom she means upper-class women as decadent as those of the French court, asserting that middle-class women "appear to be in the most natural state." By positing her audience as representative of the natural state for women, she can then critique those social institutions that have caused such women to degenerate into an unnatural condition unworthy of mothers of citizens. Middle-class women's self-absorption, manipulative behavior, and lack of social responsibility she squarely sets down as the results of inadequate education, social practices that keep women in childish relation to their spouses, and the material pampering that makes women happy with their lot.

> Women are, in fact, so much degraded by mistaken notions of female excellence that I do not mean to add a paradox when I assert that this artificial weakness produces a propensity to tyrannize, and gives birth to cunning, the natural opponent of strength, which leads them to play off those contemptible infantine airs that undermine esteem even whilst they excite desire. (Wollstonecraft, 1975: 83–4)

The fact that Wollstonecraft struggles so hard, chapter after chapter, in a full-fledged attack on the institutions that sustain women's objectionable status indicates the importance of the stakes. Her *Rights of Men*, succinct by comparison, only has to argue against monarchy; the *Rights of Woman* has to argue against patriarchy itself. Her choice of titles clarifies this difference: "men" is a present and known entity composed of real people; "woman" is an objectified and timeless one, an idea not a person, "woman" not "women." The historically favored way to attack women's rights issues has been one that plays on this distinction, usually by identifying all women with the ahistorical concept of "the mother." Wollstonecraft cannot escape the inevitable association between "woman" and "mother," but does her best to use it to her purpose by lucidly pointing out the reasons why a good citizen is necessarily the offspring of a responsible and well-educated mother. Yet the full implications of Wollstonecraft's argument could not be absorbed by her readers despite her various strategies and reasoned discussion. And because she cannot devote the main part of her argument to women as citizens themselves (an argument not possible in Britain until women get the vote), her treatise is less radical than it could be, but it was, even so, considered dangerous by many. Even her focus on motherhood did not satisfy deeply conservative readers who saw any attack on the status quo as alarming.

In this sense, Wollstonecraft failed to convince others of what she saw so clearly. However, her use of motherhood to make a political argument allows us to see how women understood politics. Motherhood is an unstable conceptual model for feminists of the Romantic period to use; it functions equally well for both the conservative and the radical point of view, and can be easily turned from a radical argument into a convincing conservative one. Wollstonecraft's analysis of motherhood was intended to indicate women's true subjectivity, but conservatives found the concept equally useful for reducing women to an inconsequential political status. Moreover, the concept itself gained such political overtones during the period that it too easily hid the difficult issues Wollstonecraft and other feminists were critiquing. During the Romantic period motherhood had many overt uses: to bring nations together, put women in their place, dispel all talk of women's rights, and vilify powerful women such as Marie Antoinette, Josephine Bonaparte, and even Wollstonecraft herself.

The following section discusses the multiple uses of the maternal metaphor to promote Romantic interests, whether nationalistically or artistically. Because the maternal metaphor both plays into, and resists, women's struggle to use rhetoric effectively to present themselves as thinking as well as feeling individuals, it becomes a powerful Romantic device. For instance, in Wollstonecraft's *The Wrongs of Woman, or Maria* (1798), it is the heroine's love for her infant that allows her tyrannical husband to trick her into unjust but legal incarceration in an insane asylum. In Mary Shelley's *Frankenstein* (1818), it is the absence of the mother for both creature and creator that produces the novel's destructive denouement. As both a presence and an absence, the maternal metaphor provides women writers with a way to discuss intellectual issues without being interpreted themselves as immoral or sexually transgressive. It also provides them with ways to reposition themselves and the female figure away from the weakly passive idea of woman or the destructive idea of her. But it was also a weapon against women because it enforced their biological difference from men, and therefore it also assisted men's use of metaphorical language and associative logic to silence women intellectuals. As we will see, the metaphor and its associative possibilities can swing both ways in the political pendulum of women's real and literary roles.

Maternal Nationalism and Children's Literature

Motherhood as a metaphor for nationalism seems to meld the private role of woman as mother with her positive public role of mothering the nation, but in a way that is reassuring rather than transgressive. During the initial phase of the French Revolution, women writers in France and Britain responded enthusiastically to the promise that it held out to them of an integration of their private identities and responsibilities with public affairs and activities. But, in the aftermath of the revolution's destruction of the private individual's experience, women writers began collectively to see such integration as dangerous and fatal. This action and reaction is just one of many stories about the making of the Romantic nation. Part of this story includes how women writers came to see the role of the mother not as a radical one, but as a conceptual re-dressing of revolutionary disintegration. This refashioning of nationalism takes one of the dominant symbols of the revolution, the protective and nurturing mother, and turns it into a British idea of the nation that is still protective and nourishing, but also educative: what will be termed here "maternal nationalism." Maternal nationalism becomes the concept through which future British citizens would be produced, nurtured, and properly educated into political loyalty and social responsibility. Wollstonecraft's radical idea of motherhood, as that which benefits the mother, is here turned into a conservative and disarming one that benefits the male child. It is an idea that assures all alarmists that rights discourse can no longer be associated with motherhood, and motherhood, like Mother Earth, underlies and promotes society and supports male dominance of the public sphere. Thus revolutionary writing becomes tamed,

91

especially in the last half of the Romantic period, through the application of a powerful metaphor.

Yet women found ways to transform even this reactionary trend to their own purpose: maternalism could also produce a positive and protective way to imagine women's role in the new national ideal by responding to and translating earlier Romantic images of the mother as destitute, mad, or otherwise unsound or absent. These images were most often found in the works of the male Romantics, but all Romantic literature, in fact, is populated largely by orphans, siblings without families, or families missing one parent. The idea was that the hero could no longer define himself through "normal" or integrated social groups; instead, his quest is to find himself, with the help of separated others, through a union with Nature. Nature's bond with the heroic-poet figure replaces the unity of the family in order to magnify the experience of the individual, and to project the poet into the cosmic world beyond the physical. The poet can then heal the fragmented family unit, which represents a sick society at large, through the bonds he will forge with Nature herself. To emphasize Mother Nature's importance in this quest, the human mother of the family is often the missing or lacking parent.

Recovering motherhood from this characteristic representation, then, required that women writers create a way for maternity to be politically necessary, and for a conceptual model to be created for it. If maternal nationalism was one of the ways radical and non-radical women alike responded to the political problem of the missing mother in literature, another was the new genre that we now term "children's literature." By focusing simply on women's roles as mothers, and ignoring Wollstonecraft's complex approach to motherhood, female authors could address politics in non-revolutionary terms, emphasizing children's status as future citizens and de-emphasizing women's own relation to the political. In this way, children's literature follows the safer path for engaging politics chosen by Seward, yet it still allows women a way to assert their views publicly and to effect political change. One way the new genre aids these goals is through the author's adoption of the mother function to teach the child the alphabet, reading, morals, and respect for nature; children's literature thus reveals the author as maternal, transforming the absence of the mother in adult literature into a literary presence for child readers. If the adult literature displaces the mother from the quest narrative, children's literature firmly replaces her for a young audience just forming its mental and social attitudes. And, although men and women both experimented with this genre, as William

Blake does in *Songs of Innocence and of Experience* (1789–94), women were by far the greatest producers of this material. Through their use of rhetoric these women writers produced what we might call the "literary maternal" – an appropriation of the maternal metaphor for educative purposes. They address child readers directly rather than writing about them or imitating their emotions and voices as men writers like Blake and William Wordsworth tended to do for the adult reader. (For a detailed account of education and children's literature, see Richardson, 1994). Women writers were more clearly focused on the future citizen, men writers on the Romantic child. Yet women's very attempt to subvert charges of radicalism, while correcting negative images of the mother through the medium of children's literature, produced its own drawback by making possible a hostile interpretation of literary maternalism as the capacity to write for children only. Like radical women, conservative women also found their solutions to their own representation being used against them.

Before examining maternal nationalism and children's literature, we need to understand that a more basic issue than women's control of their representation was the use to which such representation was put, as when the maternal metaphor underpins a nation's character. We need to ask why the maternal as a Romantic concept became a way to grapple with important issues such as the identity of the nation. To appreciate this, we need first to understand that, after Britain's entry into the Napoleonic Wars, the seemingly clear division between English monarchy, with its parliamentary structure, and the chaotic democracy of revolutionary France suddenly dissolves when Napoleon becomes emperor. The idea of empire is deeply threatening to the old idea of the kingdom (since empires swallow others' kingdoms), and to the modern idea of the nation (which is democratic and, so, antithetical to empire). Because nationalism becomes the largest question of identity to grip the popular imagination, it became important to devise a sense of national identity strong enough to fend off the threat of imperial absorption. If the paternal has failed the nation through the role of the monarchy, Romantic England can still rely on the promise offered by Mother Nature to support and nurture her chosen ground.

Clearly, maternal nationalism offers a useful associative concept for several Romantic ideas and themes. In her *Letters Written during a Short Residence* (1796), Wollstonecraft claims that imagination is the "mother of sentiment," that without it our affections are untouched. For her, imagination gives life to man in a form that Mary Jacobus (1995: 66–7) has characterized as the "maternal spark." This is the Promethean spark as delivered by the mother to her child, a vastly different characterization of the usually masculine spark that is so important to Romantic conceptions of creativity. Here, four years after writing the *Rights of Woman*, Wollstonecraft still sees the role of the mother as more than biological and domestic, but rather than identifying a political goal for motherhood, she offers a non-revolutionary one as imaginative and creative. This definition of the maternal is quite different from her earlier one, shifting the public role of the mother back to the personal and individual. The mother is now she who produces the new subject rather than the new citizen, a view much more in line with Romanticism's general emphasis on the individual and the imagination. It is in this shift, from rights discourse to imaginative discourse, which we also find in women's literature for children, that maternal nationalism provides a way for radical and reactionary thinkers alike to project the new national identity, and the new British subject. Moreover, such a projection provides a revised and female-centered context for the dominant themes of Romanticism. This revision cannot be viewed as a feminist victory, however, for by centering themes (rather than concepts) in the female, women were forced into a more conservative perspective, while men could co-opt aspects of the female for the male-oriented conceptual frame of High Romanticism. However, such themes did provide women writers with focal points for their critiques and alternative visions.

The first of these dominant themes is the Romantic paradox of the child as father to the man. This is promoted most intensely in Blake's and William Wordsworth's use of the child figure. Secondly, we have the notion of the child as a subject who must be educated as a citizen. As noted above, this, in combination with a reaction against the popular representation of an absent or passive mother figure, gives rise to children's literature, a genre that many women including Dorothy Wordsworth and Charlotte Smith tried their hand at. Thirdly, it allowed a way for later women writers like Felicia Hemans to envision alternatives to the larger issues that children's literature and the Romantic child represent, such as a domestically centered state. These themes, particularly that of the Romantic child and Romantic citizen, provide a way for women writers to interact non-radically with the important thinking of the day, while also re-working these themes and attempting to push thought away from a completely male perspective.

It is important, then, to understand the difference between a "male" focus on the individual self and a "female" focus on the family. (These are somewhat gross exaggerations, and we might rather say, "a radical

94

focus on the individual self and a conservative focus on the family";
neither set of characterizing terms is quite accurate, but they give an
indication of the broad lines being drawn.) The individual self is a highly
Romantic concept. Historically, as the first moment of real political
activism for feminism and women's rights, as well as of the birth of
liberalism and socialism, the awakening consciousness of the working
class, and the foundation of modernity, Romanticism holds important implications for a modern understanding of the self. Because
Romanticism's location of women in the social world made all other
constructions of selfhood difficult to imagine, women's maternalism and
maternity came to be the primary way that women could find themselves
as selves. It was also the only political claim they had available to them,
and, even so, their husbands had legal rights to their children, until
nineteenth-century activists like Caroline Norton successfully fought for
women to be legal guardians of their own children. At the same time,
"motherhood" as a conceptual birthing or nurturing of the nation offered French revolutionaries a powerfully cohesive symbol for re-knitting
a society fully or nearly at war with itself. The maternal breast became
identified with a nurtured nation; women suddenly had a new symbolic
role that connected them with the embodied state (a republic of citizens),
while disconnecting them from the legislative making of that state
(see Landes, 1988; Outram, 1989; Gelpi, 1992). This political use of the
maternal metaphor in turn became a useful aid when the British needed
to strengthen their own sense of national identity.

But how does the "male" view of the individual correspond to the
family? We have already seen that for Romantic writers it was desirable
to eliminate or fragment the family, producing motherless heroes who as
orphans were self-dependent. But still, the family must be accounted for.
Patriarchal belief systems take the nuclear family as its smallest integral
unit. This unit works both in large (the state as family, with monarch as
father and queen consort as legislatively powerless mother, aristocrats
as eldest children, and populace as younger and helpless children) and
in small (the main wage-earner as head of his family). The Romantic
depiction of this nuclear family identified each role in this unit – father,
mother, eldest son, eldest daughter, younger children – either by political
function or by economic function. Under the growing influence of the
bourgeoisie and petit bourgeoisie, the mother and her daughters came
to represent consumerism, leisure, and amateur hobbies (see Campbell,
1990). Women who sought to use their amateur skills to gain an income
were opening themselves up to criticism and social devaluation. The
father and eldest son had for several centuries enjoyed a possible connec-

tion to court patronage and a certain status elevation due to their ability to own land (younger sons usually did not inherit the family estate, and so enjoyed a lesser status). Under the growing influence of the bourgeoisie's interest in liberalism and democracy, father and sons held a less essential relation to the court, itself more symbolically than legislatively important, while their social relations to other citizens, especially through business-dominated relations, increased their local political influence.

However, the literary and political importance of the family unit lies largely in the way the Romantics imagined motherhood. It is the single most persuasive element in how women writers thought about themselves as poets speaking to men, and so to the nation. In the right literary hands, Romantic motherhood can provide women with a subjective self that is otherwise denied them under patriarchal law and religion. It provides an individualizing and unique status for the mothering body that creates the family, thus offering writers a way to recreate the woman as self, and accord her a potency within society. Yet working against this goal (so similar to the one Wollstonecraft had earlier envisioned) is the prevalent concept of womanhood *as* motherhood, in which motherhood, from the purely biological and social definition, means that larger social understandings of women's permitted and prohibited activities and dreams are limited. In this negative model, all female behavior that takes place outside these restrictions is construed as deviant or exceptional; such behavior accrues to the individual herself in order to reform her achievements into a story of her body, and to revise her individuality into an acceptable stereotype of femininity. Thus Romantic motherhood could be construed as liberating or restricting, opening up or diminishing women's individuality through its obsessive focus on the idea of the child in order to highlight the mother's special status and ritualized importance *in relation to* the future citizen.

When this stereotype is not challenged but is systemically reproduced by women writers themselves, the constraints are both difficult to perceive and to avoid, particularly when the antithetical emblem of the bluestocking (the woman intellectual) is there to warn women away from non-maternal roles. Mary Wollstonecraft's *Thoughts on the Education of Daughters* (1787) and Catherine Macaulay Graham's *Letters on Education* (1790) were some of the early attempts to ward off and redistribute the symbolic weight being invested in maternity, but they were ultimately unsuccessful. A more powerful approach was to write as mothers to audiences of children. Charlotte Smith, her sister Catherine Anne Dorset, Dorothy Wordsworth, Mary Lamb, Anna Laetitia

Barbauld and others all used the new genre of children's literature to enter into or add to the literary field. The difference is that the maternal metaphor provided men writers with a way to think about the child's place in the world, while it provoked women writers into thinking about the child as a reader. For male writers, the child is still essentially an object to contemplate, but for women writers the child is an experiencing subject to whom the poet can address her words.

When Mary Shelley writes her first novel, *Frankenstein, or The Modern Prometheus*, nearly three decades after Blake's visionary poems about children, she plots her story around the experiences of childhood. But her real theme is maternal nationalism and the Promethean spark her own mother, Mary Wollstonecraft, associated with motherhood in her *Letters Written during a Short Residence*. Mary Shelley (1797–1851), the daughter of Mary Wollstonecraft and William Godwin, eloped to Switzerland with the poet Percy Bysshe Shelley when she was 17 and he was estranged from his wife, Harriet. They were married after Harriet drowned herself in 1816; tragedy continued to haunt them when each of their children but one died young, and Shelley himself died in 1822. *Frankenstein* (1818) was not only her first novel but her masterpiece. Her five subsequent novels were written to support herself and her son, including *Valperga* (1823), *The Last Man* (1826), and *Falkner* (1837). She also edited Shelley's poetry and prose, and wrote short stories, articles, and a travelogue, *Rambles in Germany and Italy* (1844).

Of all her novels, *Frankenstein* is the one that most directly confronts the issues of childhood and maternity. Frankenstein's laboratory creation is, in fact, a baby: the creature has a child's enjoyment of nature, but no language, no knowledge base, no way of dealing with the world. It is frightened by its lack of parents, its lack of protection in a cruel world. Eventually the creature masters both language and cultural knowledge, and the pleasure both tools provide him clearly echoes the child's pleasure in learning. But if the creature has successfully absorbed the lessons children's literature is meant to provide, if he has at this point become the good citizen, all of that achievement is then undermined by the lack of a mother. Without a parental figure, or an equivalent of the maternal figure so often personified in children's stories as storyteller and knowledge-giver, the creature cannot belong to society. When Victor Frankenstein creates his baby himself without any female aid, and then rejects this baby (thus denying the creature its humanity by denying it parental love and familial protection), he denies his child the two elements defined by women writers as necessary to the good citizen. The creature's revenge on his "parent" is, like the destructive emotion that escalated the ravages of the French Revolution, the rage of the lower classes on their political father, the monarch who denies them their citizenship and thus their adulthood.

What Mary Shelley understands about children's emotional and physical needs provides a clear analogy for the needs of adults in a protective and nurturing social contract. And it is this rejection of the social contract that children's literature strives to protect future generations from by inculcating in its readers the principles of social bonds and ties of affection. Children's literature, in this sense, projects a vision of social cohesion that begins with the citizen's knowing participation. Writers address this mutual objective in two fundamentally different ways, depending on whether their audience is essentially adult, as for Mary Shelley, or children. Writers who take the subject of the child's experience and education often attempt to effect greater change through the reader most capable of action. Writers who see their charge as itself the education of the young are attempting the same goal through the formation of the new generation.

The politics of this domestic subject are highly charged, and two writers in particular help illustrate this difference. William Wordsworth wrote many poems about children, and his sister Dorothy Wordsworth's first poems were to children; both poets' depictions of children reflect the essential Romantic conception of the child as an entity retaining its natural purity in the face of social artifices and decadence. However, William pointedly uses the child to figure the relation between the social and the natural orders, much as Mary Shelley uses the creature to rupture this relation. Father figures are, for William, incapable of promoting or dissolving the child's relation to nature; they watch the child at a distance but do not actively teach or parent the child. For him, the child is connected neither with maternal nationalism (as it is for Mary Shelley) nor with children's literature (as it is for Dorothy Wordsworth), but with High Romanticism itself.

"To a Butterfly" (1802) exemplifies William Wordsworth's interest in addressing natural entities as a way of re-learning a purer way of being: "Stay near me – do not take thy flight! / . . . Much converse do I find in thee." The conversation the speaker finds, however, is all his own; the beautiful insect is the "Historian of my infancy" only because it recalls memories until now "dead" to him. The maternal lies nowhere in this poem and must be spun out by the speaker himself; he recreates the lost mother by inserting the maternal metaphor into his adult world. Written in the same year, "To H.[artley] C.[oleridge], Six Years Old" is William

Wordsworth's address to Coleridge's son (Wu, 1998: 366–7). It describes the child in the same naturalizing terms. As for the butterfly, this poem says nothing *to* the child except that what he says does not signify ("mock apparel," "unutterable thought"), what he does is not real ("faery voyager," "blessed vision"), and what he is, is not human ("That art so exquisitely wild"). In fact, the address can say nothing to the child because he is not the actual addressee, just as the butterfly was not. The address becomes an elegy for the to-be-lost childhood at the very point of exclaiming on the child's exquisite wildness: "I think of thee with many fears / For what may be thy lot in future years." As in Wordsworth's extraordinary "Intimations" ode, the speaker's concern is a meditation on the human experience and not what the child may learn about his own humanity.

William Wordsworth's poems take their task to be the production of the child's social place. They function as a kind of mediating agent that thinks through how the child will transfer itself from a natural to a social being – and in the process to think through what this means to the poet's own imaginative existence. Dorothy Wordsworth's poems supplement this philosophical exercise by beginning at the moment of social being, taking the child as already in residence in the social world. Dorothy Wordsworth (1771–1855), who published little in her lifetime, is best known because of her working and domestic relationship with her famous brother. She not only aided William's own writing in a variety of ways, but she kept several journals of exceptional quality (particularly the *Grasmere Journals*), wrote poems that have only recently been redis-covered, and maintained a voluminous correspondence with family and friends. Much of this is now published and available, but during her lifetime the only poems to be publicly printed were those included by William in his poetry volumes.

In these poems, mostly addresses to children, we see a poet who respects the Romantic vision of poet toward pure child. But at the same time the poems ensure that the real child, the child safely situated within the family unit of relations, be protected from that vision; this is the very protection that Mary Shelley's creature lacked. Dorothy Wordsworth's poems addressed to children invite them to explore their imaginative space, and to connect natural elements to their own subjective experi-ence. She uses the maternal metaphor both to authorize her own poetic voice and to teach real children to be subjects in their own right. For her, the poet is the maternal pedagogue, the one who mediates between the human mother and Mother Nature, helping the child to understand its relation to the human and natural world.

Dorothy Wordsworth's earliest verses, which exclusively address dependent children, offer a strongly contrasting conception of the child's
poetic role. William included these poems in his collected works, with
notes indicating her authorship, and his act of inclusion implies that he
felt their poems contained some similarity of theme and focus. But his
retitling of the earliest of her poems, "To my Niece Dorothy, a sleepless
Baby" (composed 1805), as "The Cottager to her Infant; by my Sister"
(published 1815) reveals the difference between them; she approaches the
infant as an active and willful being while his focus is solely on the
poem's speaker. The persona that William installs in Dorothy's poem is
a protective device that divides her from the maternal role, but Dorothy
Wordsworth does not accept this public and impersonal poetic relation
to the child. In this sense her children's verse intensifies the politics of
poet and addressee that children's literature in general reveals.

"Address to a Child" (composed 1806, published 1815), written a
year after "To my Niece," acknowledges the role of the child's voice in
storytelling, and the poet's responsibility to the child's creative facility.
The poem attempts to cajole the child into obedience through
storytelling, a narrative method that responds to the child's voice in a
way that reveals this to be a true address in which the response is both
anticipated and integrated in the poetic utterance. The poem begins,
"What way does the wind come? What way does he go?," a ritualizing
device that plays with the rhythms and repetitions that engage children's
imaginations. At each turn in the story we sense a change in the direction
not of the wind, but in the child's attention and his possible questions.
More is at stake than following and redirecting the child's attention, for
this is also a poem about the Romantic wind. But agency is ascribed to
the wind, not just as a symbol of the creative power of imagination, but
in order to activate and animate what it might be in its own creative
right. The child's imagination and the wind are linked through the aid
of the speaker, who does not herself represent the visionary mind of the
poem but rather the child's nurturer and guide. And the stress on the
domesticity of the address's setting ("Here's a *cozie* warm house for
Edward and me") unseats the solemnity and divine power normally
ascribed to the Romantic wind without distilling from it its creative and
inspirational drive. In these poems Dorothy figures the child, rather than
the wind, as the subjective self. (See Shelley's "Ode to the West Wind"
(1819) for a contrasting and more standard vision.) To focus on the child
as simultaneously subjectively present and yet also becoming, growing
into someone else, provides an imaginative opportunity, a projection into
the better-parented future with its new generations.

Because the Romantic period was also the blossoming of children's literature as a genre and as a marketplace commodity, the Wordsworths' poems to and about children provide an interesting light on this newly popular form. They themselves did not publish specifically in the children's literature market, but Charlotte Smith and Catherine Anne Dorset did, as did Charles and Mary Lamb. William Godwin and his second wife, Mary Jane Clairmont, established a children's press, the Juvenile Library, in which even the young Mary Godwin (later Shelley) published. Against the Wordsworths' poems, Smith's poems written for children offer an interesting and certainly more self-consciously focused contrast.

Smith's *Conversations Introducing Poetry* (1804) was so popular that it was republished and reissued until 1863. The work uses an experimental form to combine teaching with amusement by interlacing poetry and prose. Based on the cultural assumption we still believe today that children have a natural affinity for lyric songs, Smith uses verse to gain the child's interest and then weaves them in with prose "conversations" between a maternal figure, Mrs Talbot, and her children, George and Emily. Like Dorothy Wordsworth's poems to infants, Smith's lyrics purport to teach children about nature and the proper ways to care and feel for nature. As complex as these weavings seem, they are further complicated by the real intrusion of the fictional children's aunt, whose parts are written by the real-life aunt of Smith's own children, Catherine Dorset.

Although the two children, and by extension all children readers of the work, are Smith's addressees, the prose conversations between the poem lessons allow Emily and George to become an active part of the text. This tactic frees up the question of subject and object, self and other, that comes between poets like William Wordsworth and the Romantic child. Smith is able to connect to the child as Dorothy Wordsworth does in her poems, and similarly allows for another subject, such as nature or a natural entity, that needs to be understood and cared for. Such beings would seem to resemble William Wordsworth's natural addressees like the butterfly, except that Smith does not take the natural entities to have a mystical relation to divinity. The individual poems are much more pragmatic than William Wordsworth's in their addresses to insects ("To a Green-chafter," "Invitation to a Bee," "The Early Butterfly," "The Moth"), to animals such as the hedgehog, and to flowers, birds, and trees. These addressees are not symbols for something else, but representatives of their species; as such, they connect the child directly to nature, without a sentimentalized intercession of the speaker and his emotional

101

experiencing of the connection. But perhaps more significantly for im-
parting a Romantic attitude to the child, certain strategic poems are to
a scenic landscape: "A Walk by the River," "An Evening Walk by the
Sea-side," "The Heath." These poems address the children rather than
nature, in order to teach them how to appreciate what they are seeing,
and how to understand the emotions attached to the land and water.
These children are being taught by the maternal figure to feel the High
Romantic aesthetic, but they are also being taught to feel the connecting
emotion arising from the land, and to value their national identity.
Smith's emotive pedagogy is Romantically connected to the nostalgia for
a more honest and heroic past bred out of the faked antique poetry of
Macpherson and Chatterton, but it is also a maternal reaction to the
destruction in France of the land and of a past during this period. By
bonding the child to its natural and national matrix of emotions, associations, and ideas, Smith can educate the new generation into a love of the
land and the nation that will prevent future revolution at home.

It is clear from Smith's "conversations" that nationalism as a Romantic invention has special pertinence to women. Women express this
pertinence in terms of what children need to know before they grow up,
and they see educating the child as citizen as a promotion of the ideal
of the virtuous republic. And it is because the rhetoric of nationalism
uses the family and home to symbolize what are in fact economic and
therefore nationalistic interests that women felt compelled to write into
being a more caring nation. There is also a potent ideological pull that
women must face between a nostalgic depiction of the home as a place
of privilege and love, and the drive of the modern with all its promise
of political and intellectual equality. By the time a writer like Felicia
Hemans was publishing in the 1820s, High Romanticism had peaked,
Napoleon was dead, and Wollstonecraft had long been a dirty word.
Britain had passed through a reactionary response to revolution and by
1824 was in the reform era. It was in this period, in which reform
legislation was seriously proposed, that Britain made its belated and
moderate political response to the French Revolution. Despite political
initiatives for reform, however, women found themselves in an increasingly conservative environment. Writers like Hemans found safety and
even acclaim in focusing on the domestic, the family, and the preservation of social institutions that concern the family (see McGann, 1993a;
Sweet, 1994). Like Mary Shelley, Hemans does not engage child audiences or children's literature, and instead returns us to our discussion of
maternal nationalism through her use of the home as political metaphor

to produce an agenda for adults similar to the one we saw in children's literature.

Felicia Hemans (1793–1835) was born during the years of French revolutionary tumult and came of age during the last years of Napoleon's reign. She published her first volume of poems in 1808 with her parents' help, and her *Domestic Affections and Other Poems* in 1812, the same year she married. After having five sons, she was deserted by her husband, and Hemans wrote to support her family. Her many poetic publications include *The Forest Sanctuary* (1825), *Records of Woman with Other Poems* (1828), and *Songs of the Affections* (1830). Her poems about the home reveal how nationalism is especially pertinent to women because of the almost allegorical use of the family's relation to the home to exemplify the economic and political interests of the nation. In Hemans's "The Homes of England" (1828), this focus clearly dictates the oddly nostalgic tone of the speaker. The poem projects into the future a longing for the past, while it breaks down the different classes of homes present in England. First the "stately homes of England," or country homes of the upper class, are described with their "ancestral trees," deer and swans (Wu, 1997: 574). But the wealthy homes are described in terms of their picturesque appearance, and it is not clear that anyone lives there. More than anything, these homes are symbolic of the proud power England is capable of. Next comes the "merry homes of England," and these are where families live. With a woman's voice in song and the telling of children's stories, these homes are described in terms of daily life and familial love ("What gladsome looks of household love / Meet in the ruddy light!"). The "blessed homes of England" describe the home of clergy and the religiously minded, and here again the symbol of the house is more important than who might live there ("How softly on their bowers / Is laid the holy quietness / That breathes from Sabbath hours!"). Finally, the "cottage homes of England," which she locates by the "thousands on [England's] plains" round up the catalog of house types, and again the cottage is described symbolically rather than by those who inhabit it. The cottages "are smiling o'er the silvery brooks / And round the hamlet fanes. / Through glowing orchards forth they peep," we are told, and the only hint of inhabitants comes from the line "And fearless there the lowly sleep."

It takes the final stanza to pull together what it is that these different classes of home represent of – or to – the nation: "The free, fair homes of England!" It is in the sum of these homes that nationalism itself, constructed as a nostalgia for a perfect past, infuses the hearts of the populace: "Long, long, in hut and hall, / May hearts of native proof be reared / To guard each hallowed wall!" All these homes will produce the defenders of the nation, and each can do so precisely because of that mother's song and the children's stories heard in the "merry" or middle-class homes, with their reversions to "Merry Old England" understood. It is because of these uses of the poetic voice – poetry as applied to maternalism, the instruction of children, and the creation of national nostalgia and pride – that each home can contain the seeds of a Romantic belief in the purity and destiny of the child. But against the earlier Romantic doubt about how the child will preserve its purity as it enters the public world, Hemans depicts a different vision of the Romantic child. Her child represents a healthy continuance between the nostalgic past and a nostalgically projected future that the very child safeguards. How the nation is to be reproduced as healthy and safe depends very much on the maternal voice and the stories children are told, the same message Smith inserts into her "conversations." Strikingly, the poem ends with: "And green for ever be the groves / And bright the flowery sod, / Where first the child's glad spirit loves / Its country and its God!" What had been an evocation of the naturalized rural landscape, differing only from a Wordsworthian landscape by being peopled in its middle-class rather than its lower-class referents, changes abruptly into a political anthem. The "child's glad spirit," alludes to the gladness of Wordsworth's "Ode" on immortality (Wu, 1998: 375–80). Coleridge's "Dejection: An Ode" (Wu, 1998: 507–11) urges joy on the child Edmund, but here the joy urged on the child is not to preserve its connection with nature, but to create a connection with the nation. Once the nation is itself maternal, the need for nature as a mediating agent between the individual subject and the divine no longer applies. Here the child has already been properly educated, and therefore the nation is safe from external invasion and internal transgression. With the health of such relational ties in place, there is no need for anxiety over female transgression, individualist selfishness, or revolutionary foment. In such a land, the women writer can be free to create; Hemans's healing of the public–private divide produces a counter and framing utopia to Sarah Scott's *Millenium Hall*. These two works, one written before and the other after the revolutionary and Napoleonic devastation that so violently mark the period, both envision a place where the private is the only political available.

Hemans, the most published woman poet of the century, lived when the overt political writing that had been possible in the 1790s was no longer conceivable, when public female transgression was far less tolerated, and when the feminine approach to republican virtue was the most acceptable frame for women's writing. She was a writer who understood philosophical as well as artistic traditions, but, unlike Scott, she also understood that in order to sell her work she would have to incorporate an approach to art by which the artist is her own artwork, as in the spectacular case of Letitia Elizabeth Landon (L.E.L.) who was also writing during this latter part of the period. Hemans's solution, very much in the footsteps of William Wordsworth, was to combine philosophy with aesthetic embodiment by crafting her poems so that she, like Wordsworth, became the voice of the nation. Writing during the period when Wordsworth is not yet poet laureate but is clearly writing as, and even received as, the voice of the nation, Hemans takes over the female charge of that role. She converts the temper of the times into the kind of narrative she wants to be witness to. This is a type of culture-making that is transformative rather than conservative, and it provides Hemans with a philosophically grounded authority seemingly not of her own making.

The strategy of this discussion so far has been to analyze women's and men's writings as both contributions and reactions to a specific historical cultural moment and its effects. Chapter 3 will change the focus from one on a cultural moment to an exploration of how a single genre represents that culture. The explosion of the popularity of the Gothic has usually been accounted for by representing it as a woman's genre that both women writers and women readers took undue and even degenerate delight in. But men writers explored the possibilities of the Gothic equally assiduously. Again, the division between men's and women's writing blurs when we consider the textual evidence. Again, the divide is political rather than artistic, a matter of critique *as* a Romantic attitude versus a more recognizable Romanticism, so that this divide is often politicized more by our own modes of reading than by the writers themselves.

Further Reading

E. J. Hobsbawm, *The Age of Revolution, 1789–1848* (1962). A detailed overview of the complex historical forces that produced the formative revolutions of the eighteenth and nineteenth centuries.

Joan Landes, *Women and the Public Sphere in the Age of the French Revolution* (1988). Landes's research opened the debate concerning women's role in the French Revolution and in the formation of the modern public sphere. Essential background for anyone researching Wollstonecraft, Hays, or Williams.

Chapter 3

Women and the Gothic: Literature as Home Politics

Figure 3   *The Ghost Story!*, by R. W. Buss. Lithograph, advertisement for Dr Jayne's
Expectorant. Undated, private collection

Queen of the solemn thought – mysterious Night!
Whose step is darkness, and whose voice is fear!
Thy shades I welcome with severe delight,
And hail thy hollow gales, that sigh so drear!
Ann Radcliffe, The Romance of the Forest, *p. 83*

The novelistic genre that came to fruition in the Romantic period and that best captures the popular imagination of Romantic culture is the Gothic. The Gothic is escapist fiction that explores the threshold between the real and the supernatural, between what is knowable and what is known. It does so by exploiting characters' and readers' fears about the unknown and it compels us by promising mystery and intrigue. The Gothic usually centers on a patriarchal villain or a patriarchal institution such as the Catholic Church. It is typically set in the past and in another land, such as Germany or Italy, and it tends to focus on the beautiful and desirable heroine whose fate is to be victimized by the villainous father figure.

Some writers at the time were aware of the implications of a genre that too expressly captured the fantasies of popular culture. In *Northanger Abbey* (1818), Jane Austen's satirical treatment of the rage for Gothic romance, Austen is less critical of the Gothic genre itself than of readers' obsessive reaction to it. Her argument centers on the rational achievements of the Enlightenment against all belief in supernatural forces. How can this genre be so excessively popular when it insistently revives superstitious terror, the abuses and horrors real and purported of the medieval Catholic Church, and irrationality: all objects Enlightenment thinkers struggled to eradicate through scientific reason? Austen's most specific criticism, which she places in the mouth of her hero, Henry Tilney, concerns the improbability of imaginatively importing these anachronistic and entirely fictional terrors onto home ground:

> "Dear Miss Morland, consider the dreadful nature of the suspicions you have entertained. What have you been judging from? Remember the country and the age in which we live . . . Does our education prepare us for such atrocities? Do our laws connive at them? Could they be perpetrated without being known, in a country like this, where social and literary intercourse is on such a footing . . . Dearest Miss Morland, what ideas have you been admitting?" (Vol. II, ch. 9)

Henry's reminder of the difference between reality and fiction is instructive for the novel's heroine Catherine and for us as well. As she realizes that all her suspicions of Henry's father are of her own manufacture, we too realize we have been in suspense to discover the secret to the "mystery." We are forced to laugh at how willingly irrational we can be even as we laugh at Catherine.

We are usually less self-conscious about this willingness to be drawn into an irrational world, and more ingenuous in our desire, as strong as Catherine's, to be frightened. The Gothic itself does not aspire to either amusement or self-recognition, but rather uses our willing fear to explore the realms of transgression within an apparent or approximate realism. The Gothic makes evil believable so that we realize its appearance even in our own lives, or even in ourselves. It forces us to recognize that transgression does indeed exist, despite Austen's warning, on home ground.

Unlike most types of novels, the Gothic tends to focus on a heroine, an innocent like Catherine, who must actively seek her own rescue from tyranny and supernatural events, rather than a hero. It is an odd aspect of this genre that the typical Gothic hero who attends the heroine is a Romantic poet figure like Henry whose sensitive personality combines both Enlightenment reason and Romantic emotion. Nearly all Romantic literature puts this figure at the center of its narrative, but the Gothic subordinates the sensitive man to a minor status who is necessary for plot resolution only. This lesser role is that normally cast for literary heroines. The Gothic's inversion of major and minor roles for the protagonist makes it unusual as a Romantic genre and at the same time representative of the questions about gender and limitations, patriarchy and institutional control, that are at the heart of the Romantic movement and Romantic culture.

When Austen ridicules this inversion of gender roles, she does so in a way that still speaks to Catherine's qualities as a heroine. As a heroine, she is more imaginatively and sensitively inclined, and is thus more susceptible to the Gothic's dark imagination than Henry is; it is she who can actively investigate the mysteries she encounters, and whose interruption of the Tilneys' home purges the darkness that inhabits Northanger Abbey. Austen's critique does not attack the idea of a female protagonist but rather supports her belief that female characters, like real-life women, need reason as much as do men to solve what are, to her, not supernatural or Gothic problems but the problems of real life. Her ridicule, then, is directed not against men or patriarchal society (the usual target of the Gothic). Rather, she attacks the very women who promote the ideal of a sensibility-laden heroine who must act on intuition and emotion rather than logic: the women writers who provide and women readers who demand this kind of fiction. Austen's attitude is not typical of Gothics by women but it helps us to see how the Gothic's structure makes it difficult for the woman writer interested in Romantic critique to pursue critique clearly and without complicity. One point in particular is helpful in seeing this: Henry's rationalism is preferable to Catherine's gullibility most obviously when the reader is made to realize the dangers of a fiction that centers on the incarceration and abuse of women, as the Gothic does. As Austen points out, it is because such acts are illegal in reality that they can be titillating in fiction, but she worries that such fiction can negatively affect women's sense of self and their rational processes. She is therefore less concerned with what we might call "home politics," the patriarchal practices prevalent in the domestic sphere, and more with the way in which Gothic fiction targets women readers, seducing them with the heroine's vulnerability rather than exposing the political dangers of abuse to women.

But helpful as this point is, the home politics of the Gothic is more complex than Austen admits, and its feminist motivation needs to be understood. Sexual politics in the home has two fundamental impulses. One is external, and drives inward in order to intrude on the privacy and supposed protection of domestic space; the other proceeds from the internal in the opposite direction, expanding the privacy of imaginative psychic space outward to fill and distort the dimensions of the home. The first impulse is driven by the demands of the public or state on privacy itself that force past our personal barriers and defenses, while the second pushes our private selves outward so that we realize how little protection the walls of our own homes actually afford us. The first makes us realize how politics affects the personal, but it does not rob us of our sense of identity or individuality; the second begins by undermining our sense of identity through terror and paranoia until the personal can no longer be distinguished from the political. Such situations of domestic abuse – whether perpetrated by family members or state leaders – put in place a different definition of the individual's experience. In either case, when a fictional home becomes unsafe or imprisoning, then there is room to explore how one can experience the self more fantastically and more politically.

The issues raised by the debates over individual rights and women's rights, particularly in the 1790s, gave rise to such exploration. Despite Austen's protestations, domestic abuse and paranoia are immediately present, familiar, and believable in the period's patriarchal culture, and such abuse has its own seductive appeal. Literature that structures its narratives on the very "domestic ideology" which makes appealing women's subordination to men's rule even in the home must either reproduce that ideology or critique it. Broadly speaking, the Gothic form itself necessitates both responses because its popular appeal and market-ability are based on the seduction and titillation of the reader. It thus makes authors participate in this domestic ideology by promoting even when they are trying to critique it, as Austen complains.

Whether they are conscious of this double-bind or not, Gothic women authors often attempted to write themselves out of it, and one way they did so was by distancing the narrative either by historical period or by culture. However, these devices serve to hide the problem – protecting the text from seeming too political by offering the pretense that the fiction does not apply at home. This allows the reader to experience thrill and mystery, horror and terror as vicariously pleasurable emotions rather than dreadful experiences. How the writer employs these inescap-able aspects of the Gothic that are also aspects of High Romanticism – mystery and terror, emotions and individuality – and to what purpose, will focus questions about the genre in general and sharpen the gender analysis of this chapter.

Interest in the Gothic was initially a response to several new elements in late eighteenth-century British culture: the increasing awareness of middle and far Eastern cultures due to colonial rule and trade; the popularity of sentimental literature and the Cult of Sensibility; scholarly and hobbyist interest in antiquity and language origins; and spreading enthusiasm for aesthetic theories of the sublime and the picturesque. Late in the Romantic period, when the initial enthusiasm for Gothic fiction had waned, it regained momentum as a vehicle for critiquing society after the macabre – and even Gothic – French Terror was over. However, even the early Gothic texts explored the same inherent dangers of a patriarchal society and its potential for abusive relations, decadence, and irrespon-sible leadership that preoccupied the late texts. Both men and women writers exploring the imaginative dimensions of the Gothic found it provided several different lenses through which to view contemporary British society. Literary scholars often divide the resulting modes into two categories – the masculine and the feminine Gothic – although this is a simplistic view of the genre. It is fair to say that men and women Gothic writers do exhibit narrative tendencies that are marked by culture as gendered: women tend to shape their text around a love plot; men tend to model theirs on a failed hero (such as Faust) or Prometheus theme. But what complicates these categories is that women also treat the Promethean project, as for instance, in Mary Shelley's Gothic critique of the Prometheus myth in *Frankenstein*, while men treat the love plot, as does Walter Scott in *The Bride of Lammermoor* (1819). It will be more helpful, therefore, to classify the differences in the Gothic by distinguishing between internal versus external Gothic perspectives, following the two fundamental impulses of home politics described above. This produces three categories for us to examine: one external, *the social critique Gothic*; one internal, *the psychological drama Gothic*; and the third a feminist blend of the external and internal, *the radical critique Gothic*. Our concern here will be to discover the complexity of the highly popular Gothic: how it reflects issues central to Romantic culture and values central to High Romanticism; how it describes aspects of women's experience; and how it provides women writers with several outlets for revising that experience.

Defining the Gothic

Some of the most popular British Gothic authors of their day are names we still recognize: Ann Radcliffe, "Monk" Lewis, Charles Maturin. Many more writers were producing Gothics, including Clara Reeve, Charlotte Dacre, Charlotte Smith, whose names also belong to Romantic studies. But many names have been lost from view. Austen's heroine Catherine Morland is given a list of Gothic authors to read by her friend Isabella, and the list is one of popular novels that did not survive the test of time: *Midnight Bell* (1798) by Francis Lathom, *The Castle of Wolfenbach* (1793) and *Mysterious Warnings* (1796) by Mrs Parsons, *Clermont* (1798) by Regina Maria Roche, *Orphan of the Rhine* (1798) by Eleanor Sleath, *Necromancer of the Black Forest* (1794) by Peter Teuthold, and *Horrid Mysteries* (1796) by Peter Will. Besides other Gothics by these authors (Sleath, for instance, also wrote *Who's the Murderer?, or The Mysteries of the Forest*, 1802; *The Bristol Heiress, or The Errors of Education*, 1809; *The Nocturnal Minstrel, or The Spirit of the Wood* 1801; *Pyrenean Banditti*, 1811; and *Glenoven, or The Fairy Palace*, 1815), there are many more authors whose novels have not survived. It is important to recognize how widespread the Gothic was both in the literary marketplace and in the social consciousness of the period. Although we will be focusing on novels considered to be of literary as well as historical importance, and therefore representing "original" rather than stereotypical literary aspects, the popularity of the Gothic is due in great part to its predictability, as Austen's short list of titles implies.

It will be helpful to see what is original if we know what the stereotype is, and Eleanor Sleath's four-decker *Orphan of the Rhine* provides a good example of the type. In the first paragraph of this novel we learn that in the year 1605 the Catholic Julie de Rubine dwells in a cottage in the hills near Geneva (the same location as for Mary Shelley's *Frankenstein*). By the fourth paragraph a stranger introduces herself as an emissary from an aristocrat, the Marchese de Montferrat. This woman brings both a letter and an infant girl, and we learn that the Marchese has searched Julie out, intending that she raise the orphaned baby. Julie's startled emotional response to the Marchese's name alerts us that she has known him previously, and we immediately suspect that her own history is as mysterious as the infant's. The imminent death of her mother soon leaves Julie an orphan also, which binds her symbolically to the baby. By chapter 5 Julie must chose if she will accept the attentions of a Protestant suitor, and by chapter 7 she has to defend herself against a cruel aunt, "the unceasing visits of Vescolini, who seemed determined to persevere in his addresses . . . [and] his persecutions," and the increasingly apparent interest of the Marchese. The rapid pace of events, and the combination of mystery, sexual "persecution," and cruelty from a female family member all contribute to intensify our readerly need to discover how Julie will manage to maintain her honor and virginity through the next 37 chapters. Yet all of these elements, introduced so early in Sleath's novel, are standard fare: German location (or location in a Catholic country to make use of Catholic superstition and church abuses); earlier historical setting; mysterious past of an impoverished heroine; an orphan; cruel relatives; aristocratic sexual predators; their ruinous castles where the heroine is brought to live; and the inserted poems and stories of additional characters that help add mystery and atmosphere. Even though Romantic period readers were eager for more of the same, serious writers could use these elements in new ways to create works that have something unique to offer. Feminist critics are even more interested in how writers, particularly women writers, use these elements imaginatively to create works that critique society and sexual politics. However, before we think about these different ways of defining what is of value in a Gothic, we need to consider how such works may be distinguished by category. In doing this, we will see that value becomes attached to how successfully a work fulfills the requirements of its category.

In traditional accounts of the Gothic, critics have tended to divide the literature into at least two types, as mentioned above. The first is the feminine "terror" Gothic as defined by Ann Radcliffe, which should have an elevating element to it. The second is the masculine "horror" Gothic, which should simply scare you to death, as found in Horace Walpole's *The Castle of Otranto* (1764) or Matthew Gregory Lewis's *The Monk*

(1796) (see Ellis, 1989: ix–xviii). Ann Radcliffe produced her critical distinction between different classes of Gothic mystery in a posthumously published essay in the *New Monthly Magazine*. Here, Radcliffe explains that terror and horror are opposites, so that "the first expands the soul, and awakens the faculties to a high degree of life; the other contracts, freezes, and nearly annihilates them." She claims that Shakespeare, Milton, and Burke all focus on terror to elevate the reader to a sublime state, and that terror is a state of "uncertainty and obscurity" that is aligned with mystery rather than the superstition of horror (*New Monthly Magazine*, vol. 7, 1826: 149). Notably, she herself does not connect either class of Gothic to a gender. This equation was one her readers inferred based on what many considered to be the feminine characteristics of her own novels. Although Radcliffe bases her distinction on the difference in aesthetic emotion the reader feels on reading a Gothic, the validity she finds in terror as an "expand[ing]" emotion makes it the ideal vehicle for the external approach of social critique, a finding shared by Wordsworth in *The Prelude*, Shelley in *Mont Blanc* (1816), and by other High Romantics. The experience of "contract[ing]," by contrast, provides a physical expression for the psychological drive of the "internal" Gothics, and for High Romantic works that explore the inner psyche such as De Quincey's *Confessions of an English Opium Eater* (1821), or Coleridge's "Dejection: An Ode."

Montague Summers provides a slightly different classification: the "terror Gothic" (which is Radcliffe's "horror" Gothic), the "sentimental Gothic" (or love plot), and the "historical Gothic" (which is not clearly differentiated from the first two, but has elements of the historical romance in it) (Summers, 1964: 29–30). Summers's classification does seem to confirm that, in general, women writers of the Gothic did gravitate toward a style that uses aesthetic distance to avoid terrible consequences for the heroine (the "feminine" or "terror" mode). Men, by contrast, tended to employ a style that emphasizes the psychological to produce fictional devastation and a confrontation with death (the "masculine" or "horror" mode). But if we choose to follow either Radcliffe's or Summers's classes, we are stressing a too easy interpretation of sexual difference among writers that does not allow us to account for atypical but important cases. For instance, writers like Walter Scott or, later, Emily Brontë and Charles Dickens combine the "masculine" and "feminine" forms to produce a radically unresolved critique of individual will, inheritance, history, and social construction. Such critiques are powerful statements and need to be accounted for rather than ignored by a feminist interpretation, which is why the terms "external" and "internal" will be more helpful to us than gendered terms like "masculine" and "feminine."

One aspect of the traditional attempt to divide Gothic literature into a masculine and a feminine form is helpful to us, however, and worth retaining. It clarifies why the home politics of the Gothic helps to interpret the new ideology of the home as a safe haven from the public sphere of commerce, as well as its ever-threatening ruin. Home politics, then, is integrally related to the new middle-class sense of the home as both a refuge from the hostile world of commerce, and as a center of consumption that can prove ruinous to the family's income. Houses need repairs, furnishings and servants, while the ladies of the house want fashionable clothes and expensive parties. Both these representations of the home are based on the idea of marriage as an economic exchange of lands and money between the man and the bride's father, and of the place of marriage (the home) as a site of investment (good or bad) and protection (successful or failed). The home is in many ways the focal point of all Gothics because protagonists are either thrown out of their homes or incarcerated in them. This reveals why these two ways of viewing the home orient women readers' fascination with the genre, and it suggests a reason why earlier critics have wanted to associate those Gothics focusing on the home with women writers. For instance, in *Northanger Abbey*, Austen portrays the abbey as threatening rather than protective, controlled by Henry's father and lacking any feminine touch of the mother. Catherine is invited to the abbey when Henry's father believes her to be an heiress, but she is rudely ejected when he learns she is not. We then understand that his true personality is harsh and vindictive as we watch him throw Catherine out of his house in a manner befitting a real Gothic. This, Austen indicates, is not the stuff of Gothic, but the stuff of real life: the home can be the site of consumption or privation, protection or violation. Whatever Henry may claim for the English legal system and civilized life, Austen lets us know that the economic exchange of women, and their precarious relation to the home that is so essential to Gothic plots, is a fact of ordinary life as well.

Austen's seriousness about this particular point highlights the central importance of the home to women's safety and happiness. But it is not just women who are so affected, as is proved by many plots in the literature of the period that dwell on the difficulties of younger sons who cannot inherit and the possibility of an older son's disinheritance. The division of Gothics into "male" and "female," then, is not supported by this examination of the home even though such a division points us to it.

115

In many ways, it is the home itself that creates the categories of the external or social world, and the internal or psychological world. The external and internal are, remember, the two key terms for the classification of Gothics we will use here. And such terms, which stress the state of the social world and the experience of the individual, are more connected to Romantic themes than are "male" and "female" or even "terror" and "horror," with the concern with how the mind works, with social issues, political justice, and population theories. These concerns, one of which leads to the modern study of psychology and the other to sociology, provide the relevance of these internal and external divisions to the modern mind and to the way we think about the world today.

The external, or socially oriented, Gothic has its foundations in the earliest works we can properly term Gothics: Horace Walpole's *The Castle of Otranto* (1764) and Clara Reeve's *The Old English Baron* (1778). Notice that by pulling these into the same category, we have already side-stepped whether these works could be categorized as "male" or "female" Gothics. Indeed, Walpole's novel could be considered a male or horror Gothic, and Reeve's a female or terror Gothic. But by discussing them as such we would not pay proper attention to the way in which each examines its world and pronounces judgment on it, and how very similar these two works actually are. Both of these works are highly anxious about the lineage and patrimony of the hero, his rejection and disinheritance at the hands of a now decadent patriarchy, and the intrusion of phantasms and the marvelous to establish the origin of the true son against the distortions imposed by the usurper. These novels are both about the home, but here they are more concerned with the man's relation to it and the issue of inheritance. This early identification of the Gothic form with the home as a male problem of inheritance will turn increasingly in later Gothics to an identification of the home with the economic vulnerability of women. This very different vulnerability is one that leads to potential or actual sexual abuse of women in order to gain control of their fortune. Gothic novels concerned with the external or social world will use this focus to critique current inheritance and marriage laws, while Gothics concerned with the internal or psychological will emphasize the feelings such vulnerability and threatened abuse arouse in the imagination. It is often the case, although not always so, that women writers will favor the external approach because it allows them to critique laws that do not provide women with rights and do not protect women from abusive practices. Furthermore, such writers attempt to stress women's innate rights by creating scenes that reveal female characters' natural affinity for the highest forms of nature as revealed in sublime landscapes. This connection of the heroine to the sublime implicitly supports social arguments for her right to better legal protection. Thus we see the clearest way in which the terms "external" (or social critique), "female Gothic" and "terror Gothic" could be considered synonymous. But if we do use them interchangeably, we run the risk of ignoring important exceptions in Gothics by men or Gothics that do not employ the sublime to invoke terror. The same argument applies for "internal" (or psychological drama), "male Gothic" and "horror Gothic."

However external it is, *The Castle of Otranto* also contains the seeds of the internal kind of Gothic, the psychological drama, which Reeve recognizes but strongly criticizes. The most important of these seeds in Walpole's *Otranto* is its mythic dimension that has the potential to extend into the demonized psyche. Examples of such are the murderous *doppelgänger* James Hogg produces in *Confessions of a Justified Sinner* (1824) or the seductive vampire of Bram Stoker's later *Dracula* (1897), and his forefather, the monster of Polidori's *Vampyre* (1819). These nightmare figures allow authors to explore a negative relation to nature that is the very opposite of the sublime: the abject. The sublime allows the human imagination to transcend, but the abject forces it into a humiliating recognition of its own capacity to degrade itself. This form of Gothic is also related to the Romantic closet drama, particularly works like Byron's *Manfred* (1817), a character whose name reminds us of the tyrant of *Otranto*. When a writer combines the inner explorations of the abject with the political implications of social critique – not so much with its promises of women's connections to the sublime, but with its promises of romance and of a utopian resolution for the heroine – then we have the radical critique Gothic. Such works exploit both the idealism of the social critique Gothic and the nightmare vision of the psychological drama in order to point out how real life can and does contain elements of both these extremes. Mary Wollstonecraft's *The Wrongs of Woman, or Maria* (1798) and Joanna Baillie's play *Witchcraft* (1836) both explore how real social restrictions on women's behavior or their imaginations can lead them into literally life-threatening situations that are historically plausible, such as imprisonment and accusations of witchcraft.

Ann Radcliffe and other women working in the social critique Gothic seek to oppose the psychological drama Gothic with an ennobling "terror" drawn from the aesthetic sublime. Reeve, whose *Old English Baron* anticipates Radcliffe's social critique tradition, begins somewhat differently with an insistence on both a rational and moral universe, while Radcliffe is willing to use the supernatural to keep her reader in suspense but eventually reveals all as historical and explicable phenomena. Where these two writers really differ is in Reeve's very Christian medieval world, where plot twists are narratively worked out as the result of providence and divine intervention in clear antithesis to the medieval superstition that infuses Walpole's Gothic tale and is exploited by all subsequent Gothic writers. It is superstition rather than belief that allows for the paranoid universe of Monk Lewis, James Hogg, and Charles Maturin, where religious figures are the servants of self-interest or of human evil, if not of the devil. If Radcliffe uses religious belief or superstition, it is in the aid of plot and suspense, not narrative morality. Here we see that Reeve would not clearly fit into either the old "male" or "female," "horror" or "terror" categories. Reeve's need to instill a Christian morality into her tale *The Old English Baron* comes from her criticism of Walpole's *Castle of Otranto* that his heavy use of "machinery" emphasizes a plausible paranormal activity. This she finds to be too close to the medieval superstition that the Enlightenment sought to eradicate. Walpole's use of horror threatens her view that literature should portray a rational and realistic world. Walpole, however, is less interested in exploring reality than in moral and psychological limits. In *Otranto* he portrays the extremes of personality and of appetites, and in doing so also turns the non-literal stories of nightmares into literature. Reeve prefers to relegate dreams to the realm of divine influence, and rejects the power of the unconscious to determine human behavior. Radcliffe then turns Reeve's version of the dream into the heroine's sublime and uplifting experience of nature. This essential difference in the role of the dream determines the division of the Gothic into external and internal.

So far we can see that by distinguishing exteriority and interiority (to ignore, temporarily, the third type of Gothic which blends them together), we can cut across the difficulties caused by both male and female writers invoking domestic novel traditions. When Romantic texts cement both these forms together, as in Coleridge's "Rime of the Ancient Mariner" (1798) and Mary Shelley's *Frankenstein*, then we have something that is grounded in, but extends beyond, the Gothic. Clearly, the Gothic must be viewed not as a minor genre, but as something that, in its component parts at least, is central to the Romantic project. This is particularly apparent in its natural–supernatural explorations that can also be discovered at the foreground of Wordsworth and Coleridge's *Lyrical Ballads*, Byron's Oriental Tales, Robinson's verse, Blake's mythology, Keats's romances, and Mary Shelley's fiction.

But how did the term "Gothic" come to be used for this particular genre? The term was not initially used to refer to literary works, but to the Goths and their language; it was later applied to a period of late medieval architecture, or to signify the barbarous in reference to the "Dark Ages." As a casual historical distinction, the term was used to differentiate the "romantic" or romance aspect of the medieval period from the earlier classical era. *Gothicism* was used by Thomas Gray to refer to his friend Horace Walpole's fake castle, Strawberry Hill, rather than to his horror novel, *The Castle of Otranto*. The term "Gothic" was not yet in vogue, but the thriller tales imbued with elements of the old romances are what we normally think of as Gothics. Nevertheless, Gothic architectural ruins from Henry VIII's destruction of the monasteries dotting the British landscape were becoming an important visual element for aesthetic theory, especially the picturesque. It was not a far step to imagining being in the ruin itself and of seeing ghosts of the original inhabitants. Such ghosts would have to have been in life the originals of the old romance heroes, their beloveds, and the villains that attempt to destroy them. Indeed, the old medieval romances that are the literary inheritance of the Gothic were narratives of knightly quests that involved supernatural agents, knights with false honor, and feats of chivalric heroism. A more recent source for Gothics was seventeenth-century French romances, especially those of Madeleine de Scudéry. Writers of Gothics had plenty of material already in the literary tradition to draw on, and the reading audience was already well prepared to like Gothics and to be thrilled by them. And because of this background, the Gothic was perceived to be a native form rather than a classical one; to embrace it as authentic and native is to emphasize British over classical or ancient culture. The Gothic is therefore more real to the average Romantic reader's imagination than classically inspired literature, but its native origins and its popular appeal also make it a "low" art form compared to the "high" art of classical artworks. This, as well as the preponderance of women writing Gothics during this period, has made it difficult until recently for us to see how representative of Romantic culture and literature the Gothic actually is.

We turn here to an overview of the novels that constitute the literary tradition of this genre. The Gothic is usually said to begin with Horace Walpole's *The Castle of Otranto*, although Walpole's intent was merely to extend the illogic of the sentimental novel with the nightmare logic of superstition. As he put it in his preface to the second edition, he wanted "to blend the two kinds of Romance, the ancient and the modern." Clara Reeve more fully develops the form with *The Champion of Virtue: A*

Gothick Story (1777), reissued and better known as *The Old English Baron* (1778). Reeve recognized the possibilities of Walpole's novel for exploring women's social and legal situation but deplored its masculinist violence; he, likewise, found her emphasis on the feminine aspect a distinct undermining of his artistry. Although both writers focused on the external impulse, Walpole's use of violence and the supernatural was to develop into the internal or psychological drama Gothic, while Reeve's interest in the external would be redirected toward a story about women in Radcliffe's hands. Thus the Gothic developed into two more or less distinct strands that would then together produce yet a third.

The external strand or social critique Gothic takes a positive and idealistic perspective that resembles in part the domestic romance. It consists of sensational love stories, such as those written by Ann Radcliffe and Charlotte Smith, and involves active heroines who detect and explore in order to counter both their attackers and the supernatural. By the novel's end, they have managed to heal the poisoned home in order to create a healthy one in which to live out their future. The point of these love stories is for the narrative to prevent or prolong as much as possible the lovers' meeting. In this way the reader's desire for this constantly deferred event acts as a lever into seeing the villain's intervening patriarchal privileges as equally arbitrary to the deferral of the hero or heroine's (and the reader's) desire. However, the social critique is not entirely a women's genre, and was also chosen by some men writers because it resembles so highly earlier sentimental writers like Samuel Richardson in his novel *Clarissa* (1747–9).

The internal strand of the Gothic, the psychological drama, was usually engaged by men writers like Matthew "Monk" Lewis, Charles Maturin, James Hogg. But it had its female adherents as well, such as Charlotte Dacre. These were writers interested in the horrific machinery of the supernatural of Walpole's *Castle of Otranto* that so aggrieved Reeve, and because of this it is usually fatalistic and negative, in contrast to the idealism of the first strand. The psychological drama is also concerned with patriarchy, but in a much more individual and psychologically disturbing sense. Not a critique at all, this strand explores the limits of individualism. Therefore, the less important heroine becomes passively imprisoned or murdered (often by her father or lover) or represents a diabolically seductive force, while the hero, more often an anti-hero, is exiled from the idealized home and wanders the earth as an inversion of the spiritual quest characterizing High Romantic poetry. This strand also invokes a strongly Romantic play with guilt and improper passions; Lewis's hugely successful *The Monk* (1796), for in-

120

stance, involves cross-dressing, sexual relations within the monastery, incest, murder, and Satan himself. The machinery is both supernatural and superstitious, involving the worst imaginings of the medieval, and using fantasy to create a warped world that matches the warped mentality of the anti-hero.

The romance of the first strand and the fantasy of the second both bring to the Gothic genre the correlation between the social body and psychological pain. This is the connection between the relations that produce the social body (the marriage of the heroine and hero) and those mental evils that can get in the way of these relations (nightmares turned into real abuses such as incest and beatings or the pain of paranoia, hysteria, madness). Romantic literature often emphasizes the connections between motherhood and pain, whether bodily (imprisonment) or mental (madness). Examples are Walpole's play *The Mysterious Mother* (1768), which Radcliffe quotes for chapter epigraphs in *The Italian* (1797), and the Gothic selections of the 1798 *Lyrical Ballads*, including Wordsworth's "The Mad Mother" and Coleridge's "The Dungeon." The essential link between motherhood and pain, with its biblical connotation of Eve's punishment in childbirth, is the absent presence of the Gothic. The mother is nearly always absent or dead when the narrative begins and the heroine must strive to discover her or her story, or the heroine's own maternal identity, before the narrative can resolve. The Gothic, then, is a purposeful disconnection of the domestic triangle, an exploration of what can go wrong in a patriarchy so strong that the mother is unnecessary to the story, the home is governed by the father, and the future generation is at stake. Mary Shelley's *Frankenstein*, although more properly classed as science fiction, is often considered a Gothic precisely because it focuses on the death of the mother and the consequences of non-maternal generation. Charlotte Dacre's *Zofloya* (1806) begins with the recognition of the domestic-destruction imperative when the libertine villain Count Ardolph is described as one whose energies were devoted to "the savage delight to intercept the happiness of wedded love . . . to blast with his baleful breath the happiness of a young and rising family" (Dacre, 1997: 43).

In response to the genre formulation of the disconnected domestic triangle, women writers who were more concerned with political change than with the Gothic genre in and of itself, used the genre to critically evaluate social injustices. These writers employ a more political approach to the question of interior and exterior in the third form of Gothic that we are calling the radical critique Gothic. As I explained above, this third class of Gothic blends the social and psychological aspects of the first two

121

classes in order to more fully critique particular institutions or specific social practices.

Now that we have our three classes of Gothic – social critique, psychological drama, and radical critique – how are we to think about them in relation to Romanticism and to feminist concerns? We might begin by saying that, in general, the Gothic interrogates the interrelations of the domestic triangle, a specifically Romantic act that strongly interested feminists of the time. The need to cut the maternal parent out of the bond between father and son, to repress her until she becomes evanescent, mysterious, supernatural, produces both the mystery of the first strand (as in *The Mysteries of Udolpho*, 1794, by Radcliffe) and the guilt and paranoia of the second (as in *Melmoth the Wanderer*, 1820, by Charles Maturin). Questioning her absence is an essential social act in the social critiques and the radical critiques because without her the home becomes an unstable center for the heroine. The mother's absence is less questioned than fearfully accepted in psychological drama Gothics as an almost Freudian depiction of the deep fears of rejection and desertion that underlie our dreams and nightmares. Alternatively, if the mother is too present as the evil mother or stepmother, that is, as the woman who resists being cut out or who displaces this absence onto her daughter, then she becomes the embodiment of mysterious evil. Often she turns into what men fear to be the full expression of female rage against the perverse use of patriarchal law. For instance, witches are often used to represent female rage at abusive male privilege. This is a fear that Sir Walter Scott delineates fully in *The Bride of Lammermoor* (1819) where the witch Ailsie Gourlay is hanged on North Berwick Law ("law" means hill: the witch is executed on the line where the legal and the geophysical meet). The centering focus on the mother's absence or evil presence provides us with one clue as to how to begin interpreting Gothics.

We can find another clue in how the Gothic uses the romance tradition, particularly in terms of the heroine and sentimental or sensational representations of her. In sentimental depictions, such as in Scott's *Bride of Lammermoor*, the heroine is passive and unable to defend herself against the evil machinations of others. Here, the victimized heroine of Scott's radical critique resembles the passive heroine of the psychological drama Gothic, although she is less sentimentally portrayed there. In sensational depictions, such as in any of Radcliffe's novels, the heroine actively investigates the evils that threaten her, and plays a leading role in defeating them by the novel's end. There are a number of reasons why this split developed in the Gothic between the female victim and the female investigative hero, some having to do with the literary traditions of romance and the sentimental novel. But most relevant to our interests is the relation between this development and the events of the French revolution (a reminder to us that the Gothic genre itself is not static but is affected by and reflects historical influence).

For the Gothic, romance must relate either literally or by analogy to the novel's representation of domestic and public space, both before the French Revolution and after the Reign of Terror. It is in this sense that the Gothic is one of the most representative and exemplary genres of the Romantic period. This is because of the way in which the revolution changed people's conceptions of the public and the private, the nation and the individual, the social and the psychological. The oppositions between these terms were transformed by the devastating ways in which their boundaries were blurred and diminished by revolutionary acts. Earlier novels either emphasize the element of possibility and of active heroism, or the destructive aspects of old laws that need to be revised because they turn potentially active heroines into victims. Later novels tend to increase the sentimental element of romance, with the effect that eventually the heroine becomes fully passive, retaining none of the active detective trait that is such an essential part of her role in the social critique Gothic. For instance, Burney's and Austen's last published novels, *The Wanderer* (1814) and *Persuasion* (written 1815), are heavily sentimentalist and pessimistic, although both authors wrote several domestic novels idealizing the love romance previously. They also incorporate certain elements of the Gothic, particularly the victimized heroine, even though they are not Gothics themselves. These two late novels take to heart the dangerously ambiguous signs emanating from Napoleon's Europe, and signal social fear on the heroine's body and spirit through rigorous constraint despite all persecution. Romance here is despairing rather than ideal, and reflects the way romance is treated in radical critique and psychological drama Gothics. By contrast, women novelists are generally determined in the early stages of the revolution to treat romance in an ideal fashion. Such novelists, particularly Ann Radcliffe (whose most positive novels, including *A Sicilian Romance, The Romance of the Forest,* and *The Mysteries of Udolpho,* were published between 1789 and 1794), mediate this romance by presenting a working map for women of how to behave during occupation by the French. Simultaneously, they carefully map out just how dangerous all but the most self-disciplined male behaviors could be, and dispose of the rake, the untutored heir, the selfish bourgeois, the arrogant patriarch one by one. Only the aristocrat by nature rather than by birth (like the chivalrous Theodore against the decadent Marquis in Radcliffe's *Romance of the Forest*) can out-sustain the vigilance of the heroine. Together they prove themselves capable of buttressing the new world no matter what its perils may turn out to be. This act of mapping, which is particular to the social critique, provides a positive response to the exigencies and possibilities that social upheaval offers to women. Clearly, we need to pay especial attention to how the heroine is portrayed, whether she is active and sensational or passive and victimized. And we need to analyze whether the novel is portraying her as such because of its Gothic category or because of the author's response to the pre- or post-revolutionary spirit of the times.

We have now two clues to follow in reading Gothics as feminist critics: how the mother is portrayed and how the heroine is portrayed. Moreover, we will have to pay attention to the opposed perspectives of external and internal, each showing the other as insufficient, that provide the two bases of Gothic literature: the "purity" of medieval virtue at one pole, and the nightmare fatalism of the unconscious at the other. Of particular interest from a feminist perspective will be the radical critique, which mediates the difference between the virtuous idealism of the social critique and the fatalism of the psychological drama Gothic.

Interestingly, of the three types of Gothic, the radical critique Gothic was the least appreciated by readers. It mediates the external and internal as a warning against both the daydream of purity and the nightmare of solipsism, and as such attains a greater degree of realism that appeals to today's reader. But for the Romantic reader the realism of this mode readily supplies the answer: it too pessimistically assesses a woman's ability to defend herself in real life, and readers were more interested in a heroine before she was seduced or fallen than afterward. Nevertheless, the relation here between social realism and romance focuses critique in a way we must recognize. The social critique attained a high popularity, partly because it so strongly resembled the quest romance (like novels by Henry Fielding and Scott) and the domestic romance (like novels by Burney and Austen) that were favorites with readers. We must recognize in this genre as well, despite its willingness to satisfy popular demand, the extent to which it broaches certain aspects of social reality (inheritance and marriage laws, for instance) and critiques them. Indeed, all three forms of Gothic reveal weaknesses in the social fabric, and it is this tendency that makes Gothic, in fact, central to the Romantic imagination. But it is the social critique Gothic and the radical critique Gothic that most carefully carry out the feminist critical agenda.

The Gothic as Domestic: Social Critique Gothics

Ann Radcliffe is the best-known writer of Gothics during the Romantic period and it is her formulation of the genre that provides the model for the social critique Gothic. But Radcliffe's own development of the terms and attitudes she uses in her distinctive novels owes much to the work of Clara Reeve, both in her early Gothic *The Old English Baron* and in the romance genre. Since Radcliffe and Reeve originate the terms of the external strand of Gothic, it is best we know something about their lives and literary careers.

Clara Reeve (1729–1807) was educated by her father, and was encouraged to read both classical and English history. Her first publication was a volume of poems, *Original Poems on Several Occasions* (1769), but she is best known for her novels *The Old English Baron* (1778), *The Two Mentors* (1783), *The Exiles* (1788), and the Gothic *Memoirs of Sir Roger de Clarendon* (1793). She also wrote extensively about education, as well as her work of literary criticism, *The Progress of Romance* (1785). Ann Radcliffe (1764–1823), born 35 years after Reeve, grew up in Bath. She married an Oxford graduate who worked as a journalist in 1787, and there is some speculation that his long work hours gave her the time and inclination to attempt novel writing. Her novels include *The Castles of Athlin and Dunbayne* (1789), *A Sicilian Romance* (1790), *The Romance of the Forest* (1791), *The Mysteries of Udolpho* (1794), *The Italian* (1797), and *Gaston de Blondeville* (written 1802, published posthumously). She also wrote poetry (collected after her death in *Poetical Works*, 1834) and travelogues, including *A Journey Made in the Summer of 1794 through Holland and the Western Frontier of Germany* (1795).

Much of the relation between these two authors has to do with their attitudes toward romance. Clara Reeve's *The Progress of Romance* is a meditation on the difference between the traditional romance and the more realistic novel called the "domestic romance." In considering Reeve's treatise on romance, it is important to understand the medieval and Renaissance forms of romance to be a genre written by men, about men, for men. Women characters appear as supernatural agents of good or evil, and as helpless victims with little relevance to the real goals of the hero. In Sidney's *Arcadia* (1590), for instance, regal women suffer misrecognition, rape, and harsh sentences. Reeve's argument in *The Progress*, however, is that the romance genre is amenable to women's imaginations and experiences. To strengthen her argument for a female

125

genre of importance, she also claims that romance developed out of early epic poetry and that it is the equal of epic. She argues its *natural* presence in cultural legacies in terms that Wordsworth echoes in his 1800 Preface to *Lyrical Ballads* for the natural and ancient practice of poetry. This is both a claim about authentic origins and about the originality of romance and Reeve presents her case by citing numerous scholarly treatises on the subject.

Radcliffe builds on Reeve's distinctions for the importance, naturalness, and femaleness of romance by calling her mode of Gothic "the romance or Phantasie." These terms were used in her original title for the *New Monthly* essay, although the title was editorially changed to "On the Supernatural in Poetry" to emphasize the more sublime aspect of her poetic work. Radcliffe's original choice provides a classification that defines her "sublime" fiction against horror novels like Walpole's *Otranto* or Lewis's *The Monk*. In taking the fantasy element of romance more seriously than its thriller elements, Radcliffe was, like Reeve, purposely distinguishing her work in terms of its moral quality. Radcliffe's insistence that she was writing fantasy hid the fact that her plots often focus on attempts to rape or forcibly marry heiresses; such attempts were a very real danger as proved by the passage of the Hardwicke Act of 1753, which proclaimed such deeds illegal (see Ellis, 1989: xi). If we look at Radcliffe's novels in this light, we see that domestic romances depicting non-inheriting heroines marrying wealthy gentlemen, such as Elizabeth Bennet's marriage to Darcy in Austen's *Pride and Prejudice*, are more fantastic than the plots of social critique Gothics. But by disguising the criticism her fiction performs by calling it fantasy, Radcliffe makes both her version of the Gothic and her critique of society less threatening, more of a daydream, and more palatable. In this way she can continue the traditional danger of romance for women, with its representation of abduction or imprisonment as the prelude to meeting the lover knight, as both a realistic and a critical device that hides its real intention behind the screen of fantasy. If Radcliffe's continuance of this disguise provides her novels with the readerly thrill and seductive quality that made her such a popular author, it also allows her to criticize social conditions in a non-threatening way. Furthermore, she can continue the fantasy by providing social utopian endings. However, in saying this we also have to understand how strong an inheritance the romance was for both the Gothic and for Radcliffe, and how difficult it was for her to break away. Her first successes, *The Romance of the Forest, A Sicilian Romance, The Italian . . . A Romance*, all indicate by their titles that she considers their romance element to supersede their Gothic mode. *The Mysteries of*

Udolpho, however, foregrounds Gothic mystery over romance, and other authors will increasingly resist and transform the Gothic–romance connection to provide an artistic opposition to changes in what Charlotte Smith calls "The Romance of Real Life."

Another aspect of Reeve's work that Radcliffe borrows is her emphasis on the real – what can be explained – and her resistance to the darker forces of the inexplicable. Romance as "phantasie" produces Gothics that are as earth-bound in their rationalization of supernatural occurrences as Austen's domestic novels are in their rationalization of unlikely love matches. Radcliffe, in particular, uses the explicable mystery as a way to reduce the threats to her heroine, and to increase interest in her love plot. This was important to do, since for women "nightmare" is a much more likely term than "phantasie" to represent the old romance form. Even in late medieval and renaissance verse epics or prose tales such as Sidney's *Arcadia* (1590), Ariosto's *Orlando Furioso* (1532), and Malory's *Morte D'Arthur* (1485), the rape, theft, or seduction of female characters is a recurrent plot motivator. Women writers who invoke the romance tradition, then, need to distinguish between the romance that emphasizes the hero's desire, and the sentimental fantasy of true love that redirects plot elements in the interests of the heroine. These are antithetical conventions even though both belong to or are derived from the romance.

Where Radcliffe fully differs from Reeve is her distinction between terror and horror. She follows aesthetic theory to do so, using Edmund Burke's definition of terror as that which leads to the transcendent experience of the sublime, and horror as that which stops the reader and character dead in their tracks. The first is the ecstatic leap out of the body that promises revelation, the second is the dreadful entrapment in the body that threatens fatal pain. Radcliffe equates terror with the sublime as an aspect of nature appreciation, and uses it to help her heroines imaginatively escape domestic thralldom, whereas horror defines the psychological thrill of the mysterious. Radcliffe stresses the importance of terror for her vision of the Gothic by closely differentiating between the picturesque, the beautiful, and the sublime in her popular *Romance of the Forest*, while leaving horrible incidents untheorized and not overtly discriminated. This allows Radcliffe to refuse real power to either the supernatural or the abject. When Radcliffe differentiates between horror and "positive horror" in her posthumous article, the "positive" she intends is a "source of the sublime" that is closer to terror and the compelling power of natural phenomenon. Horror in itself is marked by "uncertainty and obscurity, that accompany [it], respecting the dreader

127

evil" as well as by a dread of bodily decay and other horrific aspects of the natural world.

These aesthetic distinctions provide an index to the personalities and integrity of characters in *Romance of the Forest*. For instance, Radcliffe's heroine Adeline is contrasted with the more impetuous and undisciplined Clara. Clara has received a Romantic education from her father, in which sensitivity to duty and the needs of others have supposedly overcome her natural self-centeredness; instead, she has become a creature of emotional responsiveness, unable to be a moral guide or support to male others as Adeline is. Adeline, whose education was aristocratic as a child and then severe and monastic from the death of her parents, retains the inherent nobility of her birth that overcomes selfish dictates and allows her to exert self-control when in the company of family or strangers. She is deeply affected by the sublime aspect of landscape and of music, and we know her noble character from her appreciation of nature – but we learn from her by watching her actions, which are modeled themselves on the absolute integrity of romance chivalry. This integrity is depicted as inherent, a natural quality of the noble born that is accompanied by a native sensibility. The chivalrous young men who court Adeline are also men of sensibility, and Radcliffe depicts these attitudes in opposition to the superficial courtly manners of the patriarchal villains, and especially of the libertine and decadent Marquis.

Scholars have understood this novel as an illustration of the differences between the Marquis's patriarchal degeneracy and the "natural" or Romantic paternalism of Clara's father, the Swiss La Luc. Supposedly the Marquis and La Luc offer Adeline (or the reader) two opposed aesthetic modes: hedonism and naturalism. Yet Adeline is not unmarked clay awaiting the potter's cast, and she is specifically held up as a spiritual aristocrat against the Marquis's sophistry as well as against the undisciplined Clara. Radcliffe's novels offer part of their social critique by implication: literary villains are neither too exaggerated nor too empowered when compared to real persons. The self-indulgent Marquis, for instance, might be read as a figuring of the very real Marquis de Sade. At the time of the *Romance*'s composition Sade had already been incarcerated at Vincennes for more than a decade, imprisoned rather than executed for his crimes through his wife's influence at court. But Radcliffe's critique does not extend very far: if the villain is real, the heroine is idealized. Adeline is strong, but she had been raised to suffer and serve after knowledge of her aristocratic birth was suppressed by the Marquis himself, not to rule. Radcliffe pictures her as incapable of true action, but strongly resistant to evil forces.

In the subsequent *Mysteries of Udolpho*, Emily St Aubert is a more active and determined character, presenting a more assertive role model for female behavior. Her ability to hold the despotic Count Montoni at bay through several hundred pages, and to sustain encounters with ghosts, terrible portraits, and mysteries concerning her lineage present her as courageous and competent, a hero who overshadows the more fragile character of her lover Valancourt. Women readers adored this novel while critics reacted negatively to this novel's implicit critique of women's place in society.

Another way in which Radcliffe implicitly critiqued the social roles of women was her use of romance daydreaming. Although noted for her deployment of deferral and excitation, at the heart of Radcliffe's art is her ability to exploit the tremendous stretch available in daydream (the romance–fantasy equivalence) that produces the structure for sexually nuanced suspense. Daydreaming employs the subject's imagination in order to go beyond or escape the realistic limits of diurnal life; the heroic energy is an active sexual identity that directly contrasts the passive sexuality of imprisoned victims awaiting their fate. It usually involves exploits of dangerous, even mortal situations where the self can act as hero and rescuer, an active agent who not only survives but combats and triumphs over evil beings and their traps. Where nightmares explore the fear of death, pain, and capture, daydreams use an interactive mixture of imagination and conscious control to try the possible, rather than absolute, limits of mortality. Through romance scenarios Radcliffe can explore the possibilities available to women in the extended limits allowed by daydream, transforming the negative or horrific possibilities of both nightmare and realism into a realm of positive achievement.

Despite Radcliffe's refusal to analyze the finer points of her distinctions, her novels model the structural heroism of daydreams and imagine how an active yet sentimentally attuned heroine could not only survive the villainy of patriarchal tyrants, but come out the heiress and determiner of her future. Radcliffe's heroines purify their homes by remaining pure themselves despite all attempts at forced marriage, abduction, seduction, and rape. In addition, her heroines usually end by owning several homes, multiplying the effects of their purification of society several times over. Other writers used this impulse to register the forces pulling on women. Felicia Hemans, whose conservatively toned poetry does not generally invoke the Gothic, uses it as a device in her *Records of Woman* (1828) to dramatize such forces. "Arabella Stuart" is a lengthy poem based on fact but devoted to exploring the psychological dilemma of a royal lady whose near relation both to Elizabeth I and James I made her a threat to them if she married. She was kept imprisoned in the Tower and single, a veritable Gothic victim. When, like a Radcliffean heroine, Arabella attempts to escape with her lover, the plot goes wrong and she is recaptured; she goes mad and dies in prison, her lover having unchivalrously escaped to Flanders. Hemans does not put the mad scenes to poetry, which would have made this a psychological drama Gothic; instead she opts for the optimistic scenes in prison before the escape venture, thus invoking an external Gothic mode. The pathos of Arabella's apostrophe to her Seymour (" – I wake, / A captive, and alone, and far from thee, / My love and friend!"), however, depicts a more pessimistic and sentimentalized version of the external Gothic than Radcliffe's novels. Had Hemans included the mad scenes in the implicit criticism of women's social and political vulnerability in her plot, and had she made her political criticism explicit, we would have had a radical critique Gothic. Nevertheless, Hemans's use of sentimentality in her social critique allows readers to feel angry on behalf of the victim-heroine, and thus compels them to think harder about such injustices.

Other women writers who were themselves familiar with the real possibility of Gothic life found Radcliffe's solution, as well as Hemans's later sentimental one, untenable. They instead produced novels that revealed how desperate women's choices were in a society where their legal rights were minimal. Such novels might contain elements of social critique to exploit the paradoxical relation between the romance of the Gothic and women's experience of real life as an anti-romance with very Gothic-like features. Women writers familiar with the anti-romance elements of real life included Charlotte Smith, who turned to writing after her marriage of convenience was soured by her husband's extravagance. Her ironically titled *Romance of Real Life* (1787), a collection of tales based on French criminal trials, was written while she was in France to escape her husband's creditors. But her Gothic *Montalbert* (1795) more fully incorporates the external Gothic in order to confront less publicly acknowledged forms of crime, such as the domestic abuse with which she was herself familiar. Smith's other novels of domestic romance continue to use Gothic conventions because of their reminders to readers that the home can always be construed as a space of tyranny, imprisonment, and abuse. Montague Summers (1964: 12) comments that even in *The Old Manor House* (1793), "Mrs Smith has presented her rambling old Hampshire mansion, its mysterious sights and sounds, its antique and deserted rooms, its secret passages haunted by smugglers . . . with as fully

Gothic a flavour as though it were a frowning castle in the awful heart of the Apennines." Other women authors made even fuller use of their immediate knowledge of real-life abuse to critique it, as Charlotte Brontë does in her later novel *Jane Eyre* (1847). But Smith generally prefers a more subtle approach, using nuances to intimate the threat of violence rather than the shockingly violent acts typical of the Radcliffe line of Gothic romance.

The Old Manor House provides a good transition to our next section because it uses aspects of the social critique Gothic, mixed with psychological drama Gothic, in order to create something that is not a Gothic at all, but that, like *Northanger Abbey*, critiques what the Gothic celebrates. Smith conceives of a dark and troubled narrative atmosphere rather than the optimistic romance we find in Austen's novel, allowing her to challenge romance. Yet she does not grant a fully Gothic (and unreal) world either, forcing her hero to confront very real-life situations while his love is continually imprisoned and abused by her aunt. This contrast of plot treatments makes us see the impact of Gothic on real life without letting us fall into the fantasy world that Gothic provides.

Unlike the standard Gothic setting, *The Old Manor House* is set in a nearly contemporary historical period, and its location is not a foreign or Catholic country, but at home in the familiar landscape of southern England. Smith thus sets up a paradoxical relation to the Gothic that is the same one Austen uses in *Northanger Abbey*, but Smith does it to critique the Gothic's unhealthy representation of the individual's relation to society, while Austen does it to critique the Gothic genre itself. (Although the earliest Gothic writers, like Clara Reeve, also set their novels in England, Smith does so after the tradition of extra-national locales has been firmly established for the specific purpose of creating an alternative, non-realistic narrative universe.) Like Reeve, Smith chooses to center her story on a male character and, like Austen, chooses not to write a true Gothic, but she pulls features of the Gothic into her more realistic novel in order to highlight those aspects of a diseased society she wishes to analyze. These very features – patriarchal tyranny, gloomy atmosphere, secrecy, general paranoia, and a fantastic universe – are common not only to the social critique, but to all types of Gothic. The psychological drama Gothic, however, exaggerates these particular features; this fact allows us to see how pointed is Smith's choice to create an alienating and internalizing aspect in her novel that disturbs the normal novel structure. Her implicit argument is that psychological drama threatens the individual's normal external social relationship with others, and that this unhealthy threat spreads easily outward, ruining the chances of a utopian society that the social critique Gothic promotes and that her hero and heroine clearly desire.

Smith's novel shows how aspects of the psychological drama can be appropriated by women writers wishing to reveal how negative a force internalization can be for both individuals and society. Because of this, the narrative's extension to such contemporary events as the war with America, American Indians, and slavery, makes more sense than it would in a typical Gothic: Smith is using contemporary examples of "otherness" to emphasize her critique of Romantic individual subjectivity. However, it is interesting that she considers it necessary to choose a male protagonist instead of a female one in order to make her point. Clearly, the plight of her heroine might make a good social critique Gothic but Smith's interest is too political to stop there, and her use of a male protagonist means that she has already overstepped what the social critique Gothic can accomplish. What she wants to reveal is how the Gothic focus on the psychological absorbs any sense of realism into a paranoid internalized world where the (usually male) individual is completely subject to larger, unknowable forces that rob him of his identity. This form of Gothic revels in a negative rendition of Romantic subjectivity, exploring the psychological depths possible when an individual loses control over his own destiny.

Psychological Drama Gothics

While the social critique Gothic imagines ways in which women can succeed in a patriarchal and corrupt society, the psychological drama Gothic imagines what the Reign of Terror (or its corollary, the Spanish Inquisition) will do to the patriarch – or his son. This focus on the father–son inheritance depends on an absent or fallen mother, whose loss weakens the son's ability to perform heroically against a powerful father-tyrant. This form of the Gothic thus becomes a highly subjective, internalized fiction that imagines the horror of victimization, the psychological dimensions of awaiting torture or death, the emotions of the innocent, and the emotions of the guilty. The extent to which horror and superstition are exploited in this mode makes the inspiration for the psychological drama a medieval one. Horace Walpole, for instance, wrote his *Castle of Otranto* out of his memories of sleeping in medieval houses as a child, as well as from a nightmare about his own fake medieval "castle," Strawberry Hill.

The psychological drama Gothic might best be classed as an anti-romance because it turns inward, driving the imagination and aesthetic sense into the inner realms of nightmare, paranoia, and a schizophrenic fragmentation of the self. It is a drama rather than *merely* an internalization of the Gothic effect because there is an intense awareness of the self's place in the story that is like one's experience of nightmares. But it is also like the actor's awareness of himself on stage playing a part that is both his own and not his own. It is this aspect of self-dramatization that makes the psychological drama relate to High Romantic poetry. However, this relation is one of inversion: the psychological drama drives inward the Romantic visionary quest that Wordsworth, Blake, Coleridge, and Shelley all specifically describe as an upward or transcendent escape of the self. This form of the Gothic, then, is not a critique, but the underside of Romanticism. It seeks the negation of sublime joy, an abject lowest point of feeling that uses our weaknesses to descend (rather than transcend) the self.

Horace Walpole willingly credits the psychological reality of dreams, and it is this realm of dream, nightmare, paranoia, and neurosis that constitutes what Radcliffe terms "horror fiction." Male Gothic writers tend to work within this paranoid universe that typically involves dreamscapes, receding galleries and staircases, labyrinths, and walls that close in and threaten to crush the victim. The very first imitator of Walpole, however, was not male: Anna Laetitia Barbauld wrote a short fragment four years earlier than Clara Reeve's *Old English Baron* which follows Walpole's example of the horror or psychological drama Gothic, "Sir Bertrand: A Fragment" (1773). (There is some disagreement over Barbauld's authorship, and the tale may indeed be by her brother, John Aikin. For over two centuries, however, the tale has been believed to be by a woman, making it worth a brief mention here.) This early Gothic tale was published in *Miscellaneous Pieces in Prose*, a volume by Barbauld and her brother that included her essay "On Romances." Walpole, who also took the tale to be by her, was flattered by it, writing to a friend that "Her *Fragment*, though but a specimen, showed her talent for imprinting terror" (quoted in Summers, 1964: 48). Leigh Hunt, radical poet and essayist, and editor with his brother of several radical journals, however, insisted, and went to great lengths to prove, that the powerful "Sir Bertrand" was written by John Aikin and not his sister. Hunt's need to credit the tale that so impressed him to a male rather than a female writer indicates that the psychological drama Gothic has a very masculine imprint, one which is deeply connected to Romantic visionary poetry.

The dream-vision nature of both *Otranto* and "Sir Bertrand", represented by the narrative device of translation or fragment, indicates the relation implicit in Gothic between the inability of language to represent horror and mystery, and the literary text as a symbol of this incompleteness. As Vijay Mishra (1994: 23) notes, those writers influenced by Kant saw a connection between the Gothic and that moment of sublime transport when "discourse itself breaks down as reason struggles with imagination." The resulting fracture is often represented by eighteenth-century and Romantic writers as fragmentary texts, translated texts, found texts, and transcriptions of dreams (as for *The Castle of Otranto* and *The Old English Baron*, for instance). What the struggle also leads to is a "ruptured discourse," which explores the consumerist society's fear of death (Mishra, 1994: 23). The horror tale compels us through the unease we have about being ourselves disposable by making us face death itself.

One way the horror tale manipulates this unease is to use the Gothic's stereotype of another land, another religious atmosphere (that is, Catholic rather than Anglican), and another historical period to contradict the sense of safety these distancing devices create in the social critique Gothic. Instead of distancing, the reality of the hero's psychological torture makes this "other" world seem frighteningly real, just as nightmares are indistinguishable from real life while we experience them. The purpose is to allow Anglican authors to show the superstitions promoted by the medieval Church – its excess, its corruption, its Inquisition, its use by priests and monks to gain an earthly luxury – as evils that threaten the individualism promoted by contemporary Romantic society. But they are also evils that, like the threats that motivate social critique plots, can be very seductive to readers.

Charles Maturin's *Melmoth the Wanderer* (1820) exemplifies how conservative Anglican and Protestant authors use Catholic settings and mental attitudes to criticize the threat of an erstwhile Catholic France which, having turned revolutionary, is merely another version of the same threat. The novel is less about the evil Melmoth than about the embedded narratives that primarily recount the paranoid experiences of a resistant novice within a Spanish monastery. The embedded accounts, each of which reflects a diseased narrative that successively inflicts more and worse torture on the victim protagonists, finally can only end in torture at the hands of the Inquisitors, and a salvage through the physical collapse of monastery walls. A series of deaths, or anticipated and then deferred deaths, fill the "found" text of the narrative until we finally discover the secret of the tale: not the identity of Melmoth, so much as the truth about his undyingness. In a novel obsessed with death, the title character lives beyond death to haunt ordinary persons. The Gothic horror tale is so nostalgic for death precisely because it cannot imagine that transport through the Romantic sublime, and so it imagines the inverse experience.

Melmoth owes certain of its plot devices to predecessor novels such as "Monk" Lewis's fabulously popular *The Monk* (1796) and Radcliffe's *The Italian, or The Confessional of the Black Penitents: A Romance* (1797), but Maturin actually suffers for his choice of models by borrowing too heavily. His Preface acknowledges this: part of the novel "has been censured by a friend to whom I read it, as containing too much attempt at the revivification of the horrors of Radcliffe-Romance, of the persecutions of convents, and the terrors of the Inquisition" (Maturin, 1968: 5). And, like Lewis, Maturin focuses on a universe driven by Catholic guilt that has no explicable basis and is thus exactly like a real nightmare. Maturin exploits to excess the psychological drama Gothic's capacity to allow readers to vicariously experience persecution, victimhood, guilt or the powerful feeling of inflicting this guilt on others, and debasement. The anti-social nature of the psychological drama contrasts sharply with the critically social aspects of the other two Gothic forms. How women use this form of the Gothic is therefore instructive. For instance, in "Sir Bertrand" Barbauld explores feelings of victimization in ways that warn women readers away from such fantastical horrors. Perhaps more instructive, however, is Charlotte Dacre's use of the form since she finds the psychological drama Gothic liberating for her radical imagination.

Charlotte Dacre (?1771/2–1825) was the daughter of a notorious moneylender and blackmailer who divorced Charlotte's mother to marry a countess, only to be arrested for bankruptcy a few years later. Dacre's novels and poems use sentimental and Gothic themes with a terrible poignancy, and her popular *Confessions of the Nun of St Omer* (1805), also written in response to Lewis's *The Monk*, reflects her own Gothic awareness. It focuses intently on the psychological drama Gothic in order to flesh out her own unstable social status and patrimony in the individualized terms of the Romantic outcast rather than the general terms of social injustice. Dacre resolves her troubled position in patriarchal culture through a demonized subjectivity. Her novels *The Nun of St Omer* and, even more so, *Zofloya* (1806) provide a feminized version of the psychological drama Gothic, and are powerful examples of the exploration possible in this type of the Gothic.

Set in Renaissance Italy, *Zofloya*'s aristocratic heroine Victoria begins a series of transgressions against society through her own mother's seduction and sexual fall. Victoria then chooses, seduces and eventually marries another aristocrat of her home city. When her husband's brother visits, Victoria desires him as well. But it is his servant, Zofloya, a Moor, who becomes the most important sexual conquest for Victoria. He is her dark "other," her opposite in race and color and sex, but her semblance in pride and a vengeful personality. They both rebel against society's constraints on her sex and his race; both seek out many kinds of transgressive acts, pushing all imaginable boundaries. These identical souls become lovers, which in terms of the psychological drama Gothic means that Dacre has inverted the dynamics of victimization and guilt so necessary to the structure of that form. She does so to empower her heroine past such terrible reductions of personal and emotional liberty as Maturin and Lewis depict. She has also rewritten Shakespeare's *Othello*, turning the Moor into Iago (as Zofloya), and making Desdemona (as Victoria) as sexually disobedient as Othello comes to believe she is. Dacre thus exacts her fictional revenge both on her own age and on literary tradition. However, she is herself caught in the structure of the psychological drama Gothic; she must account for Victoria's sexual relations with a black servant, and she chooses the guilt and paranoia of the psychological drama Gothic to do so. Victoria is responsible, with Zofloya's help, for three deaths, and her guilt puts her in his power; like Iago with Desdemona, the servant now has the upper hand of the aristocratic lady. But Zofloya's blackness and lower class at first represents only physical and psychological abjection to Victoria. She must learn to see things differently, to escape the abject experience of victimization in order to see Zofloya both as a lover and as another version of herself. Even when she does so, the conclusion of the novel punishes her, reverting to the ending of Lewis's *The Monk*, with Zofloya turning into Satan himself and viciously killing Victoria. Nevertheless, she has enjoyed a freedom to do whatever her wild will dictates – something real society allows no woman to do – and she never experiences the torment, beatings, and emotional pain that her fallen mother continues to suffer throughout the novel. (For different interpretations of this novel, see Craciun, 1997; Hoeveler, 1997.)

As *Zofloya* illustrates, in the hands of a free-thinking woman writer, the psychological drama Gothic's super-emphasis on the individual self can verge on radical critique through the power such novels allot to women characters. This different perspective on selfhood explodes the psychological drama to politicize it in terms of gender and otherness.

Emily Brontë's late Romantic *Wuthering Heights* (1847) also uses the psychological drama Gothic combined with Dacre's use of sexual and racial politics to create a heroine so strong that death proves no barrier for her hauntingly passionate spirit which must always return to her dark "gypsy" other and lover, Heathcliff. Like Dacre, Brontë turns this form of the Gothic back on itself, but her heroine Catherine Earnshaw is so compelling a romance heroine that the narrative's internalizing quality overrides any overt political criticism it contains. In contrast, the radical critique Gothic reverses this order, giving priority always to the critique of political injustice over the psychological or romance elements of the tale.

The Romance of Real Life and Radical Critique

Radical critiques do their work by incorporating the most realistic aspects of the social critique Gothic into the more traditional domestic romance novel. The domestic romance during the Romantic period, most ably practiced by Jane Austen and by Sir Walter Scott, represents real life in a recognizable rendering of social interaction and of personality that precedes the development of modernist realism. The radical critique Gothic often begins as a domestic romance, but uses Gothic elements to critique either the romance as a genre inappropriate for depicting real-life experience, or the Gothic as a vehicle inadequate for interpreting real-life experience. Either way, the radical critique provides a tool for disillusioning readers who take their fiction too seriously. This section begins by revisiting Austen's *Northanger Abbey* and then examines Scott's *The Bride of Lammermoor*. These two works, with a brief look at Joanna Baillie's *Witchcraft*, will provide the background for what the radical critique can achieve. We will then be in a position to understand two of the most powerful radical critiques of this period, Mary Hays's *The Victim of Prejudice* and Mary Wollstonecraft's *The Wrongs of Woman, or Maria*.

Most readers of Jane Austen remember vividly her parody of the Gothic in *Northanger Abbey* (1818). Austen's heroine, Catherine Morland, is visiting Bath through the generosity of friends of her parents; there she meets the hero, Henry Tilney, but she is too naïve and inexperienced to know how to flirt, or even how to analyze her own feelings about him. Her world has thus far been the circumference of a happy family, and she interprets her new friends in Bath as more sisters and brothers. However, this domestic approach to the larger world cannot work when young women visit Bath, a spa town, for the primary purpose of meeting eligible young men. For instance, Catherine's new friend Isabella has purposefully set out to capture Catherine's brother, but Catherine cannot see this because she accepts her friend as a sister. Catherine also views her new friends Eleanor and Henry Tilney as her own sister and brother, even though Henry is clearly interested in her. Catherine's domestic perspective, with its emphasis on sibling relations, reflects dominant Romantic attitudes. But the tangle of friends engaging each other as siblings, at the same time that sexual attraction makes them view each other quite differently (particularly Isabella toward Catherine's brother, and Isabella's brother toward Catherine), allows Austen to show how such idealism does not combine well with the real world. Furthermore, Isabella's and her brother's interest in marriage is motivated not by love but by the mistaken belief that Catherine and her brother are adoptive heirs of the rich friends who have brought her to Bath.

The motivation of economic gain typical of the domestic romance (Austen's more usual genre choice), and of real life itself, is also one of the main plot motivators of the Gothic genre. Austen adds to her portrayal of Isabella's mercenary behavior her reading of fashionable Gothic literature to show Isabella's superficial taste and temperament. But it is just this reading that allows Isabella to capture the gullible Catherine's richer imagination, and the two girls devour Radcliffe's *Mysteries of Udolpho* together. They are more thrilled by the eventually explained "mysteries," such as the black veil in the portrait gallery, than by the moments of sublime terror that Radcliffe hoped would uplift her readers. The girls' reading is prompted by their love of the "horrid" elements rather than the sublime or marriage plot elements. Austen's point is that Catherine, as a more naïve reader than Isabella of both the text and the current situation, succumbs to an imaginative hysteria related to horror that is unfit for everyday life. Stemming from a practice of reading by titillation learned from Gothic novels, it leads Catherine to respond to normal situations in inappropriate ways when what she needs to learn, as Henry later points out to her, is objective distance and critical thinking.

Life, Austen implicitly argues throughout, is not a Gothic novel. Yet Austen also acknowledges that real life itself contains recognizable elements of Gothic, such as Catherine's first visit to the Assembly Rooms at Bath. For Catherine, who at this point has not even encountered Isabella's Gothic novels, this experience is a hysterical one in which the rooms are too small for the press of people, the air too hot and claustrophobic, the movements dizzying. Hysteria is an appropriate psychic state for Gothic reading and for imagining oneself into the Gothic, as Catherine then proceeds to do when invited to stay at the Abbey, but it was real life that made hysteria part of Catherine's personal experience. Austen's point is that the uncritical Catherine has not learned to differentiate real threats from fictitious horrors. At the Abbey, she is terrified by a fragment text which turns out to be only an old laundry inventory, she explores "secret" galleries that are not, and imagines a terrible fate for the dead mother of her new friends.

Yet Austen's parodic critique is pointedly double; as much as she mocks such self-titillation by hystericizing the rather ordinary ballrooms at Bath, Austen also alludes to the everyday possibility of Gothic plots in women's lives. Henry's teasing tutoring of Catherine is tinged with a cruelty borrowed from his patriarch father, and when he points out that the law does not allow present-day men to murder or incarcerate their wives, we are reminded by his very arguments that men nevertheless continue to do so. We never learn how Henry's mother died, and certainly his sister Eleanor is treated too repressively by her father for us to feel sure that the parents' relationship had been a loving one. As victims of spouse abuse, women can be confined to their rooms, prevented from visiting their families, committed to insane asylums. In fact, Austen's later novel *Mansfield Park* reveals the small ways in which a young woman is denied, stifled, manipulated, repressed, and confined within the grounds of a house regardless of her wishes. Although *Northanger Abbey* is a light-hearted and dismissive example of the radical critique, it provides a helpful starting point because of its illuminating comparison of real life, the ways in which real life can be viewed as a romance, and the pitfalls of romance that Gothic fiction exaggerates.

Walter Scott also engaged in a critique of the Gothic and its influences in his novel *The Bride of Lammermoor* (1819). *The Bride* exemplifies the blend of interior and exterior vision of the radical critique by refusing complete credulity in the supernatural while, like Reeve and Radcliffe, also pitting the explicable against darker mysteries of the psyche. Radcliffe's novels, rather than Reeve's, are critically acknowledged to be influential for Scott because he takes Radcliffe's rational approach to the supernatural (Duncan, 1992: 141), or because of the psychological approach of explaining the demonic as the delusive effects of a powerful imagination (Robertson, 1991: pp. x–xi). But it is more true of *The Bride of Lammermoor* that he moves beyond Radcliffe's social critique by putting into radical conflict the supernatural, as something one can rationalize, with medieval superstition or witchcraft, as things the individual psyche can be so convinced of that inexplicable events can actually occur.

The Bride of Lammermoor concerns the domestic tragedy of Lucy Ashton, the daughter of the bourgeois first Lord Stair of Edinburgh: her secret betrothal to the aristocratic but impoverished Ravenswood after her mother arranges a marriage of convenience for her to Bucklaw, and her fatal wedding night. In standard Gothics of the first two types, the aristocracy is generally depicted as morally, politically, and sexually degenerate, while the middle class, representing the new social order, is first victimized and then morally triumphant when the bourgeois heroine successfully fights off the depraved aristocratic tyrant. But in this novel Scott critiques this standardized perspective, questioning whether the new order cannot be just as depraved, just as corrupted by power and money as the old, and whether the old order might not have been a better system after all. Beginning his plot with the problem of inheritance – the estate inhabited by the Ashtons is the ancestral seat of Ravenswood's family – Scott uses Ravenswood to represent the honor of the knightly old order, while the Ashton family of lawyers turned politicians represents the decadence and abuses of the new order. Although this reversal of a standard Gothic scenario involves the two heads of family, Ravenswood and Lucy's father, Scott makes it clear that the real struggle over old and new orders is between Lady Ashton and Lucy. Lucy's mother wants her to marry the middle-class, pragmatic, and realistic Bucklaw, while Lucy wants to return to the old order (and the old owners of her home) by marrying the noble romance hero, Ravenswood. This struggle over the destiny of the family and its home is first fought through law as Lady Ashton forces Lucy to sign a legally binding marriage contract with Bucklaw, and then through old superstitions when Lady Ashton employs a local witch, Ailsie, to help her weaken Lucy's resistance.

Legal contracts belong to the new order, superstition and witchcraft to the old. But Lady Ashton's unloving and manipulative behavior make her as much a "witch" as Ailsie is. Through the medium of the witch, a figure of the evilly powerful mother who represents the absence of the good and protective mother, *The Bride* bridges romance and history. But the novel's dual depiction of the witch figure – both her abusive treatment of Lucy and society's treatment of the witch herself when she is hanged – provides a radical critique of society. The witch figure is the transgressor in whom social law and psychological perversion meet as a representation of nature and romance. For Scott, she replaces the absent or dead good mother as the evil mother who focuses the Gothic; the monstrous woman whose desire for power allows her to manipulate the patriarchal law that should subdue her. The evil mother is the reverse of the patriarchal tyrant: she is the mother as both life-giver and destroyer of her children, while the tyrant father is the law-giver and desirer/destroyer of his offspring. But Ailsie, the witch who is finally punished by the law for her part in the tragedy, is only a scapegoat for the evil mother and real witch of the novel, Lady Ashton.

But why does Scott focus his critique of society on the mother? Remember that all three types of Gothic rely on the absence of the good mother, and the destruction of the family as common themes. If Scott is using the Gothic genre to produce a radical critique, then he needs to engage these themes in order to say something about the injustices of present society. But the multiplication of and emphasis on the evil mother in this novel goes beyond the usual use of that theme, and the question is why such an emphasis?

One clue might lie in the way Scott uses this figuration of the mother as a central part of the legal elements of *The Bride*. This novel is filled with lawyers, contracts, and execution hills (in local dialect, "laws"), and its actual written source is a seventeenth-century text by Robert Law. If the forced husband Bucklaw represents a disruption of the patriarchy by his very name, he cannot succeed in such a nightmarishly legalized world. Lady Ashton, the heroine's mother, uses the law in a way Bucklaw and the noble lover Ravenswood cannot, to manipulate events according to her own designs. Her willful manipulations are focused on mercenary gains and her desire to increase the family's social standing through her daughter's marriage. The legal system is open to just such manipulations. Lady Ashton will risk anything, including Lucy's sanity, to achieve her ends: she employs the witch Ailsie to help her increase Lucy's mental instability and emotional dependency, contrives the marriage contract, and commits other non-maternal acts in order to frustrate Ravenswood and encourage Bucklaw. What is interesting about this destructive female relation, which Scott sets at the heart of his novel, is that it is more real, more true to life, than the ideal romance between Ravenswood and Lucy. We can say this not only because we all know families where such destructive relationships exist, but because Scott reveals in his Introduction that he based his plot and characters on a real, historical event and the family of the real first Lord Stair. True love, as we know, is the stuff of fiction, but greed and manipulation are part of everyday life. By giving these destructive and very real human behaviors to women, however, Scott is doing something more than simply destroying romance; he aligns the destructive power of mothers with patriarchal law here. He understands that patriarchy cannot function without women's cooperation and complicity. The law is the social and political institution that denies women the right to be guardians of their own children. It denies them the status of citizen, and arranges inheritances so that they are often excluded as heirs to an estate. Lucy is the female victim of all these legal possibilities. But it is her mother, and not a patriarch tyrant, who makes her so and who calls the law down on her. Scott implies that women are as much to blame as men for the social injustice of women's lack of rights, a radical thing to claim. This is Lady Ashton's own form of witchcraft: to be able to manipulate the law (a patriarchal tool) to her own will. Scott is saying that witchcraft need not be supernatural, it can exist in everyday life too. Similarly, Ailsie's form of witchcraft also needs no supernatural element to be effective. She merely spends her time with Lucy telling her ghost stories, engaging her naïve and gullible imagination in the same way that Austen's Catherine Morland was engaged by reading Gothic novels. By fictionalizing Lucy's daydreams, Ailsie can turn her daily experience into the stuff of nightmares simply by manipulating her imagination. However, the result of these explicable acts of evil and imagination produce the moment of abject horror when Lucy's wedding night ends in a bloody struggle that the narrative refuses to fully describe or explain. We are left with the sensation of horror, and of the presence of the supernatural. This is Scott's most explicit critique of the damage done by psychological drama Gothic novels, and on the Gothic in general as a female genre. Scott not only blames witch-women for social injustices, but blames women writers for romanticizing these injustices in Gothic novels. At the same time, his strong advocacy of his fated heroine Lucy reveals that Scott also wants to defend women from political and social injustice.

Scott's conflicting attitudes toward women and their social role in *The Bride* highlights the question of why the novel is filled with such strong female and weak male characters instead of his usual heroic male characters and masculine subject matter. This contradiction makes more sense if we realize that there are two kinds of critique in *The Bride of Lammermoor*: a radical *and* a conservative critique. Scott's anxiety over the female origins of his narrative – both the historical Lady Stair and Scott's great-aunt's version of this story that was his original contact with it – reflects a *conservative critique* of female authorship. By extension this is also a critique of women's Gothic novels. Despite the strong tones of this critique both in his other writings and in *The Bride*, however, Scott's Gothic narrative focus on the hapless Lucy Ashton reflects a *radical critique* of the laws and social customs that allow her parents to victimize her for their own gain. That Lucy's father is himself a lawyer, and her mother well versed in legal manipulation, shows Scott's apprehensions about the current legal system and its susceptibility to miscarriages of justice. Moreover, by taking a true event and using what little is known about the Stairs' history, Scott gives his radical critique a historical authority that powerfully strengthens its criticism of an unjust system, and that subdues the force of the conservative critique. Although by the end of *The Bride* we certainly hate Lady Ashton and her abuse of parental authority, we can also see in the execution of Ailsie a woman victimized (like Lucy) by the political system's hatred of real or imagined female power. Scott further supports his radical critique by making us realize that, of course, Lady Ashton is the real witch, and that she triumphs over the legal system by using her female power to protect herself from its punishment. "Lady Ashton lived to the verge of extreme old age, the only survivor of the group of unhappy persons, whose misfortunes were owing to her implacability." By both combining and defeating the Gothic strands, as many radical critique Gothics do, Scott sets up self-collapsing oppositions: history with romance, legal fiction with Gothic fiction, public or national with private or domestic abuse. It is an attempt to end the Gothic and its strong female influence at the same time that it is an exploitation of the Gothic tradition to reveal social wrongs. Although *The Bride* aims to expose the evils of female power, Scott's two opposing critical agendas mean that his novel can only mourn the harm caused by both kinds of evil, but even such mourning becomes a strong political statement. If understanding Scott's novel from a feminist perspective is fraught with difficulties, it is worth the effort in order to see how women's issues were never simple or clear cut. We can also see from Scott's novel that women readers could appreciate a conflicted perspective of these issues and yet still experience the text as a radical message.

In Joanna Baillie's unperformed play, *Witchcraft* (1836), a young girl is also tormented by seizures and seeming madness, and appears to be the victim of witchcraft despite all attempts to bar her sickroom thresholds from witches and demons. Like Scott, Baillie is content to mourn the victim of false accusations, but in such a way that her radical critique is effective and uncompromised. She sets her play, as Scott does, at the historical crux in which the persecution and sentencing of witches was ending, and she is concerned, as was Scott, with rational explanations for people's belief in witchcraft, as well as with the motivations of those (like Lady Ashton) who manipulate such belief to gain their ends. Rationalized sorcery in *Witchcraft* is used to illuminate the evil Annabella's

143

jealousy as an all-consuming passion that drives her to use superstitions about witchcraft to impeach her rival. The heroine is accused of having used witchcraft to torment the sick girl, evidence is planted against her, and she is eventually executed as a witch. Yet, as with Lady Ashton, it is Annabella who is the real witch, and Baillie makes it clear to the reader that Annabella's manipulations are a much more potent and life-threatening witchcraft than that for which the heroine dies.

Far different is the powerful *Victim of Prejudice* (1799) by Mary Hays. Hays (1760–1843) was a Dissenter and an influential feminist radical. She belonged to the political circle of Joseph Johnson, which included Joseph Priestley, William Godwin, and Mary Wollstonecraft. Her first novel, *Memoirs of Emma Courtney* (1796), reveals the frustrations of a woman eager for romance but living in a realistic world where love is not always returned, and where marriage without fortune is rarely a basis for finding love. This novel made Hays not only famous but infamous because her heroine tries to resolve the romance dilemma by eschewing marriage and offering to live with the man she loves. Hays's second novel, *The Victim of Prejudice* (1799; see Ty, 1994), contradicts each element of her first novel that caused her such trouble with her readers: she replaces romance with Gothic, a reluctant lover with a villainous tyrant, and hope with despair. It is important to note that in this novel and the other great radical critique Gothics of the period, the mother either *is* the heroine of the story or the narrative centers on her, and her experiences create the conditions for the critique itself. When the radical critique accepts the absent or evil mother of romance fiction as a device, as does Scott's *Bride*, this focuses the critique against the mother rather than against the social forces that victimize her.

Like many other Gothics, *The Victim of Prejudice* uses a nightmare (but here, one concerning the mother) as its initializing moment, manuscript dissemination to indicate secrecy, and a paranoid world to heighten the abusive patriarchy against which the heroine struggles. More tellingly, however, it begins by invoking the victimization of its romance-minded protagonist for its narrative rationale:

> A child of misfortune, a wretched outcast from my fellow-beings, driven with ignominy from social intercourse, cut off from human sympathy, immured in the gloomy walls of a prison, I spread my hands . . . And thou, the victim of despotism, oppression, or error, tenant of a dungeon, and successor to its present devoted inhabitant, should these sheets fall into thy possession, when the hand that wrote them moulders in the dust, and the spirit that dictated ceases to throb with indignant agony, read. (Ty, 1994: 3)

Hays's novel employs elements that are recognizably aligned with the psychological drama Gothic, especially its elements of the paranoid nightmare world, the victimized protagonist, and the Gothic patriarch tyrant. But she sets her tale in the contemporary world where women are urged to dream impossibly, and molds her plot around a stringent critique of social norms. The heroine is illegitimate, and her mother, the victim of a seduction rather than of free and equal love, is hanged. The protective barrier established in the social critique Gothic and the psychological drama that allow the reader to pleasurably experience daring exploits or abject depths is not provided here. The abuses become too realized, not analogous but realistic and too unpleasant for comfort. Hays, the radical thinker, uses *Victim of Prejudice* to expose through a radical critique the hypocrisy and injustice of everyday life that victimizes women and prejudices the world against them.

Mary Wollstonecraft, who met her husband William Godwin at Hays's home, created an even more clearly delineated critique of domestic ideology through the Gothic in *The Wrongs of Woman, or Maria* (1798). Although this is the earliest of the works discussed in this section, it provides a fitting final example because it works out so powerfully the explosive potential of the radical critique Gothic. Wollstonecraft draws on her own adolescent experiences for her novel, of attempting to protect her mother from her physically abusive and alcoholic father, then helping her sister escape from a tyrant husband, and later of being deserted herself by Gilbert Imlay, the father of her first child. *Maria* was left unfinished and was published posthumously by Godwin; it attempts to fictionalize Wollstonecraft's *Vindication of the Rights of Woman* by delineating the legal ways in which men can abuse rather than protect the women of their families. Because she has such a strong political agenda for her novel, Wollstonecraft chooses a plot that is closer to Hays's version of the radical critique Gothic. She similarly foregrounds the Gothic elements of her novel, while using domestic romance elements to show how unsuited real life is to romance when male lovers can so easily court a woman only to desert or betray her.

The novel opens with Maria realizing she is a prisoner in a Gothic ruin that has been turned into an insane asylum, the incarceration theme that Hays uses a year later in *Victim of Prejudice*. Although the narrative attempts to go beyond Gothic horror by realizing the real horror of imprisonment, the effect remains a distanced one of romance: "Abodes of horror have frequently been described, and castles, filled with specters and chimeras, conjured up by the magic spell of genius to harrow the soul . . . [But] what were they to the mansion of despair, in one corner of

145

which Maria sat . . . !" Maria's vicious and avaricious husband drugged her, took her infant and had her abducted during the night to force more money out of Maria's uncle. The marriage contract gives a husband the ownership of his wife, their children, her money and estates; the law gives him the right to dispose of her as he wishes. Yet Maria is not a pure victim; in her prison she befriends her nurse-warden Jemima who remains constant to her, and falls in love with Darnford, a man who has been similarly abducted and imprisoned for money by his relations but who later also deserts Maria. Even though men can also be victimized under the law as subjects of patriarchal will, no man can be trusted in matters of the heart within the Gothic logic of Wollstonecraft's critique.

Finally, Maria attempts to divorce her husband in a dramatic ending, but Wollstonecraft is unable to resolve the tensions between Gothic critique and social accountability that she has set out to explore. Instead of a single triumphant or dreadful fate, we are presented with four alternative conclusions to her story, each more fated and dreadful than the last. While Maria was incarcerated in the Gothic asylum, she was physically distanced from her home and normal life and so resided in a Gothic analogue world that resembled the imprisoning worlds of domestic and psychological Gothics. But once she and her new lover escape their prison, they are returned to the real-time world where thrilling mystery and terror are no longer permissible textual pleasures. The fragmentation of Wollstonecraft's ending seems to belong to the Romantic fragment text or the nightmare of the psychological drama Gothic, but, in fact, *Maria*'s multiple endings sustain the power of the novel's radical critique. The endings produce a potent anatomy of social ills designed to elicit anger rather than titillation, emulation, or sentimentalism in the reader. We can discuss this multiple effect because, although most critics assume Wollstonecraft would have resolved the conclusion had she lived, the beginning of the novel predisposes us toward the tortured yet realistic ending(s): "surely there are a few who will dare to advance before the improvement of the age, and grant that my sketches are not the abortion of a distempered fancy, or the strong delineations of a wounded heart." The use of the term "abortion" in relation to anger and insanity binds together the maternal body and the abuse of this body in patriarchy, as well as the analogy of a rejected bodily creation to an artwork distorted by disturbed emotions. It is a matrix of images that her daughter Mary Shelley masterfully employs for the non-maternal creation of her "wretch" in *Frankenstein*. And it provides an astute analysis

146

of the function of the radical critique Gothic to portray women's role in society and to expose the potentially destructive conception of such a role.

Wollstonecraft's and Hays's novels resemble Baillie's *Witchcraft* in that all three authors use internalization to show how patriarchal society is itself psychotic, and that individuals are caught up in its paranoia despite all struggle. Austen, in contrast, grounds her novel in the domestic romance to show how the Gothic imagination has only a small and too easily exaggerated role in real life. Scott gives the Gothic more power than Austen through his critique of the political and legal systems, but only because he sees the Gothic as having a historical hold on the human imagination. For him, the Gothic backgrounds real life in a way that romance itself – as a wistful and escapist flight of the imagination – cannot do. These are subtle differences, but understanding them allows readers to analyze more competently the achievements of these authors.

In conclusion, we can see that the adage "a man's home is his castle" takes on a new and more literal meaning in the Gothic. By tracing through the distinctions in psychologically and socially oriented uses of the Gothic, we elicited some of the difficulties that arise in talking about the Gothic or about romance and realism as one-sided literary objects. Women's concern about social restrictions was relieved by their use of the social critique Gothic to explore positive role models for active female behavior, remarkable as a contrast to the nightmare visions and individual pain of the psychological drama Gothic. Novels that cross borders, such as the radical critique Gothics, defeat such contrasting positions in order to erase the fiction that realism or real life can be Gothic-like, or that Gothic heroines can effectively role model behavior for real women. The Gothic develops into several different forms after the Romantic period. Its continuation shows how powerful a hold it had on the artistic as well as popular imagination: the Gothic tale, made famous by Le Fanu and Poe; the social problem novel of the Victorian period, such as those of Charles Dickens and Elizabeth Gaskell; as well as melodrama, sensational literature, and detective fiction. It continues to be an extremely popular genre today, although in the twentieth century it has lost its critical and political force. Chapter 4 will treat the themes explored here somewhat differently by examining how women writers thought about their intellectual abilities, their legal rights, and their social position within the patriarchal culture that the Gothic so well analyzes and exploits.

Further Reading

Chris Baldick (ed.), *The Oxford Book of Gothic Tales* (1992), and Jeffrey N. Cox (ed.), *Seven Gothic Dramas, 1789–1825* (1992). These collections each focus on a different sub-genre of the Gothic, but together with individually reissued Gothic novels such as those by Radcliffe and Maturin, they provide access to a range of Gothic writing that will give the student a basic conception of the literature.

Kate Ellis, *The Contested Castle: Gothic Novels and the Subversion of Domestic Ideology* (1989). Ellis's study provides a thorough grounding for the issues that a feminist inquiry into the Gothic must address. Provides an interesting contrast and companion volume to Summers.

Montague Summers, *The Gothic Quest: a History of the Gothic* (1938, 1964). An early treatment of the Gothic, *The Gothic Quest* provides a good historical base for investigating Gothic, as well as insights into late nineteenth-century attitudes toward this genre.

Chapter 4

Women and Thought: Intellectual Critique

Figure 4 Mrs Elizabeth Montagu, engraving by J. R. Smith after the painting by Joshua Reynolds

149

Lord Lyttelton's History is not yet ready to appear . . . His delicacy in regard to characters, his candour in regard to opinions, his precision in facts, would entitle him to the best palm history can claim, if he had not added to these virtues of History (if I may call them so) the highest ornaments of style, and a most peculiar grace of order and method . . . I shall send you a treatise on the "Sublime and Beautiful," by Mr Burke, a friend of mine. I do not know that you will always subscribe to his system, but think you will find him an elegant and ingenious writer.
                                      Elizabeth Montagu to Elizabeth Carter, January 24, 1759

This chapter will survey the exponents of women's intellectualism from the late eighteenth to the early nineteenth century to reveal women writers' interest in critical, scholarly, and philosophical thought as an aspect of their literary consciousness, and as part of the Romantic formulation. Inclusion of this subject allows us to account for material not usually discussed or acknowledged in Romantic period anthologies, but to assert that there actually exists something we could call Romantic period women's intellectuality. Moreover, by reading such material for its literary Romantic qualities, we can begin to extend our understanding of women's participation in Romantic thought and the production of culture, and realize that this has not been the entirely male endeavor scholarly tradition claims it to be. We need a recuperative strategy for this material, a way to put it in the context of men's intellectual writing. We need this strategy to help us re-place women's intellectual labor and activity in relation to the metaphysical thought that grounds the male Romantic poet's struggle to understand his own relation to history.

Even a cursory look at Coleridge's notebooks and essays, Wordsworth's prefaces, Keats's letters – standard reading for students in Romantic literature courses – reveals this intellectual ground and its relevance for the imaginative efforts of High Romantic poetry. But we do not place the same value on Dorothy Wordsworth's journals or Mary Shelley's notebooks, which are sometimes included in course reading lists, but usually for contextual purposes rather than (as for the men's prose) to illuminate the workings of great minds. In part, our refusal to take their intellectual activity seriously in the notebooks and letters, as we do for men, is because women writers tended to restrict themselves to those kinds of publications that would not reveal their inadequate educations. Those rare women, like Elizabeth Carter, who were educated at home in the classics had the necessary support to write scholarly or intellectual texts rather than literary ones, but their readers did not

always accord them the same respect as for male writers. Literary women
like Dorothy Wordsworth, who wrote without the experience of university or classical training, found themselves restricted by an uncertainty of
what they should know or should seem to know, and so avoided any
appearance of philosophical engagement in their writing. Even their
personal writings reveal a consciousness of how they should appear as
women, reflecting their family preoccupations, the more fragmentary
thought rhythms of domestic life, or the belief that they should not
participate in philosophical debate even in their own journals. Literary
women were forced to face the fear that if their art were to be considered
artful rather than natural (that is, philosophical rather than imaginative)
they would be marked as unnatural, and as available to public censure
and critical attack. These fears worked on several levels, at best urging
women to produce literary experiments to more accurately reflect their
ideas, at worst restricting and trivializing their private thoughts. Men
writers, in contrast, could confidently and knowledgeably combine their
philosophical thinking with their poetic composition. And so we read
both kinds of texts for male authors as a part of literary studies, but only
certain texts for women writers. But if we accept women's need to divide
their talents and interests, rather than combine them as men writers were
able to do, we can then examine non-literary writing by women for what
it has to tell us about women's intellectual life, which we cannot easily
deduce from their literature. This also allows us to realize that women
were more than consumers and emotionalists, and did produce textual
evidence of sustained ratiocination during this period.

An additional supposition will help here: that women's poetry and
fiction, as much as their essays and letters, can also reveal the presence
of intellectualism, conscientious rigor, and an ethical imperative usually
only associated with male writing, despite women's attempts to suppress
or disguise such activity. For the purposes of this discussion, then, the
body of women's late eighteenth-century and Romantic period prose can
be suggestively augmented with those literary efforts that through careful
reading reveal similar philosophical effects. Finally, an implied thesis
might help organize the following material further: that women who
used their intellects to produce written works during this period did so
under the sway of Romantic aesthetics and philosophy. Therefore, what
women chose to direct their intellectual energy toward, as well as how
they imagined themselves as thinkers, was influenced by the same dominant conceits and modes as male Romantics. Women thought themselves
into relation to classical civilization (Elizabeth Carter), British history
(Catherine Macaulay Graham and Jane Austen), political theory (Mary

151

Wollstonecraft), education (Anna Laetitia Barbauld and Jane Taylor), all of which were dominant centers of interest for Romantic literature and thought.

We now have the basis for examining why women writers chose to pursue certain paths and not others; however, this basis does not account for the emergence of that thought in its particularity. The next section begins the thread of such an explanation with the Bluestockings. Seeing how they provided the opportunity for such an emergence through their advocacy of women's education allows us to pose women's thinking in terms of class, intellectual identity, and social background. Thinking women believed that their best efforts should be toward helping others to think, and it is important to see how widespread the utopian vision of improved educational opportunities was for different groups of women. This is not just an Enlightenment and a feminist goal, but a Romantic one as well.

The Bluestocking Circle in London

Women's intellectuality in the Romantic age was made possible by two cultural phenomena of the eighteenth century that were diametrically opposed on the social scale but shared a similar political agenda: the intellectual salon and the Dissenting academies. The salon was an upper middle-class institution, usually hosted by high-ranking or well-connected women, that imitated court culture, while the Dissenting academies were created for those who resisted the Church of England and who were thus barred from Oxford and Cambridge universities. On the face of it, these two phenomena have nothing in common, but in fact the salons were interested in increasing educational and intellectual opportunities for women, while the academies believed in educative and political equality. Both were important forces for the increased emphasis on education in Romantic Britain.

The salon originated in Paris where it brought socially important women and intellectual men into the hostess's home for witty and entertaining debates. When the salon became fashionable in London, it had acquired a more sober character and a greater emphasis on debate. It provided the perfect vehicle for bringing the political and philosophical discussions of the coffee-house, where men went to read the newspapers and to discuss government and revolutionary politics, into the home where it could belong to women as well as men. This in itself allowed for a change in attitude toward women's intellectual ability, the salon providing middle-class women with the opportunity and motivation to educate themselves beyond the ordinary matters of households, marriage, and fashion. The woman who most effectively realized the potential of the salon for stimulating intellectual activity was Elizabeth Montagu (1720–1800), and the circle she presided over became known as "The Bluestockings" or the "Bas Bleu." Members of her circle included Frances Boscawen, Elizabeth Vesey, Catherine Talbot, Mary Delany, Hester Chapone, and her early friend the Duchess of Portland (see Myers, 1990).

Montagu was responsible for supporting and encouraging many women in their scholarly and artistic endeavors, behavior that reveals the Bluestockings' serious interest in women's education and intellectual achievements. Chief among those patronized was a brilliant classical scholar, Elizabeth Carter (1717–1806), who was famous for her important translation of Epictetus, but who had also been publishing poetry in *The Gentleman's Magazine* and as separate volumes, essays in *The Rambler*, and contemporary translations since she was 16 years old. Of all the women connected with the Bluestocking circle, Carter was the most highly regarded, and her achievements have never been dismissed altogether. Montagu, on the other hand, was regarded more for her social status, her ability to make culture through her salons. This is perhaps understandably a consequence of her social connections that made her a central figure in high society, and of the flirtatious relations that men and women used toward each other in that social plane. For instance, in a letter to a Dr Monsey she writes of her intellectual friend Benjamin Stillingfleet, a member of her Bas Bleu circle, that he has left off his blue stockings and has taken to nightly visits to the comic operas and assemblies. About four months later, she tweaks Stillingfleet by writing that, "You must know Sir, Dr Monsey is fallen desperately in love with me, and I am most passionately in love with him, the darts on both sides have not been the porcupine's, but the grey goose quill." But she then resolves "never again to fall in love with a man who is a grandfather."

In the context of Montagu's witty epistolary persona, we can see why it is easy to judge her intellectual work, most importantly her literary criticism on Shakespeare's plays, subjectively, while critics have remained more objective about the serious-minded Carter, best known for her translation of a classical male text. Dr Johnson, whom Montagu had considered a friend, judged quite harshly her *Essay on the Writing and Genius of Shakespeare* (1769). Critiquing a man's text was not entirely approved. By contrast, translating certain kinds of men's texts, as Carter did, was deemed an appropriate task for women, and Greek (unlike the male-owned Latin) was particularly available to brilliant women like the French translator Anne Dacier (on whose *Iliad* Pope had based his version) and her successor Elizabeth Carter. Supporting male talent was best of all, a social rather than intellectual effort, and Montagu notably promoted James Beattie and Richard Price, as well as her two famous female protégées, Hannah More and Fanny Burney. Both Burney and More were young women when introduced to the Bluestockings' salons and are often considered "second-generation" Blues even though both soon rejected the affiliation.

Although the Bluestockings might be said to have prepared the ground for the later forms of Romanticism (such as those Burney and More took part in) through their promotion of a social interest in intellectual ideas and in aesthetic concerns, this rejection was to be a sign of the times. By the 1890s, Bluestockingism would become associated with an affectation of scholarly and intellectual interest in women, a detriment rather than an accomplishment like singing or painting that women could use to promote themselves in polite society. But in the 1790s Bluestockingism appeared a conservative intellectualism compared with the impassioned political thought of women like Mary Wollstonecraft and others stimulated by the French Revolution, and a confined one compared with the work of women poets like Mary Robinson and Elizabeth Landon who used their intelligence to portray themselves as an embodiment of a female poetic principle. The Bluestockings offered a middle road of rational thought and social concern, stimulated by sensibility but not by more politicized emotions. By the 1810s, however, their reputation had already declined such that Jane Austen can portray Mary Bennet in *Pride and Prejudice* as aspiring to a bluestockingism that is so self-promoting and affected that she is ridiculous, a young woman who cannot properly judge or understand the philosophy she reads. The demise of the Blues' cultural importance during the Romantic period may well be a reaction to their significance as a ground or foundation for women's rights. It is also likely that they represented something of the old cultural order that the French Revolution intentionally destroyed, and, as women, they would be more likely to be stigmatized for that association. However, it is important for us to understand the relation the original Blues established between gender, intellect, and community, as well as something of the ways in which this relation could be misunderstood by later generations.

Montagu and Carter, as perhaps the most intellectual of the Bluestockings, worked hard to develop this relation. But their effort was then drastically undercut by later satirists who, like Richard Polwhele with his *The Unsex'd Females* (1798), worried about the connection between women's rights and the rights issues that prompted the French Revolution. Such attacks as Polwhele's helped terminate women's overt intellectual efforts, yet the road was already prepared by secondary members of the circle like Hannah More. More supported Bluestockingism in her early works as an impassioned rather than intellectual movement in her celebratory poems "Bas Bleu" (1786) and "Sensibility: A Poetical Epistle to the Hon. Mrs Boscawen" (1782, see Wu, 1997: 24–34). By emphasizing domestic emotion claimed by the Blues as something closer to sensibility, More promoted precisely what Polwhele found to be so dangerous since the sensual is always also associated with the sexual, a connection that negatively impacts on women's relation to intellectuality. In "Sensibility," for example, More writes that sensibility is a "soothing pow'r" whose blessings are "fairy favours" beyond the ability of art to imitate. By emphasizing the association of sensibility with an innate sensual femininity, More establishes in a few lines the disconnection between women and intellect. Sensibility is an "untaught goodness," who has little need for language to express herself ("To those who know thee not, no words can paint / And those who know thee, know all words are faint!"). Such a definition puts into antithesis the celebrated object ("Thy subtle essence") and intellectuality, with its dependence on language and learning. Sixteen years later, Polwhele uses more emphatically this distancing of women from intellect in his tirade against intellectual women. Mary Wollstonecraft is the main target of *The Unsex'd Females*, but it also targets Anna Barbauld, Mary Robinson, Charlotte Smith, and other women writers not as politically motivated or as radical as Wollstonecraft. And although Polwhele focuses on contemporary women, ignoring the important female figures of prior decades, such as Montagu and Carter, his attack reflects back on them in a way difficult to ignore, while by not naming them he is all the more insulting. When women ignore intelligent argument to celebrate sensuality, as More's poems prove, they aid attacks against female intellectualism.

Like Polwhele, modern literary historians and anthologists have long neglected or trivialized the Bluestockings. Their writings are not easy to locate, and have been dismissed as incompatible with a definition of mainstream Romanticism. Samuel Monk (1960), in his important study of the Romantic sublime, does engage the Bluestockings to an unusual degree but ultimately finds them to have failed in their attempts to discover and analyze the Romantic sublime, while the male poets, he argues, succeed in this task. Even those scholars who study the Bluestockings are more likely to write of their lives rather than their works. Byron's wife, Annabella Milbanke, for instance, was given an extensive education and considered herself of the bluestocking mold, and her intellectual bent was what appealed to Byron when they first corresponded. But the many books that treat of her on library shelves focus on her biography as it relates to Byron, not her own thinking (see, for instance, Mayne's interesting yet restricted *The Life of Lady Byron*, 1929). We might profit from this focus, by changing the direction of such women as domestic centers for literary men to one that supposes, since their writings are unavailable or difficult to come by, that we might nevertheless find their thoughts preserved in the home. Such has been the case with Montagu and Carter, whose scholarly works are much less available than some of their correspondence: specifically, Elizabeth Carter's domestic letters to her friend and patron.

The Bluestocking circle in its most intellectual aspect can be contained in the relation between Elizabeth Montagu and Elizabeth Carter as well as their critical and scholarly productions. They shared a friendship that was both strengthened and betrayed by their uneasy relation to the public–private ratio of their work and lives. The sense of history they strive toward in their intellectual work is necessarily undercut by the timeless quality they must give to their creation of a masking female community. This mask displays female scholarship as one of many harmless and time-occupying hobbies women can undertake to pass their days harmoniously. Montagu begins her first known letter to Carter after a visit from her by writing, "What must my dear Miss Carter think of the signs of brutal insensibility which I have given in not answering her obliging letter? . . . I look upon my introduction to your acquaintance as one of the luckiest incidents of my life, if I can contrive to improve it into friendship." Beginning here, their writings and letters create a female community of the mind that expresses itself socially and publicly through salon evenings and publications. Nevertheless, they must clothe their intellectual community with something that makes it acceptable for women to have such pursuits. Hannah More's poem "Sensibility" is clearly a reflection of the very defense mechanism Montagu and Carter found it necessary to employ: their writings must take on the rhetoric and configuration of a friendship of sensibility (as against the "brutal insensibility" of not having written). This is something that Carter especially strives for, particularly after the rumors that her migraine headaches are caused by mental strain relievable only by giving up scholarship altogether. Such rumors, a point on which Carter is endlessly reassuring to Montagu because she needs her friend's support in continuing her work, reflect the complex relation of illness to women's intellectuality, and the fear that overuse of the mind will lead to madness and sexual barrenness. Medical and educational authorities had long stressed the negative effects of mental effort on the female physiognomy, and these beliefs placed a double burden of unnaturalness or illness, and sexual failure or deviance on women intellects. Wollstonecraft, Hays, and Dacre suffered from these accusations, but Montagu and Carter sheltered themselves behind staid positions, and strong husband or father figures. Nevertheless, Carter's letters reveal enough anxiety about the relation between migraine and mental endeavor to show how difficult it was for women to engage scholarly work.

Carter, in keeping with her intellectual interests and her anxiety about barrenness, retreats from the feminine in her correspondence with Montagu. The first letter of the series, dated August 14, 1756, begins with apologies for her headache:

> I was obliged to supply the deficienc[i]es of Tacitus by having recourse to Suetonius . . . I join with you in regretting that we have lost the fine lurid picture which would have been drawn of this reign by the pencil of Tacitus. It is difficult to judge of two such monsters as Tiberius and Caligula, which was the most detestable; yet perhaps there seems to be rather more excuse for the wretch who discharged on mankind part of the horrors that racked his own breast, than for the other, whose cruelties were a mere wanton sport, and were practised *con amore*. Whatever was the difference of their guilt, the self-tormenting turn that devoured the one, and the frolick devil that amused the other, were equal mischiefs to the Romans, though the last was the most insupportable, as misery must be aggravated by contempt. (Pennington, 1817: I, pp. 1–2)

In a letter that begins with her own tormented head and the disqualifications that pain lays on the intellect, Carter immerses herself immediately in the torment and disqualifications of the ancients. Suetonius is "whom one ought to respect, I believe, as a useful writer, though it is impossible not to grow tired of him as a very crabbed and disagreeable one." And the subject on which she has had to resort to Suetonius demands a finer hand than his, with its "frolick devil," "wanton sport," and cast of monsters. There is no hesitation in critical assessment, no feminine distaste at discussing Roman cruelty. Indeed, judgment is not only forthcoming, but responds to Elizabeth Montagu's proposed judgment rather than evading it.

The same letter discusses friendships held by both women, as well as a "wildly and pleasingly romantic excursion" Carter has recently taken in

Kent. It ends with a return to the Romans who so intrigue them through an acute discussion of moral health:

> Your Augustus would not have been the tool of Livia, if he had not been the slave of his own passions. A wise and great man who is seduced by the artifices of a bad woman, with whom he was originally connected in a fair and honest way, may be a pitiable instance of human weakness. But the marriage of Augustus with Livia, was in itself an act of injustice, and a wicked outrage on all the rights of civil life. (Pennington, 1817: I, p. 3)

Carter here anticipates the arguments of Wollstonecraft's analysis of sexual and marital relations by locating the wrongs of women in the ungovernable passions of men, although without Wollstonecraft's vindication of women's inherent right to passionate being. Nor does Carter connect Livia's evil to an unjust social system that encourages feminine manipulation and masculine abuse of power. If she disallows a similarity between Roman decadence of the late period and contemporary society, Carter's analysis shows her engagement with the domestic side of scholarly interests.

Carter maintains a similar discontinuity between contemporary French and British culture; this is a dissociation that male visitors to the Bluestocking salons, such as Horace Walpole, could not agree with, at least in terms of his presence at continental salons. "I will not trouble you for the fashionable French quarto," she writes in a later letter (January 13, 1759).

> Too many of the French writers I fear are of the same character as you represent this to be: they affect to introduce a kind of gay morality so tricked out in plumes and clinquant, that an incautious reader will not presently discover, that all this finery is merely to disguise a system of wickedness and infidelity. (Pennington, 1817: I, p. 20)

Here the artifices of a wicked woman are not to blame, nor the intemperate passions of a selfish man, but the wholesale seduction of the courtly French culture – the courtier and courtesan both. Wollstonecraft would agree with this social critique as well. As Carter remarks, the courtly masquerade costumes of "plumes and clinquant" allow French writers to initiate a "gay morality" which is death to English morals. What is seductive, she further signals, is the very fashionableness of these costumed writers whose intentions are so inexact and thus corrupt.

That this passage occurs in the same letter in which Carter fears that Montagu too highly esteems her forces a juxtaposition of strong self-assertion and self-deprecation that reads rather oddly without contextual materials:

> If I have any qualifications that intitle [sic] me to a share in your esteem and affection, as some I hope I have, I owe them entirely to my being a Christian: some of the least evils perhaps that would have discovered themselves in my composition was I any thing else, are, that I should have been a stoic, a metaphysician, a bear, and a wit. Do not be frighted; I am no such beast at present. (Pennington, 1817: I, pp. 17–18)

Carter's descendant and editor of these letters, Montagu Pennington, defends the passage from possible charges of false modesty and affectation, and asserts that "This passage, if Mrs Carter may be supposed to have known herself (the rarest of all knowledge), gives an insight into her natural character . . . [part of which is] to ascribe every good quality that she possessed, to the influence of the Christian Religion" (Pennington, 1817: I, p. 18n). Nevertheless, it may have disconcerted him to have Carter begin a letter on October 2, 1764 with:

> Are you in your dressing-room alone, my dear friend, and wishing for me, with as much impatience as I am wishing for you? I am just returned from a dinner of twelve people, with a head confused by the flutter of a mixed company, and heart very little engaged by the uninteresting topics of general conversation. After this vacancy of thought, and this suspension of sentiment, how do I long to supply the one, and revive the other by a *tête-à-tête* with you? (Pennington, 1817: I, p. 241)

This passage of the letter emphasizes that its reader should be there so that they may "chat" without the interference of husbands or family. Yet it is not this aspect that Pennington feels the need to explain, but rather a subsequent discussion of Plato and Quintilian: "I have been trying to read Quintilian, because you seemed to think I should. I have looked over as much as I could, but as to going regularly through with it, I could just as soon read a book of cookery." But Pennington's note only explains that to him Quintilian is a bore ("[I] did contrive to yawn through him"), whereas Carter's complaint is the rhetorician's "impiety." The proposal of the intimacy of female conversation in the privacy of the dressing-room, however, strikes neither writer as being of interest or impious; it is not a gendered act in the sense of Augustus's undisciplined passions

159

or French seductiveness, neither is it affected nor immodest. It is merely the intensity of intellectual intercourse, and the employment of sentiment through the unwicked, unsexed, uncostumed Frenchness of the tête-à-tête.

What we should also notice about these passages to Elizabeth Montagu besides their sensibility is the continual interweaving of scholarly interests with comments on the marital, domestic, and sexual behaviors and cultural customs other than their own. This, and not a deviant sexuality resulting from misplaced intellectual energies as Polwhele and other critics liked to suggest, is perhaps the most significant difference between the bourgeois Bluestockings and the Dissenters Anna Barbauld and Jane Taylor, and those associated with Dissenting intellectuals such as Mary Wollstonecraft. The Blues kept their eyes and critical acumen focused on otherness – from other cultures to historical periods to the study of aesthetics – while Dissenters were focused on critiquing the here and now, and in particular the condition of women in the present culture. Where Elizabeth Carter mused on otherness from her closet, Wollstonecraft wrote from the thick of events. Coming from opposite directions, from opposite points of relation to the suffering subject, from contrasting aesthetic distances, both groups of thinkers discovered that considering woman as otherness or sameness still projected the same set of women's issues.

Dissent and the Rights of the Home

Any discussion of women's intellectuality during the Romantic period must be dominated by the two pillars of the Bluestocking circle's legacy and Mary Wollstonecraft's overwhelming radicalism. In Wollstonecraft's political philosophy, the state is a prime agent in individual freedom, but it viewed women as non-citizens; the reformer's task was to change the state's attitude toward women *as* individuals. Her thinking about woman's position as non-citizen is always in terms of women's relation to the home and the family, or, in other words, as a relation between the public and the private. Equally prominent, and to subsequent generations in the nineteenth century more familiar, was the Dissenting author Anna Laetitia Barbauld. Between the two positions of socially prominent Blues and politically prominent Wollstonecraft and Barbauld are the efforts and accomplishments of Catherine Macaulay Graham, Germaine de Staël, Anna Seward, Maria Edgeworth, Hannah More, and other women less literarily influential but culturally present, like the Ladies of

160

Llangollen. In their wake lay the less radical and more disguised intellectual work of Joanna Baillie, Felicia Hemans, Mary Shelley, and the young Elizabeth Barrett.

Among these writers we can find a set of possible figurations that women saw for themselves in the constitution of public and private relations to subject (the male citizen) and non-subject (mother of the citizen). Wollstonecraft was able to meet women activists in the French Revolution, like Olympe de Gouges (author of the *Declaration of the Rights of Woman and of the Citizen*, 1791) during her stay in revolutionary Paris during 1793–4. These were women who were doing much of this rethinking of how women could relate to the public sphere. But revolutionizing the home without a thorough overthrow of the state was not easy to consider or write about on the British side of the Channel, although such attempts were fairly well received if published before the French Terror ruined utopian dreams (see Janes, 1978, for the reception of Wollstonecraft's 1792 *Vindication*.) Home, state, and educational process were so entwined, as Wollstonecraft explains in her *Vindication*, that the simple act of reading romances could foster the political conditions that kept women in domestic thralldom. And the *Vindication* itself was largely viewed as a treatise on women's education, a point that shows how closely women's subjective position was defined by whether and how much they know about the politics outside their homes. But Virginia Sapiro (1992) shows how Wollstonecraft's treatise was only in the most general terms about women's education. Although she planned a more detailed future work on that subject, the *Vindication* actually treats education only as a problem in producing citizens, not as the furthering of women themselves which interested the Blues.

> Although an important chapter of the book – indeed, perhaps the most famous – is "On National Education," the use of the term "education" is not the current restricted notion of instruction, particularly in schools, but the broader sense more common in her day, more like our current conceptions of "child-raising" or "socialization." (Sapiro, 1992: 27)

Where Wollstonecraft is often interpreted as claiming formal education for girls as a solution to women's political difficulties, Sapiro argues that she is in fact taking a much more rights-oriented position. We might refine our understanding of Wollstonecraft's views to say that education largely translates as responsibility or responsible action; and responsible action is only possible where the subject understands herself as having lawful rights in relation to the rights of others.

What is perhaps more pertinent to our discussion than women's education, since that issue does take such a broad stroke in the *Vindication*, is the rhetorical strategy Wollstonecraft adopts to make her claims, a strategy strikingly similar to that in Carter's letters to Montagu. Again, like Carter, this strategy should attract our immediate notice and yet goes largely undiscussed. Opening the treatise at random, the reader can readily come upon a statement like or close to the following:

> Unable to educate her sons or impress them with respect – *for it is not a play on words* to assert that people are never respected, though filling an important station, who are not respectable – she pines under the anguish of unavailing impotent regret. *The serpent's tooth enters into her very soul*, and the vices of licentious youth bring her with sorrow, if not with poverty also, to the grave. (Wollstonecraft, 1975: 136; emphasis added)

This quote is from a chapter discussing the "libertine" mother, the same chapter in which Wollstonecraft critiques Rousseau's depiction of the education of a girl destined for maternity in his pedagogical novel *Émile* (1762) as "grossly unnatural." In both passages she addresses the effects of a male-imposed education, and attacks male educators who insist that women are innately destined to be preoccupied by dress and ornament, and to need artifice and affectation to attract male attention. This is the unnaturalness that she sees Rousseau, as well as educators like Dr Gregory, actually teaching girls to adopt because it is all they need to learn. In other words, in one stroke Wollstonecraft reveals the false logic of Romantic education for girls (that girls are naturally unnatural yet need to be taught how to be so), and then dismisses such educational systems as the curative for women's political distress.

But more important than this dismissal is the rhetoric Wollstonecraft employs, the "play on words" that both is and is not doubly intended: her strategy is at once to attack male educators and to illustrate how irresponsibility (her definition of the badly educated) can lead to distressing lives. The mother mentioned at the beginning of the passage quoted above, one who has never understood how to instill respect in her sons, is the woman who is defined sexually as instilled herself with "the vices of licentious youth," the woman who is already a play on words. In addition, her sorrow is sexually represented as the serpent's tooth, a figuration that connotes both Eve's serpent (her pain being the physical pain of reproduction and subsequent loss) and the Romantic lamia figure (whose pain is that her seductiveness can't buy her humanity). By equating the irresponsible woman's impoverishing pain with the serpentine quality of otherness, Wollstonecraft insists that such a woman is the product of male systems that devalue the female. Such a woman's mysteriousness is not sexually attractive, it is dehumanizing and unworthy of respect. Such a woman could not be a citizen, as her sons recognize. To sharpen this point, Wollstonecraft describes only a few pages earlier her response to Rousseau's educational plans for little Sophie in *Émile*: "How are [his] mighty sentiments [for male education] lowered when he describes the pretty foot and enticing airs of his little favorite!" (Wollstonecraft, 1975: 107). The connection between Sophie and domestic servitude is not long in coming. Only a few sentences further on she writes, "Rousseau declares that a woman should never for a moment feel herself independent, that she should be governed by fear to exercise her natural cunning, and made a coquetish slave in order to render her a more alluring object of desire, a *sweeter* companion to man, whenever he chooses to relax himself" (1975: 108). The step from this sentiment to the harem is not a big one, and Wollstonecraft's most famous argument soon follows: the marriage contract essentially binds women to a harem-like existence where they are slaves instead of citizens, sexual possessions instead of full-thinking and responsible people. Rousseau's description of the enticing Sophie only clothes the male fantasy with the arguments of nature, but in fact they lead to dehumanizing conditions. "He carries the arguments, which he pretends to draw from the indications of nature, still further, and insinuates that truth and fortitude, the cornerstones of all human virtue, should be cultivated with certain restrictions, because, with respect to the female character, obedience is the grand lesson which ought to be impressed with unrelenting rigour" (Wollstonecraft, 1975: 108). Rousseau's illogic provides the foundations for Wollstonecraft's literal vindication of the female position.

In her own terms, Wollstonecraft has written a treatise not on formal education or women's dehumanized status but on female rights and manners. The association of rights with manners is not one we commonly associate with the *Vindication*, but is one we should attend to because of the high importance Wollstonecraft assigns to manners as the outward show of full subjectivity. The female citizen will be known by her responsible acts, not her seductiveness: "My own sex, I hope, will excuse me, if I treat them like rational creatures, instead of flattering their *fascinating graces*, and viewing them as if they were in a state of perpetual childhood, unable to stand alone. I earnestly wish to point out in what true dignity and human happiness consists . . ." (Wollstonecraft, 1975: 81). Wollstonecraft's emphasis on manners is not unrelated to Carter's observations in her letters concerning the state of French society, but this is no mere reliance on the eighteenth-century "culture of manners" to solve modern problems. Instead, each woman looks at culture and sees that it is not sexuality but the lack of responsible action that degrades a society. Carter focused on the degeneracy that male manners imposed on society, but Wollstonecraft argues that it is when women are given excessive power over others, especially through men's courtly behavior where women's supposed weakness forces men to bow to their wishes, that they are then corrupted by that power. "[T]heir character is degraded, and licentiousness spread through the whole aggregate of society" (1975: 126). That Carter the classicist should locate the trouble in men's behavior, and Wollstonecraft the feminist find it in women's, does not reveal an illogic of approach. Rather, it shows that Wollstonecraft is arguing that women can have a greater role in the formative processes of society than even the Blues might think.

The discussion in the *Vindication* of women's abusive love of power shows that this is a manipulative behavior that relies on language that never says what it means. Her description recalls Rousseau's own attack on high-society Paris ladies who self-indulgently attend soirées rather than attend their *enfants* at home. But Rousseau's disgust and anxiety is directed at these ladies' neglect of their maternal duty only to protest that they thus produce effeminate sons who lounge lazily in private parlors rather than manfully positioning themselves as citizens in the public sphere. His worry is about the masculinity of a nation. Wollstonecraft's anxiety over women's behavior concerns the effect that manipulative patterns have on women themselves. The emotional evil of such behavior is for Wollstonecraft the opposite of Rousseau's concern: that it deflects onto sons who are so concerned with their own (public) affairs that they neglect the mother and the domestic sphere. If Carter and Wollstonecraft come from opposite perspectives, they understand the cause as a common one. Rousseau and Wollstonecraft, however, understand the case in mutually exclusive terms and it for this reason that Rousseau's great treatise on education, *Émile*, comes in for such attack in the *Vindication*.

Furthermore, Wollstonecraft's description of the effects of courtly behavior on women echoes the same charge of degeneracy of manners and morals that she had levied at Edmund Burke's courtly defense of Marie Antoinette (discussed in chapter 2). However, here it is even more linked to morals and women's participation in their own present position, to morals of the social body as well as of the individual. Carter had essentially arrived at the same nexus of ideas in her letters to Elizabeth Montagu, that incorrect manners corrupt, but Carter carries it further in a strategy related to Wollstonecraft's own when she compares the degeneracy of French courtly manners to the corruptive seductiveness of French literary style. The difference between the Bluestockings and radical thinkers, then, is not one of foresight or social critique as their similar criticisms of male writers and thinkers reveal, but one of project. The Blues believed in the advances achieved through individual education, while radical thinkers fought for changes in the larger social agenda.

In these terms, Anna Laetitia Barbauld's writings offer an interesting contrast to Wollstonecraft's polemics. Although given an extensive education by her father, Barbauld's Dissenting background provided her not with radical political sense so much as a strong belief in individual freedom of conscience. A professed liberal, she appeared to discriminate what women needed, given their class and responsibilities, from the unnecessary, such as formal education or the frivolous "education" of manners. When Elizabeth Montagu approached her to head a woman's college or academy, she declined, protesting that she knew little of the practical education of girls. But she took Montagu's proposal to apply to girls of Montagu's own class rather than her own, and believed she would have to teach manners and dancing. To a Dissenter, Montagu's elegant salons trivialized literary endeavor by mixing it with manners and entertainment, and Barbauld reflects this attitude when she writes to her brother that, "Mrs Montagu, not content with being the Queen of literature and elegant society, sets up for the Queen of fashion and splendour. She is building a very fine house, has a fine service of plate, dresses, visits more than ever..." (to John Aikin, January 1784; Le Breton, 1874: 55). And when Maria and Richard Edgeworth approached her in 1804 with an idea for a periodical with only female contributors, *The Lady's Paper* (proposed but never carried out), her reply was: "All the literary ladies! Mercy on us! Have you ever reckoned how many there are, or computed how much trash...?" She was acutely aware of the difference not only in quality but in political sentiment among women writers: "There is no bond of union among literary women, any more than among literary men...Mrs Hannah More would not write along with you or me, and we should probably hesitate at joining Miss Hays, or if she were living, Mrs Godwin [i.e. Mary Wollstonecraft]" (to Maria Edgeworth, August 30, 1804; Le Breton, 1874: 86–7).

Barbauld's middle-class status meant that her literary friendships were with writers like Hester Chapone, Maria Edgeworth, and Fanny Burney rather than radicals like Wollstonecraft, Hays, or Macaulay Graham. Her Dissent, then, was a liberal but not a radical one, and if she was unconcerned with women's rights as an issue, she nevertheless concerned herself throughout with writing texts overtly aimed at improving the education of both male and female children. She was the first to improve children's textbooks by insisting that young children needed large type and only a few words to a page. Many of her essays written for older children also reveal an intellectualism nourished by her early education and the stimulating conversations of her father with his scholars (including Joseph Priestley) to which she was privy. Her contributions to children's fiction and prose writing proved invaluable since Britain would soon decide that young girls who read rather than embroidered would be considered bluestockings, the term itself having become a deterrent to marriage. But her educational essays, which she restricts to present-day society, British culture, and the needs and realities of the here and now, are meant for boys. She considers girls to need a less pragmatic but also less thought-provoking education, unlike the education she herself received.

"Against Inconsistency in our Expectations" (Aikin, 1825: II, pp. 21–30) is an early essay usually included as the second or third selection in most editions of Barbauld's works, originally published in *Miscellaneous Pieces in Prose* which she wrote with her brother in 1773. As an almost signature essay, it becomes all the more important to notice that "Against Inconsistency" begins with an epigraph from Elizabeth Carter's translation of Epictetus, and contains classical learning of its own. Perhaps more noteworthy, the particular passage taken from Carter refers to power and powerlessness:

> What is more reasonable, than that they who take pains for any thing, should get most in that particular for which they take pains? They have taken pains for power, you for right principles; they for riches, you for a proper use of the appearances of things: see whether they have the advantage of you in that for which you have taken pains, and which they neglect. If they are in power, and you not, why will not you speak the truth to yourself, that you do nothing for the sake of power, but that they do every thing? (Aikin, 1825: II, p. 21)

Barbauld's essay takes the form of a sermon extrapolating from a text and then building a hermeneutical exposition around its essential truths. But rather than take Epictetus and Carter literally in order to discuss power *per se*, as in sexual or political or even economic inequalities, Barbauld interprets the quote more largely as referring to good and evil. Thus she begins her essay by noting that, "As most of the unhappiness in the world arises rather from disappointed desires than from positive evil, it is of the utmost consequence to attain just notions of the laws and order of the universe, that we may not vex ourselves with fruitless wishes, or give way to groundless and unreasonable discontent" (Aikin, 1825: II, p. 21). Nevertheless, Barbauld provides the subtlety missing from Epictetus's logic by pointing out that the real problem arises when we see those who do not strive, or who strive by base means, receiving rewards and profits which exceed their labor. And this is Epictetus's point: "If you refuse to pay the price, why expect the purchase?" as Barbauld puts it. In this world, "a great mart of commerce, where fortune exposes to our view various commodities, riches, ease, tranquillity, fame, integrity, knowledge . . . [e]verything is marked at a settled price." Indeed, she reduces everything to the Romantic conception of circulation, and more specifically to the Industrial Revolution's conception of labor and profit. "Is knowledge the pearl of price? That, too, may be purchased – by steady application, and long solitary hours of study and reflection." But the figural should not be mistaken for the literal; an economy of drive + energy = profit does not translate simply as work = riches. The profit gained from study is knowledge, not wealth ("Was it in order to raise a fortune that you consumed the sprightly hours of youth in study and retirement? . . . You have then mistaken your path, and ill employed your industry"). To make the distinction between reward and mere money, she adds in the form of an addressee's question, " 'But is it not some reproach upon the economy of Providence that such a one, who is a mean, dirty fellow, should have amassed wealth enough to buy half a nation?' Not in the least. He made himself a mean, dirty fellow for that very end . . . Will you envy him his bargain?" (Aikin, 1825: II, p. 24). However, the distinction between labor and the gain of power is a finer point. Wollstonecraft would have argued that such profit of mind and soul must be directed toward a change in social conditions before women can benefit. Barbauld's sermon does not distinguish the sex of her addressee, or rather assumes a male gender by dispensing with women's barriers to the use of any power gained. She cannot or will not make the connection implicit in Carter's translation between right choices and the dominant belief that for women the non-profitable, soul-enriching choices *were* the right choices. By directing her sermon at a male addressee, she works to enforce Dissenting beliefs about real labor versus avarice, but she does not make the connection to domestic political realities. Barbauld's attitude seems to be that it is radical enough to expound Dissenting ideas to children who will become citizens, without going further to consider those children who will not.

Finally, in her essay and in her writings in general, Barbauld reduces society to a catalog of types, the poet who is a poet, the tradesman who is a tradesman, the woman who is a woman, without differentiation finer than that. She is not looking to urge genius on as the Blues do. She is doing what her figurative choice told us she was doing at the very beginning of her essay: appealing to young men in terms young men can understand, such as economy, profit, types, and finally a kind of reductive thinking that makes sense out of a seemingly irrational world. The essay seeks to produce an actively thinking citizen subject (male only, however) by appealing to boys' more immediate understanding of the adult public world.

In her essay "On Education," this strategy is more fully explained for the adult reader. She was consulted by friends who wanted only the best education for their child, and she found the husband in his library "busied in turning over books of education, of which he had collected all that were worthy [of] notice, from Xenophon to Locke, and from Locke to Catharine Macauley [sic]." Her advice is to ignore such works and to focus on what "your son" needs to learn about the real world, preferably from the father's own example. "Your example will educate him; your conversation with your friends; the business he sees you transact . . . Maxims and documents are good precisely till they are tried, and no longer; they will teach him to talk, and nothing more" (Aikin, 1825: II, p. 307). Only teaching him to think, she insists, will make him a worthy man – but of girls' education she says nothing, and on the mother's role in educating a child of either sex she is silent here.

Elizabeth Carter thought about women's lives and social freedoms or restrictions in and through her classical scholarship, and Wollstonecraft turned her *Vindication of the Rights of Men* into a second manifesto for women's human rights. But Barbauld confronts the gender divide by sermonizing young men on real life while assigning to girls the pleasant and teasingly entertaining fictional lessons of the *Legacy for Young Ladies* (published posthumously in 1825). As a Dissenter, Barbauld's choice to distinguish girls' needs from boys' may seem odd, but in fact she was not as sanguine about women's education as was the financially well-endowed Montagu. Her "Dialogue between Madame Cosmogunia and a Philosophical Inquirer of the Eighteenth Century" shows a greater tendency to spoof women's education, especially that represented by the Blues, than to promote it. Barbauld presents us with the dilemma women faced in a way that is perhaps more stark than Wollstonecraft's radicalism or Carter's self-cloistering erudition: despite her Dissenting background and her sometimes abusive marriage, she still argues for male supremacy. Despite her own education and brilliance, she does not specifically work to promote that of other women. Despite the fact that she was not free to pursue her writing fully until after her husband's death, she does not see herself within a female literary tradition of women writing against gender constraints. Her goal is to promote education itself, to better its standards, to improve what is taught in the home by involving the father in its processes. Barbauld's intellectual interest in educating the mind shows a conservative approach that puts her in opposition to Wollstonecraft as well as the Blues, while the depth to which she has considered education and the emphasis she places on it puts her in the tradition of Romantic women's intellectuality.

If Barbauld is conservative in her views, her life was neither complacent nor cloistered. She even witnessed the late period of France's decadent monarchy just before the social unrest from the fall of 1785 to the summer of 1786, when she and her husband toured the Continent after he could no longer help her run his boy's academy. The Barbaulds enjoyed their tour and were in Paris to witness the newly opened museum of the king's art collection in a Louvre gallery. They also encountered the new fad of mesmerism ("'tis in France the folly of the day"), and decadent Paris fashion ("when I see the Parisian ladies covered with rouge and enslaved by fashion, cold to the claims of maternal tenderness, and covering licentiousness with the thin veil of a certain factitious decency of manners . . ." to Mrs Taylor, June 7, 1786; Aikin, 1825: I, p. 87). They were also present for Marie Antoinette's "Diamond Necklace Affair", and met and continued to correspond with de Morveau, a lawyer turned chemist who later became republican deputy to the Legislative Assembly and the Convention, and a member of the Committee of Public Safety and Council of Five Hundred. Although none of the public dissatisfaction that Wollstonecraft, Helen Maria Williams, Catherine Macaulay Graham, and Thomas Paine would later witness was apparent to the Barbaulds, they disapproved of the king's ostentatious wealth and his manipulation of the legal process:

> The affair of Cardinal Rohan [the Diamond Necklace Affair] . . . is at length decided; but we have not been able to see without indignation the decisions of the Parliament altered in almost every instance by the pleasure of the King; so that judicial proceedings are mere child's play in this country. A grocer has got himself into the Bastille by writing a pamphlet on this occasion. . . . (to Dr Aikin, June 7, 1786; Aikin, 1825: I, p. 89)

It was on their return that Barbauld herself began writing political pamphlets against governmental injustices, including one in 1793 against

Britain's war to support France's monarchy entitled *Sins of the Government, Sins of the Nation*. Her political engagement, then, like her views on education, ignores women's condition in order to consider the larger social situation.

Having said this, we must still realize that Barbauld challenges our easy categories that set women writers up in camps characterized by specific political beliefs. Against Barbauld's decent Dissent, a stand that allows her to remain a household name far into the Victorian Age, we must pit her well-known liberal pamphlets such as her *Address to the Opposers of the Repeal of the Corporation and Test Acts* (1790), her poem attacking the slave trade, "Epistle to William Wilberforce" (1791), and her last published poem, "Eighteen Hundred and Eleven" (1812), which urges Britain to look to its own nationalistic complacency. One biographer comments that the attacks on her political texts, including Southey's unsigned review of her last poem, "show plainly that, though Mrs Barbauld may have been disliked as one who held and expressed liberal, perhaps radical, opinions, she was yet dreaded as a powerful and influential champion of freedom of thought, of progress, and of humanity" (Ellis, 1874: I, p. 194). Horace Walpole himself disliked her outspokenness, and in 1791 wrote to a friend, "Not a jot on *Deborah*," his name for Barbauld, "I have neither read her verses, nor will, as . . . I cannot forgive the heart of a woman that is party *per pale* blood and tenderness, that curses our clergy and feels for negroes" (quoted in Ellis, 1874: I, p. 192). Her ability to speak out publicly about human moral issues defines her as a tough intellect whose critical abilities were honed by her unusual access to education, but she seems to have had no sense of gender politics.

In this, Barbauld can be set up against other women Dissenters who were bolder and more outspoken about women's right to education, although none equaled the decisive position of Wollstonecraft. For instance, Jane Taylor (1783–1824) produced a body of work for children and young adults that attempted to educate young readers of both sexes into a more actively assertive sense of self than Barbauld's writings do. A member of the famous Taylor family headed by Isaac Taylor, a working-class engraver and Dissenting minister, Jane and her older sister Ann made their reputation by writing highly popular verse and rhymes for children. Jane, in particular, wrote verse that made the realities of poverty come alive. Her prose tales showed her female readers how to think themselves into more active frames of mind so that they could defend themselves against social injustices, such as the marriage system that Wollstonecraft believed was one of the major oppressive forces in women's lives.

Writing during the later period of Barbauld's life, Jane Taylor offers a vivid contrast to the more conservative ideas of her older colleague. Prose tales such as *Display*, read and enjoyed by both Barbauld and Edgeworth, engage young female readers in how to view themselves properly so that they cannot be hurt when society insists that they display themselves as objects to be purchased in the marriage market (see discussion in chapter 5). Taylor's educative technique, which blends teaching with narrative while escaping the dilemmas of preachy moralism, far exceeds the denial of the self in Barbauld's texts for young female readers. Her poems, however, more typically attempt to put the young reader, often of the middle class, sympathetically into the shoes of impoverished children. Why, they implicitly ask, should two children of similar ages and appearance be so differently circumstanced? More overtly, she asks the reader to feel the necessity of the other, to recognize that the self and the other are really the same thing, and to realize the self's need to support that other. She achieves this as a literal effect in several poems with an intertwined comparison of two similar children, or as in "A Pair," a side-by-side comparison of two young men. This poem is from *Essays in Rhyme, on Morals and Manners* (1816), a volume that collects and distills the essential morality of Barbauld's contributions to the much earlier *Miscellaneous Pieces in Prose*. In "A Pair," Taylor narrates the fates of two youths. The first is so unremarkable that the poem's speaker "quite forgot his name," but "[t]o life he started – thanks to fate, / In contact with a good estate." This jocular style of portraiture makes the narrative's purpose clear once we are introduced to the second youth whose tale is given in an iambic pentameter that seems more real but more humble than the sly pony-trot tetrameter of the first portrait. The second portrait contrasts so grimly with the first that the reader is forced to make a comparison of the two lives while in the act of reading. At the same time, the more common rhythms of the second portrait makes the artifice of the first portrait less and less acceptable, and thus makes the subject less acceptable in the face of the suffering but deserving second youth. The speaker intrudes here, coming into the dark streets with the reader to both show the way and to express her own reaction to slum life: "Loathsome and wretched, whence the eye in pain, / Averted turns, nor seeks to view again." But the second youth shines out from this place as a hard and careful craftsman, his workshop adorned with one mathematics book discarded by a student ("On this it is his sole delight to pore, / Early and late, when working time is o'er"). The poem never makes the mistake of doing the comparative work itself, and its silence on this subject compels the reader all the more to match up the incongruities offered by the poem. Taylor's attack on the British class system, clearly at work in this poem, also structures much of her work, and it is this Dissenting ideology (not shared by the older Barbauld) that helps her write against gender discrimination as well.

In a poem entitled "Egotism" from the same volume, Taylor shows in terms similar to Wollstonecraft's how she views women's complicity in class and gender discrimination. Her heroine, Matilda, appears sympathetic to friends' needs but feels that sympathy is not enough to cure social evils. The speaker uses Matilda's sentiments to encourage the reader to emulate her: Matilda "Resolves to watch *herself* with double toil, / And root the selfish weeds from nature's soil." And the speaker comments on this with, "– And so should we, for we are selfish all / . . . Self-knowledge of all knowledge is the best." Finally, the reader, who she now identifies with Matilda, is given examples of how to put this new knowledge to use: "The tattered wretch, who scrapes his idle tunes / . . . The lawless nuisance of the king's highway" – both these would be honest citizens if properly housed and clothed, she argues, an end she urges her (female) reader to work toward.

Taylor's verse translates Barbauld's purely political dissent against the slave trade or Corporation and Test Acts into a domestic dissent that argues against the socialized classifying and gendering forces of the dominant culture. Middle-class girls are not usually taught to worry about homeless or impoverished others; not worrying about them allows girls to grow into the kind of superficial and self-absorbed women Wollstonecraft finds miseducated because irresponsible. Such women want to know nothing of miserable poverty, and do know nothing of the history that allowed such social and economic differences to come into being. Without a sense of history, without a viable notion of Britain's past as a nation, the present can be seen as a mere pastime, an unimportant and unmeaning expenditure of days.

Women and History

The past as an inroad into the present, particularly the classical past and its literature, was an important topic for salon discussion. But history was also a route into constructing a viable past for Britain, a past independent of ancient Greece and Rome with its own cultural and

172

linguistic roots. This was a topic of general intellectual and antiquarian interest that intrigued the Bluestockings' salons, while the Romantic poets became more engrossed in the narrative nature of historical chronicle, and the philosophical ironies this revealed about the nature of human thought. Wordsworth's *Prelude* and Byron's *Childe Harold*, for instance, both interrogate these complexities while telling the historical tale. Women poets were also interested in this dilemma, as Charlotte Smith's "Beachy Head" reveals, and as Elizabeth Hamilton's combination of history and fiction for a critique of contemporary society in *Memoirs of the Life of Agrippina, the Wife of Germanicus* (1804) also shows. But women writers also became interested in the nature of history itself.

Catherine Macaulay Graham (1731–1791), known for her radical pamphlets on republicanism, wrote her great scholarly work between 1763 and 1783, *The History of England from the Accession of James I to that of the Brunswick Line* (8 vols). Like Wollstonecraft, who reviewed the work, Macaulay Graham's historical positioning was radical and antagonistic toward monarchical rule. She strongly supported parliamentarianism and condemned Cromwell in her work, and later supported the efforts of the American colonists. Her sustained effort, a 20-year labor that covers the end of Elizabeth I's reign to the end of a king's rule altogether in 1688, represents in itself the relation of women to history. That relation, like Wollstonecraft's relation of women to political theory, is a tenuous one as Macaulay Graham's narrative and life prove. She was admired by leading figures, from Walpole, Thomas Gray, and George Washington to Wollstonecraft and Mme Roland, and was attacked by equally formidable figures. Like Barbauld, but with a utopian view of a new nation, and imbued with a stronger sense of a public voice and social consciousness, she entered into national and foreign debates such as copyright, the need for women's education, the Quebec Act, and taxation of the American colonies.

Jane Austen, who was not radical, republican, outspoken, or rights-oriented, also wrote a history of England in 1791, eight years after Macaulay Graham's last volume of her *History*. Austen's *The History of England by a Partial, Prejudiced and Ignorant Historian*, written as a brief satire at the beginning of her authorial career and not as a mature work of intellectual and polemical labor, manages to jab Macaulay Graham's efforts at every turn. However, Austen's juvenile bite is an instructive introduction to Macaulay Graham's considered thrust. "There will be few Dates in this History," she notes just before she proceeds with irreverent biographical sketches of kings and reigning queens, much of it drawn from Shakespeare. "Henry the 4th ascended the throne of England . . . having prevailed on his cousin and predecessor Richard the 2nd, to resign it to him, and to retire for the rest of his life to Pomfret Castle, where he happened to be murdered," she begins (Austen, 1954: VI, p. 139). The consequences of power interfere with domesticity and health as well as with subject identities: "It is to be supposed that Henry was married, since he certainly had four sons, but it is not in my power to inform the Reader who was his wife." Equally unimportant is the rationale behind the motives of state: "During [Henry V's] reign, Lord Cobham was burnt alive, but I forget what for" (Austen, 1954: VI, pp. 139, 140). Austen's humor lies in the knowledge that history is not about human lives, nor even about teleological forces creating the national structure of the present, but about the bonds of power. Deaths have no connection to achievements, marriages are inconsequential except for the future kings they provide, and human action provides no real cause to the effects of the continuance of power. Against Macaulay Graham's careful claims that particular genealogies determined the fate of the nation, Austen implies that the state carries on regardless of whose head is under the crown, or whose head is lost. Her adolescent vision of nationalist politics is based on a young woman's experience of domestic rule as it reflects on her own economic unimportance, adherence to impersonal rules and power constructs, and irrelevance to the (patrilineal) genealogies that matter.

Despite her recognition of domestic strictures, Austen is no feminist compared to Wollstonecraft and her political theories of the same. On the subject of Elizabeth I, for instance, Austen can only malign this important female monarch, noting that "It was the peculiar misfortune of this Woman to have bad Ministers – Since wicked as she herself was, she could not have committed such extensive misheif [sic] had not these vile and abandoned men connived at and encouraged her in her Crimes" (Austen, 1954: VI, p. 145). This queen's biography goes on at length, during which Austen reveals that Elizabeth's real crime was to imprison the beautiful Mary Queen of Scots, and that Austen's own support of Mary against her cousin is a thoroughly romantic and sentimental one.

> Yet she bore it with a most unshaken fortitude, firm in her mind; constant
> in her Religion; and prepared herself to meet the cruel fate to which she
> was doomed, with a magnanimity that could alone proceed from conscious
> Innocence . . . She was executed in the Great Hall at Fortheringay [sic]
> Castle (sacred Place!) on Wednesday the 8th of February 1586 – to the

everlasting Reproach of Elizabeth, her Ministers, and of England in general. (Austen, 1954: VI, p. 146)

Austen's assessment of the beautiful Mary turns history into romance, making a mockery of both the arguments Clara Reeve made for romance and Macaulay Graham made for history. Furthermore, Mary's execution, along with mention of Drake's explorative feats, and Devereux's loss of his head, summarizes Elizabeth's accomplishments – a strong critique of Macaulay Graham's more straitened history. Yet Austen's "history" clearly also supports the kind of intellectuality Macaulay Graham's project demonstrates even as it mocks it.

Although Macaulay Graham identifies herself clearly as a historian who defends history against literary or gender interests, other women writers often borrowed the authority of history for these very purposes. For instance, Maria Jane Jewsbury (1800–1833) uses "history" to refer to fictional lives in her collection of short novels *The Three Histories* (1830), "The History of an Enthusiast," "The History of a Nonchalant," and "The History of a Realist." Jewsbury's purpose in this series of critical sketches echoes Austen's mock history by pointing out the fictionality of any narrated historical record as history itself. Like Austen, Jewsbury uses her "histories" to reveal flaws in the preconceptions, favorite hypocrisies, and prevailing ideological blinds of the Romantic age's fashion-minded. Her enthusiast Julie, for example, resembles Austen's Marianne Dashwood, and her name recalls Rousseau's sentimental heroine Julie. Jewsbury's Romantic heroine finds her suitor to be too healthy ("Your mind is dreadfully healthy, Cecil") because he dislikes the sway that German and British Romantic poets have on her imagination ("I remain of the same opinion still, that your having wholly, and all at once, plunged your spirit into an intellectual fountain of emotion, of which Goethe and Schiller . . . and Shelly [sic], and a dozen others, are the presiding spirits, will be productive of more loss than gain," he replies) (Jewsbury, 1831: 58–9). The question of poethood in relation to history, civil rights, and action is here reduced by the satirist to mere posturing and self-indulgence, a reprise of Austen's satiric joke that takes on more serious meaning in Jewsbury's late-Romantic stab at the uses and abuses of history.

Jewsbury's use of the term "history" for her fictional analysis of social flaws resembles Austen's play with the relation of narrative to history as a critique of the domestic realm. Both lead to the question of how women writers used the intricate relations between literary portraits of women's lives and surveys of history to expose the more artificial boundaries between public and private spheres. Because women's relation to history is so deeply problematic, as Austen so wonderfully points out, they are hardly part of it. Women writers needed to find a variety of ways to negotiate the Romantic interest in history as an essential and truthful ground. To be left out of that ground would be to erase the history of women's intelligent and imaginative productions altogether. Writing literary works and producing political philosophy were problematic ways to be remembered. Certain women writers turned to literary criticism instead, in the belief that by making judgments on others' literary and historical work they could themselves become memorable.

Literary Criticism as Art

We return to Reeve's *Progress of Romance* exactly because of her decision to traverse the treacherous ground of a history deeply inscribed with gender, in the sense that romances had come to be frivolous novels meant only for idle women readers. Reeve begins her defense of the form with an impressive display of learning, using Greek and Latin and Egyptian romances to retrace the history of literary genres and to reclaim the novel for her own purposes within a historical context.

> Romances may not improperly be called the polite literature of early ages, and they have been the favourite amusements of later times. In rude and barbarous ages, they resided in the breath of oral tradition . . . In the following pages, I have endeavoured to trace the progress of this species of composition, through all its successive stages and variations, to point out its most striking effects and influence upon the manners, and to assist according to my best judgment, the reader's choice . . . While many eminent writers [she later mentions Thomas Wharton's *History of English Poetry*, *Beattie's Dissertation on Fable and Romance*, Mme de Genlis's *Theatre of Education*, Mrs Dobson's *Memoirs of Ancient Chivalry*, and the works of Richard Hurd, Bishop Percy, and Mr Mallet on romance and chivalry] have (if I may be permitted the allusion) skimmed over the surface of this subject, it seemed to me that none of them had founded the depths of it. – Of metrical Romances they have treated largely, but with respect to those in prose, their informations have been scanty and imperfect. (Reeve, 1930: iii–v)

Compare this passage to one from Wordsworth's 1802 Appendix to the Preface to *Lyrical Ballads*:

176

The earliest poets of all nations generally wrote from passion excited by real events. They wrote naturally, and as men. Feeling powerfully as they did, their language was daring and figurative. In succeeding times, poets . . . set themselves to a mechanical adoption of those figures of speech . . . A language was thus insensibly produced, differing materially from the real language of men in *any situation* . . . Thus, and from a variety of other causes, this distorted language was received with admiration, and poets (it is probable) who had before contented themselves for the most part with misapplying only expressions which at first had been dictated by real passion, carried the abuse still further . . . . (Wu, 1998: 364)

Wordsworth and Reeve are both discussing literary genres that, in their view, have been degraded from their original high position. However, Reeve understands this process as an evolution that has allowed the romance to find other outlets for what it offers its audience; Wordsworth finds this process a devolution that must be reversed if his culture is to escape a similar degradation. Reeve seeks to resurrect romance from its current low status in the arts; Wordsworth seeks to resurrect poetry and thus art as a whole, and to return it to the high status of biblical language. ("Perhaps I can in no way, by positive example, more easily give my reader a notion of what I mean by the phrase 'poetic diction' than by referring him to a comparison between the metrical paraphrases which we have of passages in the Old and New Testament, and those passages as they exist in our common translation . . . 'Though I speak with the tongues of men and of angels,' etc., etc.; see I Corinthians 13" (Wu, 1998: 365). Yet both writers defend their chosen genre by imputing the diffidence with which contemporary readers hold them in their pure form to a readerly misapprehension as to the quality of pleasure one should derive from them (Wordsworth) or to a scholarly misapprehension as to the quality of their art (Reeve). For both writers, the degraded genre, whether romance or poetry, is currently devalued because of its complicated relation to meter. For Wordsworth, poetry is degraded because readers cannot understand the underlying metrics of all language and so they falsely compare prose and poetry; for Reeve, prose romances are unfairly ignored by scholars who work only with metrical romances. Wordsworth and Reeve both feel that the form is usurping the content and stylistic qualities of the genre they are defending, but Reeve must work harder to support and defend her historical analysis, and to deflect it away from being degraded to merely a woman's genre.

What is more, both are explaining the current low state of affairs through an examination of a literary genre not only as a historical survey (as all the scholars Reeves cites have done) but as a cultural critique of the present. Only Reeve feels the need to disguise the intellectual and critical quality of her discussion, however, which she does as a series of Bluestocking salon conversations. The analysis takes the form of a three-way dialogue between the Bluestocking intellect, Euphrasia, the male salon wit and skeptic, Hortensius, and the female audience, Sophronia. Each part of the analysis is relegated to an evening's exchange, with Euphrasia setting out and defending her ideas (which she has drawn from extensive research) before the other two, both of whom question, challenge, and are convinced by her force of reasoning and clarity of explanation. This format allows Reeve to draw on the then still fashionable women's salon, in which female intellect was permissible even though challenged by male skepticism. On the other hand, the *Progress* can also be taken as fiction, read for its lively exchanges and three interesting characters alone; Wordsworth's Preface, by contrast, and despite its equal focus on the form and basis of literary pleasure, can only be taken as non-fiction critical analysis. Reeve does not claim to have authored romances and so is not defending her own art, even though she presents and defends her translation of the "History of Charoba, Queen of Ægypt" appended to *The Progress*. But Wordsworth is clearly using his Preface for a very different purpose: to defend and to claim authorship for the originally anonymous *Lyrical Ballads*, and to insist on a proper reading of his poems by his degraded public. Both of these works are challenges thrown out as critiques of culture that still ring true today.

How these challenges are backed provides another interesting comparison. In making her claims, Reeve delineates all the major and less available reference works on her subject; if she has learned from them she indicates this borrowing in her dialogue, especially when the learned Euphrasia is talking. If she has heard of or read them too late to include them in her work, she still mentions them and her lateness on coming on them in her prefatory essay. Wordsworth, on the other hand, pretends to have read few other authorities than the Old and New Testaments, and works of genius such as Shakespeare. His only reference to critical or scholarly works is a denial of intimate acquaintance with Aristotle: he pretends not to have read the great classical philosopher in order to claim an original authority expressing his own ideas over the nature of poetry itself.

Aristotle, I have been told, hath said that poetry is the most philosophic of all writing. It is so. Its object is truth, not individual and local, but general and operative; not standing upon external testimony, but carried alive into the heart by passion – truth which is its own testimony, which gives

178

strength and divinity to the tribunal to which it appeals, and receives them from the same tribunal. (Wu, 1998: 361)

This section of Wordsworth's defense of "true poetry," as opposed to the false taste of current poetic production, opposes authorities, scholars, and critics – even philosophers – to the truth that poetry evinces. To reveal this truth, which he claims a real poet can do through his own observation of men's relation to nature and to sensations, he uses the Christian notion of the individual as what we would now term an "existential" subject. In doing so he seems to be putting himself in the place of Milton's Lucifer, watching and surveying how men experience their existence. But Wordsworth substitutes the existential subject for poetry itself, making the poetic the personal, and poetic truth a shared yet extra-human truth. He puts poetry and poetic experience on trial. Reeve talks about polite literature and the taste of the times, Wordsworth talks about truth and the tribunal; she uses the polite form of fiction to discuss these issues, he sermonizes like a preacher in the guise of Lucifer.

> Poetry is the image of man and nature ... The poet writes under one restriction only – namely, that of the necessity of giving immediate pleasure to a human being possessed of that information which may be expected from him, not as a lawyer, a physician, a mariner, an astronomer, or a natural philosopher, but as a man. Except this one restriction, there is no object standing between the poet and the image of things; between this, and the biographer and historian, there are a thousand. (Wu, 1998: 361)

Such a description of the Romantic poet challenges the more humanistic assumptions present in women writers' discussions of the poet's task, but it also pits the poet against the historian and the biographer. Wordsworth believes these last to be utilitarian but the poet to be visionary. The poet is "a man" in the fullest, most divine sense of that word, not a type as in Barbauld, or an impassioned genius as in Seward. But literary history, as in Reeve's case, was sometimes the way in which women writers could couch their acts of poetry or poetic fiction – the way in which they could flesh out their careers – so as to make their poetry more viable and more truth-filled, and less simply "verse." Wordsworth's argument provides a way of dismissing what these women were producing as without authority, and he provides a strong argument for forgetting what women had been writing. One woman who fought being dismissed, sometimes by attacking other women writers if she thought their projects weak, was Anna Seward. Her attacks on Clara

Reeve are instructive, particularly in light of the kind of argument Wordsworth sets up in his Preface to *Lyrical Ballads*, when he was still an unknown in a literary marketplace largely dominated by women writers like Seward and Reeve.

Anna Seward is perhaps the one woman of the Romantic period who saw her place in literary history, particularly in the production of poetry, as rivaling any of her male contemporaries. She believed that her poems would outlive and outperform her to the same extent that Wordsworth and Keats believed of their poetry. Yet she found her arch rival not among men but among women writers: Clara Reeve. Her public yet unsigned attacks on Reeve's work reveal an interesting sense of how women writers themselves gendered literary, and more specifically critical, ground. Seward's charges are interesting to analyze because her attacks are not on the most obvious points of Reeve's productions. She might have attacked, for instance, the salon-style conversation structure of *The Progress of Romance*, which is a female-defined style that allows Reeve to adjudicate male- and female-oriented claims between differently sexed characters. It also allows her to deny that any one statement is her own belief, which Seward might have easily targeted as a cowardly approach. Yet Seward criticizes neither this nor the intellectual project Reeve undertakes in that work, an erudite reconstruction of the romance genre and its literary genealogy.

Rather, Seward assumes the place of the literary daughter, taking umbrage at Reeve's critique of male novelists like Samuel Richardson. Seward's choice for making feminine warfare, then, is itself masculine, reproducing the same tone of lineage-making that Wordsworth uses in his Preface, and more importantly, taking place in the pages of *The Gentleman's Magazine*, a periodical that constituted male turf and that was best suited for hurting Reeve's cause. Seward's shift of Reeve's choice of the female salon to the "gentleman's" periodical allows for a curious play with gender. She assumes the role of literary daughter in order to defend the male appropriation of the novel and the woman's story in it. The conflict between these two writers reveals the deep tensions women were feeling in the literary and intellectual field, and their sense that their place in that field was impermanent, contestable, and erasable. To gain the upper hand, Seward often attacked other women writers, as a way to choose the objects of erasure herself in order to ensure her own survival, a strategy that always throws the accuser's motives into doubt and sometimes beyond historical placement – as was finally Seward's fate.

180

Seward attacks Reeve (oddly giving her name erroneously as Clara Reeves) for asserting in *The Progress* that Richardson's *Pamela* is a greater work than his novels *Clarissa* and *Sir Charles Grandison*. Oddly enough, Reeve uses arguments for the originality and forceful passions of Richardson's first novel that anticipate Scott's praise for Walpole's *Castle of Otranto* over Reeve's variation on that work. But Seward claims her own admiration for *The Old English Baron* is diminished by its author's senseless critical judgments of Richardson. Seward stakes her poetic reputation on her own critical abilities, as when she notes that Reeve's criticisms of Rousseau's "Eloisa" (her title for *Julie, ou la Nouvelle Héloïse*) are Rousseau's own and not new to Reeve:

> The author himself insinuates his reasons for the composition of this work in the preface, given under the form of a dialogue, full of pretended reproach for that unfashionable philosophy, which ventures to excuse the indiscretion of a single woman, and treats the gallantries of the married ones with such unbounded severity. These reasons are also covertly given in a letter of St Preux to Eloisa from Paris, in which he declaims upon the innocence of their attachment, yet unstain'd by infidelity, compared with the inconstant libertinism of the Parisian ladies.
>
> In those passages, Rousseau covertly suggests his own apology for the most faulty part of Eloisa. There is, therefore, no new light thrown upon that work by Miss Reeves. (*The Gentleman's Magazine* 56 (1786): 15)

However, despite this strategic use of an author's self-recognition to defend questionable practice, Seward finds a stronger tactic for her purpose by beginning with a pre-emptive attack on Dr Johnson before the first mention of Reeve, in order to blame him for unsound intellectual engagement. By this complex maneuver – Johnson as straw man against which to set up Richardson and knock down Reeve – she asserts the integrity of women's intellectuality (hers) in order that it not be dismissed by male critics as irrelevant because poorly reasoned, or because of unthinking support for one's sex. And she enforces her argument by blaming the present impoverished critical skill, of which Reeve will only be one example, on Johnson himself ("the late arch-infidel to the scriptures of Apollo").

Seward's attack takes up several letters and Reeve's final response ends the exchange defensively and sharply by questioning the sexual identity of "A.S.," commenting that she hesitates to think a gentleman would attack her in this way but shudders to think a woman could be capable of such insults. What is so interesting about this debate is its questioning of gender on every level, and its public nature. In contrast to the subtle disagreements available at the level of private reading in Reeve's and Wordsworth's accounts of literary art and intent, Seward makes her disagreements with Reeve as public as possible. Moreover, she does so over a question of aesthetics and taste, which she takes, like most of the Romantics, as an indication of moral integrity. Seward's real argument, however, is not with Reeve but with the fact that it was highly unusual for a woman to dispense literary evaluations, as we saw with Elizabeth Montagu. Most women writers, in fact, did little more than praise highly but briefly or be silent when mentioning male writers, a tactic that Austen tellingly resorted to in her published novels. Reeve, then, took a chance in elevating Richardson's first novel over his others. Seward's public slap on the hand for so bold a criticism, notably, is on the question of taste and erudition, challenging Reeve on her intellectual ability. This in itself is novel, yet also unfortunate because it reveals to all involved in the literary field how vulnerable the woman writer is to public criticism, and how difficult it is to answer such criticism.

Intellectuality and the Years of Reaction

The years following France's Reign of Terror saw a renewal of conservative political sentiment that was accompanied by increased attacks on women writers by both male and female critics. The relation between this new reactionary mood, with its concurrent xenophobia, can be seen all too clearly in novels of disillusionment like Austen's *Persuasion* or Fanny Burney's *The Wanderer* (1814). These works show a formerly spirited author accepting the new constrictions of women's political and public status by portraying heroines whose beauty and moral character is no longer enough in itself to assure them of gaining the hero's heart and hand. Complex political and economic arguments have to be plotted into the narrative before the heroine can become the transformed Cinderella, and for large parts of these novels she is in great danger of remaining the Cinderella of domestic servitude.

Several examples of this new sense of disillusionment can be found in Anna Laetitia Barbauld's poetry, where she was able to more subtly interfuse her intellectuality than in her prose. Her early poem "A Summer Evening's Meditation" (1773) is an innovative appropriation of Milton's *Il Penseroso*, combining the meditative sublime with the supposedly incompatible female subjective experience to produce an inherently Romantic moment: "At this still hour the self-collected soul / Turns inward,

182

and beholds a stranger there" (Wu, 1998: 21, ll.53–4). As a precursor for the conversation poem, this might have been achievement enough, but, in fact, her contribution to Romantic poetry was also bound to her brother's literary editorship of the radical *Monthly Magazine*. The connections of this periodical helped focus her pen; perhaps most notably, Wordsworth and Coleridge had decided to compose and send "The Rime of the Ancient Mariner" to the *Monthly* to help raise money for their walking tour (see Wordsworth's account of this collaboration in *The Fenwick Notes*; Wu, 1998: 418–19). Barbauld's awareness of the Lake Poets, their early radicalism, and the scale of their intellectuality reveals itself in her poem "To Mr [S. T.] C[olerid]ge," published in her brother's magazine (Wu, 1998: 26–7). Her poem is an intellectual analysis and caveat against the dangers of High Romanticism, and it stands as an interesting counterpiece to her great poem of political disillusionment, "Eighteen Hundred and Eleven."

The dates of "To Mr Coleridge," composed 1797 but not published in the *Monthly* until 1799, indicates that Barbauld has had time to reassess the revolution as well as the current state of literary affairs. The Wordsworths' walk with Coleridge was in 1798 and produced the *Lyrical Ballads* enterprise. Barbauld's poem, then, originally addresses not this Coleridge nor the later priest of High Romanticism, but the earlier Coleridge of his periodical poems. (She had met the young poet in 1797 at a friend's house in Bristol, where he had walked 40 miles to see her.) Nevertheless, the two dates of Barbauld's composing and publication frame the budding of Coleridge's Romantic genius in such a way as to foretell it. This is a rather astounding feat to accomplish, and even though Barbauld's poem looks like what Bluestockings have long done to support men and younger women artists, it is Barbauld whose clarity of vision detects true genius at the same time that she detects its troubled grounds. Barbauld understands, even before *Lyrical Ballads* and Coleridge's responses to the revolution, "Fears in Solitude" and "France: An Ode," what he and poets like him will become and will achieve. "A grove extends, in tangled mazes wrought," she writes, clearly thinking of the imaginative mental journey that Coleridge's conversation poems are already beginning to take with their outward and inward movements (see Abrams, 1970). The grove, a pastoral figure highly favored in poetry of sensibility, is "filled with strange enchantment," "dubious shapes [that] / Flit . . . and lure the eager foot / Of youthful ardour to eternal chase." It contrasts disturbingly with the equally allegorical but productive "hill of science," a reference to her first essay "The Hill of Science" which began her own writing career. In understanding Coleridge's enthusiasm for the imaginative grove to be born of a sensibility that can overpower the intellect, Barbauld also sees the apparent likeness to opium-induced fantasies and enthusiasms: "Dreams hang on every leaf; unearthly forms / Glide through the gloom, and mystic visions swim / Before the cheated sense." And, more importantly, she forecasts the dangers of such enthusiasm, such striving for knowledge of the aesthetic and mystical sublime, and announces that each mind "Of finer mould, acute and delicate, / In its high progress to eternal truth / Rests for a space in fairy bowers entranced," yet, in fact, it is "not here, / Not in the maze of metaphysic lore / . . . The dangerous ground, on noble aims intent" that such a mind must stay engaged. "And be this Circe of the studious cell / Enjoyed but still subservient. Active scenes / Shall soon with healthful spirit brace thy mind." Finally, the truly great mind of the poet must leave the grove in order to contribute to the world's needs, an argument that Percy Bysshe Shelley will also make much later, near the end of his life, in *The Defence of Poetry* (1821). "For friends, for country, chase each spleen-fed fog / That blots the wide creation" is a recommendation whose final prayer – "Now Heaven conduct thee with a parent's love!" – will be reflected in Wordsworth's epic, *The Prelude*. Even more than Barbauld's later critical biographies, written for her 50-volume edition of literature, *The British Novelists* (1810), this poem reveals her engagement with intellectual issues and the quality of her thought. As a response to the early Coleridge, it fully presupposes Wordsworth's *The Prelude*, as brief and succinct as the other is long and developed. But the poem does not indicate any of Barbauld's later conservatism, and certainly not the negative message of "Eighteen Hundred and Eleven."

The despair Barbauld will feel in 1811, in her last poem, over Napoleonic waste and expensive self-aggrandizement, holds only the faintest echoes of her caveats to Coleridge:

> And think'st thou, Britain, still to sit at ease,
> An island queen amidst thy subject seas,
> While the vext billows, in their distant roar,
> But soothe thy slumbers, and but kiss thy shore?
> (Wu, 1997: 11)

Napoleon's or any tyrant's reign ("There walks a spirit o'er the peopled earth – / . . . No force arrests his foot . . . ") is less to be feared than the loss of a genius's attention from the pressing needs of the present (Wu, 1997: 15–16). "The genius now forsakes the favoured shore, / . . . Then empires fall to dust, then arts decay...." (Wu, 1997: 16). (For an explication of Barbauld's politics, see Keach, 1994.)

Clearly, Barbauld still believes in the warnings she gave to Coleridge so many years earlier. But the pessimism of her Cassandra's prophecy turns the promise of the earlier poem into a clear-headed acknowledgment of what the desperate devastation of the Napoleonic Wars would reap in England itself. Published in 1812, Barbauld's poem entered into the world in a depressed year of economic hardship compounded by the working-class Luddite revolts of 1811–12, localized uprisings in which textile frames were destroyed as the mechanical displacers of weavers and other traditional laborers. The trials and hangings of these rebels were a violent reminder that warfare and retribution were occurring at home as well as abroad. Like the frame-breakers, Barbauld herself was accused of anti-patriotic messages by critics of her satire; their condemnations of "Eighteen Hundred and Eleven" silenced her as effectively as the Luddites were silenced, if not as gruesomely. But if she herself had also become more conservative and pessimistic from the experience, she only reflects the general growing conservatism over women's intellectual pursuits and abilities. During these years the anxiety over whether to educate girls beyond domestic matters, and the deep-seated distrust of bluestockingism, grew even greater, and became prevalent throughout the Victorian Age.

As Barbauld's poems show, the legacy of Wollstonecraft's and Macaulay Graham's outspoken political activism forced a retreat by women away from dangerous subjects. The safest available paths were into escapist poetry and romances, like those of the hugely popular L.E.L. (Laetitia Elizabeth Landon) and Elizabeth Barrett Browning. These were writers whose poetry embodied an introspective feminine aesthetic that could counter the current disappointments of political life; alternatively, women writers chose to take a conservative, politicized sense of the domestic that made the nation seem a safer haven, as did Felicia Hemans. Both these trends, the introspective examination and the outward corrective, were late Romantic versions of how women internalized the individual's transgressions of the public sphere and what these transgressions meant for society in general. Yet each writer relied on an educated woman reader and an enlarged picture of women's intellectual capacities. Despite the cycle of radicalism and retreat, utopian dreams and their correctives, this is a significant gain. Chapter 5 will explore some of the difficulties that such retreats pose in the last, conservative years of the Romantic period by focusing on the literarily fascinating

185

dangers women faced within the supposed safety of the private and the domestic.

Further Reading

Samuel Monk, *The Sublime: a Study of Critical Theories in XVIII-century England* (1960). Monk's study provides the basic terms of the sublime, and is helpful in understanding the intellectual basis for the Romantic sublime.

Sylvia Myers, *The Bluestocking Circle* (1990). A history of the original London-based Bluestocking circle, their salons and their successors. A necessary grounding for understanding the phenomenon of the Blues and their influence.

Naomi Schor, *Reading in Detail: Aesthetics and the Feminine* (1987). Schor's study is an elegant treatment of the gendering of the aesthetic, and provides an interesting model for a productive engagement of feminist theory and Romantic subjects.

Janet Todd, *The Sign of Angellica: Women, Writing and Fiction, 1660–1800* (1989). Provides an overview of a female literary tradition that can help ground research into British women's intellectual and literary difficulties and successes.

Chapter 5

Women and Identity: Visuality in Romantic Texts

Figure 6   Mrs Siddons in the Character of the Tragic Muse, engraving by Anthony
Cardon after the painting by Joshua Reynolds

Figure 5   "A Chinese Lady of Distinction, in her Habit of Ceremony; and a Manda-
rin of Distinction, in the Habit of Ceremony," engraving, *La Belle Assemblée; or
Bell's Court and Fashionable Magazine* (1808)

188

> *"My operations are to commence thus: Act I. Scene I. Enter Ellis, seeking Albert. Don't stare so; I know perfectly well what I am about. Scene II. Albert and Ellis meet. Ellis informs him that she must hold a confabulation with him the next day; and desires that he will remain at Lewes to be at hand . . . The rest of my plot is not yet quite ripe for disclosure. But all is arranged. And though I know not whether the catastrophe will be tragic or comic, I am prepared in my part for either."*
>
> Fanny Burney, The Wanderer, *ch. 16*

The epigraph for this chapter, from Fanny Burney's novel *The Wanderer* (1814), contains a female character's stage directions for a confrontation she hopes, by ending in her own literal death scene, will prove her love for the hero. This melodramatic behavior, turning one's life into a theatrical in order to make something come true, shows how self-conscious female characters have become by the end of the Romantic period in works by women. At the end of chapter 4, I briefly discussed how the conservative last years of the Romantic period were difficult ones for women; the prevalent conservative attitude to both politics and culture caused women to be particularly conscious of how they presented themselves publicly. Because Burney's character in the epigraph is acting in too self-conscious and radical a manner for the late Romantic period, the novel condemns her for her outrageous behavior. In her better known novel *Persuasion* (1818), Jane Austen exhibits the same concern over a family's preoccupation with outward appearance or self-dramatization. Austen's narrative condemns the Elliots' attempts to make the heroine, Anne, so invisible in relation to her family's careful self-staging that she nearly disappears from view; but it also focuses on how Anne may assert herself without self-drama and therefore without blame. Both authors are concerned with how women may properly behave in a reactionary time, and both present a novelistic attitude that shows women readers the need to concern themselves with how their behavior appears to others, while making them self-conscious about themselves as objects to be judged.

We can understand this self-consciousness in terms of the exterior and interior discrimination we saw in the various forms of the Gothic discussed in chapter 3. The emphasis on the external social world meant a focus on the relationship between oneself and others; that on the internal meant an exploration of one's feelings and dreams, and on individual psychology. When the radical critique brought these opposite worlds together it was to denounce a wrong in the social system. But the other way in which the external and internal were also brought together was in the woman reader's experience of herself once she became aware, through literature, of the difference between internal and external in her own life.

There were other factors as well that encouraged women to become more aware of themselves as having an external appearance and a contrasting internal reality in the last decades of the Romantic period. The increasing connection between women and consumerism fed an accelerating market in women's fashion. Women's magazines promoted the new fashions, and new silks and muslin patterns (fabrics increasingly available through Britain's expanding colonial trade) were in constant demand. When Austen's Catherine Morland meets Henry Tilney in *Northanger Abbey*, she is wearing her sprigged muslin with blue trim, the details of her dress indicating that she wears it to attract male attention. Men could also be interested in fashion, and dandies like Beau Brummell were watched and appreciated for their costumes and stylish innovations at the same time that society ladies were chronicled in illustrated volumes (see figure 1). Those who fashioned themselves after Brummell or the leading beauties were as much engaging in a performance at a private or individual level as political activists were at a public level. The politics of the individual are obviously subdued and less noticeable that those of the public: the wearer of Brummell-style clothes might be aware that his dress indicates a racier attitude towards the worries that plagued Tories and Whigs, but he is probably not communicating anything more serious than that. Ladies who imitated Josephine Bonaparte's clingy and revealing costumes, which stinted on underclothes, revealed much of the upper body, and were sometimes dampened so as to cling closer to the body in Grecian style, were communicating their fashion sense and daring more than an express sympathy for Josephine's husband, Napoleon. Fashion could even be playful, as when it adopted aspects of foreign dress such as Turkish and Chinese costumes (see figure 5). At the same time, the visual was very serious in that it brought politics closer to home by making women's fashion in particular a way for the body to become a sexual object, and costly dress a necessary step in catching a husband.

This aspect of women's relation to material consumption, that of the woman herself as an object, was its real significance for many women writers. What we might call the "marriage market," the convention by which men sought a woman who could enhance their social standing or fortune, was based on the set of social rules for how a woman's class, rank, dowry, and beauty might make her eligible for a good match. Women were intensely aware of this marketing of their physical and social attributes, but more importantly of the limited years in which they

190

could actually compete in it. Their awareness made them acutely self-conscious of how they appeared, and of new fashions that might improve their appearance.

Women were also influenced, as our opening epigraph shows, by theater. Throughout the Romantic period this influence was increasingly felt as actresses gained renown for their abilities. Sarah Siddons, in particular, earned heroine status in the public eye through her many tragic roles; George Romney's portrait of her as the tragic muse (see figure 6) gives an indication of the popular appeal of her ability to be something other than what she seemed. Siddons also epitomized the actress's ability to put on a character the audience could fully sympathize with and project themselves into. Both Shakespearean tragedy and Gothic drama were particularly good vehicles for this emotional exchange, and by the 1790s, theater audiences were so sensitized to characters' dilemmas that they cried readily at their distress. One frequenter of the theater wrote of the "*sobs,* the *shrieks*" heard from female members of the audience at one of Siddon's plays, while from the men came "those *tears,* which manhood, at first, struggled to suppress, but at length grew proud of indulging" (quoted in Backscheider, 1993: 231). The theater provided women with a way to see, by viewing actresses on the stage, how they themselves might be viewed or how they might themselves act a part; it also alerted them to the potential male audience in their own family circles. In another sense the theater provided a public stage because people went to be seen and to see others as much as they went to see the play being staged. But as important as Drury Lane and Covent Garden were to London society, and the provincial theaters to the rest of Britain, even more theatrical – and formative for this sense of the visual – were the earlier events of the French Revolution. Many of the most important celebrations of the revolution, such as the one Helen Maria Williams witnessed (discussed in chapter 2), were purposely choreographed as public spectacles. And in several of these spectacles, symbolic female figures such as "Marianne" and the sphinx played important roles in the political symbolism such celebrations promoted. Much worse was the spectacle of public execution, and when socially and politically prominent women, such as Marie Antoinette and Madame Roland, were guillotined the terrible dangers of public drama were also revealed.

Closer to home, women could more safely imagine themselves into spectacle through the small dramas of domestic life, a behavior Austen fictionalizes in *Emma* (1816) when the heroine attempts to stage-manage the love lives of others while remaining herself the star attraction. On an even smaller scale, women increasingly practiced what began to be called "display," a conscious attempt to play a role and to dress the part in order to attract the attention of (usually male) others. The rapidity with which new fabrics and fashions began to become available only exacerbated women's self-consciousness about how they could direct the way in which they were perceived in order to create different or more alluring identities for themselves.

Finally, the eighteenth-century Evangelical movement that Hannah More and William Wilberforce helped promote for the spiritual and moral improvement of the laboring classes had gained real force by the decades at the end of the Romantic period. Middle-class women were exhorted to engage in charitable work and to be seen volunteering their time and energy in the homes of the poor, or teaching Sunday school classes. This extreme of working in the external world, extending the boundaries of the domestic to other people, only increased women's awareness of how they were viewed and how such charity work could increase their opportunities for public display.

Complicating the emphasis on external appearance, both as a fashion and a spiritual statement, was the effect women's intellectual achievements had on how women readers perceived their role in that social world. Intellectual thought turns the psychological interior into something that can be reasoned. It allows the reader to see women's role as more than physical and emotional. But it also provides a conflict, since women's intellectuality asserts a public aspect to the psychological interior. If a woman's outward appearance is so much the property of others, in that it can be judged for beauty and accepted or dismissed, the inward mind should be something private and kept from such judgment. But intellectual engagement makes the inward mind available for scrutiny, at least for the woman writer; for the woman reader it makes the possibility of such scrutiny all too real. Women readers were made all the more aware that their thoughts could be made public, and should therefore be self-consciously analyzed.

Thus the division between a woman's external appearance and how others perceive her, and her internal experience of herself and what she believes that experience should resemble, creates a double-bind that immensely complicated and constrained women's identity. I will call this psychological and social double-bind "self-perception" in order to distinguish it from others' perception of a woman, on the one hand, and from public displays and spectacles that women would have seen and imagined themselves into, on the other. The male artist's self-perception does not so necessarily include an opposition between inner psychology and outer appearance, and the more general male perception of women is that of sexual object. Women's self-perception, however, very much reflects the conflicted cultural perception of them at this time: that women are both pure and impure, aids or impediments to male goals, objects of value and objects to be dismissed. Self-perception, as a reflection of this attitude, is a double-bind that pits outer beauty against inner self-consciousness, and outer materialism against inner thoughtfulness, making it very difficult for women during the last years of the Romantic period to feel at peace with themselves or with their role in society.

In order to understand just how complicated the phenomenon of self-perception was for women, another concept that will be helpful is the "internalized view." This refers to a social process by which the public spectacle – something which is external and purely visible, but which affects the viewer by pulling him or her into the emotion of the event – becomes internalized. It can be internalized to such an extent that individuals learn to readily accept social evaluations as they have accepted the larger political and communal vision of the spectacle, over and above what they already know about themselves. Several women writers convincingly treat this psychological difficulty which can prove so detrimental to a person's sense of identity and worth, often choosing heroines whose main virtue is their ability to resist the internalized view.

Another useful term for us will be "theatricality." If self-perception is an anxious awareness about how one should best present one's "true" self, theatricality is its opposite, a suppression of one's inner self in order to perform a particular role or create a particular identity. Against the internalized view, it represents an externalized vision that does not depend on, and even represses, introspection. Theatricality represents the most violent rejection of individual personality in order to conform to some ideal or role the individual has no intention of taking seriously but merely dons like a mask. The great criticism of city life from Romantics like Wordsworth is that it promoted such masking of real identity and selfhood. Many women writers not only agreed with this criticism, but through their fiction focused it as a female problem, arguing that only a resistance to the visual can hold the possibility of a sincere regard for the self, and of an ability to see the self well.

This chapter will discuss several works by women writers that employ this focus by exploring the difficult late years of political reaction in the Romantic period, years which demanded a heroine's self-perception and consequent self-control or action. One of our concerns is the historical and literary question of women and their relation to visuality during this concluding part of the period. Behind this relation lies the cultural changes that were the consequences of the Industrial Revolution, changes such as the new consumerism, the fetishistic importance increasingly granted to material and human objects, and the questioning of women's place in the world outside the home. One result was that women were increasingly on display at home as well as in public, with the theater of the home making the husband's and father's objectifying gaze at once more critical and judgmental. Another result was that, however women chose to react to this gaze, whether by playing to it or accepting it as an evaluative medium, they could not elevate themselves to the position of citizen-subject that Wollstonecraft argued for, until they learned how to see beyond the spectacle's limitations. Women's literary works struggle with this difficulty, and in them we find the seeds of self-knowing and ways of seeing that in the next century will allow for a revaluation of women's subjective status and thus for women's political rights.

Seeing and Seen: the Writer and the Proper Lady

Mary Poovey (1984) claims that Romantic writers like Wollstonecraft, Austen, and Mary Shelley were subject to gender constraints particular to women, and she defines the major constraint as the idea of the "proper lady." The "proper lady," a feminine ideal that promotes the spiritual over the physical and that substitutes selflessness for selfishness, was a stereotype but one that came to seem increasingly natural. Individual desires and needs could all too easily be viewed as unnatural, as things to be fought off and guarded against. This provided a strong reason why the contradiction between external and internal experience should be felt and heeded by women. Women authors were often even more self-conscious about this contradiction, especially in terms of their publications. Poovey notes that Catherine Maria Sedgwick, who comments in her diary that "her 'author existence' was 'accidental, extraneous & independent of my inner self'," was only one of many who dealt with this difficulty by establishing artificial boundaries between their inner and outer selves (Poovey, 1984: 40).

Another woman who was also equivocal about her private and public identity as an author was Mary Shelley. Shelley, daughter of Mary Wollstonecraft and William Godwin, was caught between the radicalism of her mother, whose death had done nothing to stem her blackening reputation, and the increasing conservatism of her father. When Mary chose to elope with the poet Percy Shelley, who espoused many of the same principles as Wollstonecraft, she was choosing her mother over her father, radicalism over conservatism, but her first novel, *Frankenstein* (1818), reveals how ambivalent she still was about the choice. Her husband's early death several years later left her alone in Europe, estranged from her father and facing an even greater conservatism at home in England. Her novels written after Percy's death forsake the attitude of radical social critique apparent in *Frankenstein* to reflect a bleakness and pessimism that derive not only from her personal loss, but also from the more rigid attitudes of the readership she must now please.

Poovey (1984: 116) notes that even for "the young Mary Shelley, the collision between what we now call the 'Romantic' model of originality and the 'Victorian' model of feminine domesticity was particularly dramatic." The household she grew up in celebrated imaginative originality, but both Godwin and his second wife then veered away from the radicalism of sexual politics that Wollstonecraft affirmed toward a more conservative view of women's role. Poovey argues that Mary Shelley was particularly affected by the conflict between these two positions, that of her mother and of her stepmother. She was continually torn between her mother's support of Romantic theories of the artistic ego, and the increasing socially conservative attitudes espoused by her stepmother and society in general about the ability of the individual to govern imaginative energies and desires. Shelley's distrust of individual egotism, represented by Victor Frankenstein's creation of an ungovernable imaginative force in his monster, can also be seen as her distrust of her own imaginative powers in a society that prefers women to be beautiful objects rather than creative artists.

In Shelley's comments on *Frankenstein*, she indicates this ambivalence toward her writing. In her Introduction to the 1831 revised edition of the novel, she attempts to counteract the initial responses to the anonymous 1818 edition. Contemporary reviewers and readers assumed the novel to be by a male author, due to its nightmare subject and the real direction of sympathy toward the creature and the male artist figures. Moreover, a woman writer should have moralized overtly about the horror that the monster embodies and the destruction he wreaks, all a consequence of Victor's immoral attempt to play God in his laboratory. Her 1831 essay begins with the wish to answer "the question, so very frequently asked me – 'How I, then a young girl, came to think of, and to dilate upon, so very hideous an idea?'" But before beginning her explanation, Shelley shows herself to be a "proper lady" by defending herself against any impropriety as a woman who happens to write: "It is true that I am very averse to bringing myself forward in print; but as my account will only appear as an appendage to a former production . . . I can scarcely accuse

195

myself of a personal intrusion." Moreover, Shelley claims that she is herself not a great artist: "As a child I scribbled . . . [but my] dreams were at once more fantastic and agreeable than my writings. In the latter I was a close imitator. . . ." Finally, it was her husband who promoted her authorship, "from the first, very anxious that I should prove myself worthy of my parentage." In the page and a half of her essay, then, Shelley offers the three most important disclaimers for women to the charge of egotism: resistance to visibility, lack of real talent, and promotion by a husband or father.

Feminist critics have frequently examined Shelley, particularly in light of her first novel, as an author who used fiction to work out the gendered conflict over imagination and propriety she experienced even as a girl. One of the most important early feminist analyses of this novel is by Sandra Gilbert and Susan Gubar in *The Madwoman in the Attic* (1979). They argue that Shelley projected her own artistic identity into the creature, showing how monstrous she felt that identity to be. More importantly, they interpret the male scientist's creation of a living being as Shelley's reinterpretation of her own guilt at her role in Wollstonecraft's death. As the infant whose birth caused its mother's death, Mary Shelley is herself a version of Frankenstein's monster. We can extend this analysis by adding Poovey's interpretation that the monster is a creature whose egotistical desires overwhelm the ability of society to meet those needs, until he is driven to destroy every example of domestic harmony he encounters. Both mothers and entire families suffer from an individual's extreme egotism, and Shelley's creature is particularly driven to destroy the family belonging to his "mother," Victor Frankenstein. Significantly, Victor has made this creature *because* his own mother's death made him vow to create a super race that could withstand the ravages of disease and early mortality. But if the mother's loss causes the monster's birth, Victor's act of supplanting the mother's role in childbirth with a laboratory birth looses a projection of his (and, we could say, Shelley's) ego in the monster that maniacally destroys the possibility of motherhood for his immediate community.

I have mentioned Mary Shelley's *Frankenstein* in a number of contexts in previous chapters, and her important novel can provide yet another insight for us here. The plot, one of the most familiar of the Romantic period to modern audiences, concerns the young scientist Victor Frankenstein and his Promethean project to attempt the god-like experiment of creating life from body parts. What we remember less is the structure of the narrative, in which four layers of story are embedded one within another. In the first layer we encounter an explorer of Romantic imagination, Captain Walton, whose childhood education resembles that of Victor, and who rescues him as he is dying. Victor tells Walton his life's story in the second layer, the narrative of the grand experiment. Embedded in Victor's tale is that of the creature after he comes to consciousness and begins to socialize himself. Within the creature's tale is the fourth layer, that of the De Lacy family he secretly watches in order to learn social behavior. (De Lacy is the 1818 spelling; it is also spelled De Lacey in the 1831 edition, and de Lacey in the manuscript version.) The story of the De Lacys is structurally at the center of the narrative and sits, then, at the heart of the novel. It needs to be analyzed for its centrality to Shelley's text and to the male activities of watching and speculating.

Mary Poovey (1984: 128) comments that the creature only develops self-consciousness through an act of "literal self-perception." He sees the response to his face – that part of him most visibly repellant – in "[a]n old man's terror, a pool of water, a child's fear." These are all "nature's mirrors" reflecting back to him his own unnatural and unacceptable origins. Once he reads of his "birth" in the laboratory notebook he discovers, he attempts to erase these origins by rebirthing himself as a socialized person. He hides in a woodshed attached to the De Lacy's cottage, "as if [he] could be born again into culture by aping the motions of the family [he] spies upon" (Poovey, 1984: 129). It is here that he learns to hope for acceptance by society through the blind old M. De Lacy, who can only judge the monster by his kind acts and not by his appearance.

What we need to understand from these feminist analyses is the relation of the creature's own effacement (his is a face no one can bear to see, so that he must continually hide himself) compared to the faces of the De Lacy family that become so dear to him as he watches. " 'I had admired the perfect forms of my cottagers – their grace, beauty, and delicate complexions: but how was I terrified, when I viewed myself in a transparent pool!' " We also need to understand the relation of his invisible status in the woodshed to the "staged" setting of the De Lacy family. Although the creature is himself hidden and unknown, he is like a spectator in a theater watching the actors perform something he can then try to imitate. The creature is especially enthralled with the two family actresses: Agatha De Lacy, the paragon of domestic virtue, and Safie, the Turkish beauty with whom Felix De Lacy is in love. By watching Agatha, the creature learns how to love; by watching Safie, who like him is culturally alien, he learns how to be European from the lessons Felix gives her.

Shelley sets up a situation at the heart of her novel that involves a

197

theatrical experience in which someone watches others on their home stage from the safe anonymity of his theater seat. Shelley implies that the home is a domestic stage for all women. But the difference here is that the creature is aware of himself as alien, and believes the De Lacys to be "normal." The reader, however, knows they are both existing on the margins, for like the monster in his woodshed, the De Lacys live in their cottage to escape harsh social conditions (a poverty and exile brought on them by Felix's attempts to rescue Safie's father from French injustice). The reader, the true spectator here, recognizes the undeserved marginality of both watcher and watched, and must therefore recognize her or his own potential for being alien or idiosyncratic, for not quite conforming to the accepted norm. In a theater this realization is always available because the audience knows the actors are alien (that is, they put on roles or other personalities), and so the spectator is always made aware of her or his own role-playing and therefore own potential marginality.

The centrality of Shelley's staged home, and the monster's focus on the women actors of this drama, provides a way of reading the real theater stage and the relation of actresses like Sarah Siddons, Dora Jordan, or the young Mary Robinson to the public gaze. One difficulty actresses had on the real stage was that they were on view but not in a domestic (and therefore acceptable) setting. This made it easy for audiences to speculate about them and their lives off-stage, without any corresponding opportunity on their part to practice defensive self-perception as women in the home could do. Speculation, whether about a woman's morals or dowry, provides a way for the industrialist and consumer classes to produce a kind of private marketplace in the home. There the man's display of wealth could extend to the pleasing display of his well-dressed wife and daughters, and to their ability to entertain and amuse. In the theater, this speculation could escalate enormously through a long-standing disparity between men actors as professionals and women actors as self-promoting prostitutes. Both Mary Robinson and Dora Jordan became mistresses of George III's sons, for instance, but more scandalous was the famous "green room" where actors practiced their lines and gentlemen could come to mingle and arrange liaisons with the actresses. Outside the theater, and especially in the home, this speculation was also a common activity, showing how close an analogy existed between stage and home, as Mary Shelley reveals. When Mary Robinson and her new husband moved to London, for instance, he openly encouraged sexual liaisons between her and those to whom he owed gambling debts or hoped to borrow from. His behavior, enacted when she was still very young and before her public affair with the Prince of Wales, shows how clearly the bonds between sex and money were related to marriage; part of Mary's "dowry" was her beauty, which he planned to turn to his own profit. Speculation also worked for the woman's benefit, for it was a crucial way to attract good matches for the daughters of the house, as Mrs Bennet knew very well in Austen's *Pride and Prejudice*. The marriage market produced an exchange of money between the new husband and the father, and an increase of status and power for the new bride. Austen's Lydia Bennet demonstrates how much girls looked forward to this power without realizing that their husband's money would not be theirs to spend: after her marriage Lydia usurps her eldest sister's place in the family parade, saying "'Ah! Jane, I take your place now, and you must go lower, because I am a married woman.'" But such speculation on the mother's and young woman's part must always play into the father's and suitor's more obvious speculative activity. In Burney's *Evelina* (1778), the dissipated Lord Merton opines that women only have value in terms of the marriage market ("I don't know what the devil a woman lives for after thirty: she is only in other folks way"), a dark hint at how limited a woman's assets actually were (Burney, 1982: 275).

Mary Robinson's real-life and Lydia Bennet's fictional experience are actually more similar than they appear in the above examples. Both were young girls of attractive appearance with little dowry who believed that the dashing young men paying them attentions were the key to a new adult life. But in both cases the suitor insisted on clandestine arrangements that involved the real possibility that a marriage would not occur after all. Lydia faced the possibility of becoming a fallen woman after she eloped with Wickham; Mary and her mother agreed to a secretive wedding before the couple finally moved to London, but without knowing why and fearing the worst. In both cases the secrecy was part of a larger speculation that involved attempts to force the hand of a family head. For Lydia, it was her father and uncle who had to try to provide a dowry large enough that Wickham would marry her honorably; for the beautiful Mary, it was her husband's attempt as an illegitimate son to win an inheritance from his real father. Both these women suffered from the limiting effects of the marriage market, the only economic market most middle-class women had access to, and both learned that they could only too easily be the losers in it, a fate Mary Wollstonecraft points out in her *Vindication of the Rights of Woman*. Moreover, as Austen emphasizes in her novels, if marriage is uncertain, women's attempts at speculative activity can only make things worse. In *Emma*, the heroine's main fault is her propensity for speculating about others in order to indulge her love of matchmaking: "How much more must an imaginist, like herself,

be on fire with speculation and foresight!" (vol. III, ch. 3). Because Emma
ignores the economic drive behind love, she assumes that a lovely face
and good connections are enough to attract an eligible man even without
a dowry, and so she mistakenly encourages what she believes to be the
attentions of Mr Elton towards the illegitimate Harriet. Elton, however,
has fixed his sights on Emma instead, and serious difficulties could have
developed if Elton's attentions had gone further, as Emma's brother-
in-law repeatedly warns her. Austen's novel shows how dangerous any
transgression of the rules of the marriage market can be for women, but
it also reveals the advantages of speculative activity for men. Frank
Churchill, who will inherit handsomely from his aunt and uncle, falls in
love with the beautiful but destitute Jane. He speculates on his chances of
winning both Jane and his inheritance by keeping the engagement a
secret from everyone and pretending to woo Emma until he can reconcile
his status-conscious aunt to a match with Jane. Austen disapproves such
behavior at any cost, depicting Frank's plan as irresponsible and wound-
ing to Jane, but Frank does win both prizes in the end. Frank's literal
speculation is the reverse of Victor Frankenstein's idealistic gamble that
he can succeed both in his creation of a new super race and in marrying
Elizabeth, by whom he would father an ordinary family. Both Shelley
and Austen disapprove of such male speculation, pointing it out as
behavior destructive to domestic relations and the social good. Austen
uses Mr Knightley to show her disapproval by having him secretly
observe Frank to ascertain his motives. "Frank was next to Emma, Jane
opposite to them – and Mr Knightley so placed as to see them all; and
it was his object to see as much as he could, with as little apparent
observation" (vol. III, ch. 5). What he does observe is that, despite
Frank's flirtation with Emma, it is Jane – Emma's equal in all but birth
and financial standing – who has attracted Frank through her talents,
worldliness, and elegant manners, as well as her beauty.

The marriage market, the arena of Frank's speculation, insists that
girls be educated in making themselves *presentable* rather than to be
present as themselves, as Jane's story reveals. Those girls with fewer
economic means need to learn more "accomplishments" to make up for
their important deficiency. This means that they spend their adolescence
learning how to have charming and graceful manners, to be physically
and sexually attractive, amusing, superficially or actually cultivated in
music, painting, and social dancing. That is, they had to learn how to be
good actresses. Every parlor was a stage, as was every ball, theater event,
and dinner party, and women had to learn to act a part in front of each
other as much as in front of the men they were playing to, because

everyone was always under critical appraisal. This is not to say that men did not also have parts to play, particularly when they stood to gain either financially or socially; but men's livelihoods and economic security depended far less on their social acting than did women's.

We have discussed the relation between theater and parlor stages in terms of the social pressures on women to act roles, and to be seen rather than to see. This pressure also worked to suppress women's desire to be artists and writers, producers of culture. Clearly, the emphasis on the visual provided one way for society to restrict women's ability to overtly influence the direction of cultural development. But there is a deeper connection in Romantic culture between speculation and seeing, and between seeing and poetic vision that is important for us to understand before we can fully realize the gender implications for women.

To see poetically is to see well, and vice versa; to see well is the way to produce social good. This is the teaching of Wordsworth's *The Prelude*, and his various prefaces explain that the poet is a special character whose inherent vision – his discernment, his ability to see into the heart of things, and his inner vision – can teach society something of immense value. Unlike the followers of sensibility, Wordsworth did not believe that everyone could be a poet, but they could learn to see well, the poet teaching readers to value this over the merely visual. There is a moral depth to proper seeing that false poets ignore; they emphasize the external visual, and thus "encourage idleness and unmanly despair," and "talk of Poetry as a matter of amusement and idle pleasure." For true poets, "Poetry is the image of man and nature," and "a task light and easy to him who looks at the world in the spirit of love . . . the Poet, singing a song in which all human beings join with him, rejoices in the presence of truth as our visible friend and hourly companion. Poetry is the breath and finer spirit of all knowledge" (1802 Preface to *Lyrical Ballads*).

Wordsworth believed his visually oriented society needed redemptive lessons in what he referred to as the tyranny of the eye. One poet who influenced Wordsworth's attitudes toward art, Charlotte Smith, provides us with an understanding of how Wordsworth's analysis of poetry and vision takes something from the female perspective even if his argument is aimed against those who "unman" the reader. Smith made her reputation by producing poetry of a melancholic tone and pose that became her trademark, and, as we saw in chapter 3, novels of a Gothic bent that capitalized on her poetic moods. Her posture of melancholy is markedly Romantic in its view of the world and of nature's relation to the subject self, but it is also different from High Romanticism in that it refuses to be either self-absorbed or, in Mary Shelley's terms, egotistical. In a characteristic sonnet, "To Melancholy, Written on the Banks of the Arun, October 1785" (from *Elegiac Sonnets and Other Poems*; Wu, 1998: 35–6), Smith positions herself in the poem much as Wordsworth does in his best-known poems: walking on the river bank as the evening mist rises, the poetic "I" listens to the sounds of nature. Like a prior sonnet to the river Arun in the same volume, Smith evokes the spirit of Otway here, a playwright whose *Venice Preserv'd* (1682) was one of the most successful and influential plays of the period, but who died in poverty. Creating drama, then, is not the route to successful poetry, she seems to be arguing, even if the unappreciated playwright as a figure for herself produces something sweetly painful to meditate on. If "Pity's own Otway I methinks could meet," Smith's speaker does not actually conjure the playwright's ghost, but only agrees with herself that her imagination is stimulated in this direction by natural sounds. It is not Otway that she addresses or meditates on, but the pleasure that melancholy provides a poet: "O Melancholy! – such thy magic power, / That to the soul these dreams are often sweet, / And soothe the pensive visionary mind!" Her vision directs itself inward as an imaginative process that does not require others to imaginatively produce a state that replaces negative emotions with pleasure.

Even without the "other" to cast the poet into a state of knowledge, vision still plays an important creative and internalizing role in this aesthetic moment for Smith: "For at such hours the shadowy phantom pale, / Oft seems to fleet before the poet's eyes," an appearance that provides or nurtures the "pensive visionary mind." Smith's meditation on Otway's ghost by the river appears to be very similar to Wordsworth's encounters with others, such as in his poem on the leech-gatherer, "Resolution and Independence." Neither poet delineates his or her vision so that the reader can see it too, and, instead, both resort to describing the vision's effect on them so that the reader feels that he or she has in some sense also felt this effect. Both poet-speakers have seen into the heart of things to gain self-knowledge, although they differ in their objects of vision; both have plotted this envisioning as a sequence of unanticipated acts and associated thoughts; neither considers him or herself to be posing or to have staged their visionary encounter. Both even conclude similarly with a decision or supporting emotion about the poetic profession through a meditation on someone from another world (the leech-gatherer is "sent"; Otway's ghost might appear), an actor appearing on a landscape suddenly made strange or stage-like. The one real difference by the end of both poems is that Wordsworth's speaker appears to experience a transcendent moment through the leech-gather's words, while Smith's Otway ghost, who we never see, tells her nothing, only appearing to promote her melancholy and make it possible for her to write. She is not teaching the reader how to see properly, but rather offering herself up to view to show how she is authorized to write by male others. Smith's poetic positioning is a turning outward of her own self-perception; she stages herself in her sonnets as a Romantic figure of melancholy, spectral vision, and imagination in order to deflect what her self-perception tells her may be unacceptable. To mitigate any criticism, she herself takes the place of object or other, so that the reader can be the "self" who watches her. As a result the reader is invited into this scene, as Wordsworth's reader is not, so that reader and poet can meet in the moment just before the sonnet's turn. Smith refuses to "teach," but she enacts something that the reader can participate in to see better for him or herself. To some extent, Wordsworth takes this positioning of the poet as an "I" in his own work, but his speaker is the "self" who is watching someone or something else. He takes advantage of the poetic positioning she advocates, but he rejects the disadvantages it also contains, refusing to alienate his poetic self from the visionary act. Because Smith, like Mary Shelley after her, is so aware of how she may be received publicly, she cannot afford to dismiss the disadvantages that help her camouflage any unacceptable self-promotion.

Joanna Baillie provides an interesting comparison here because she kept out of sight herself while writing plays for the stage, and, by hiding behind her literary works as a kind of invisible writer, she could thus avoid the pitfalls of self-staging that Smith confronts. Moreover, few of Baillie's plays were ever performed, and instead she had a large audience of readers who preferred her plays as closet dramas, as plays to be read. Her literary strategy for self-perception, for coping with the difficulty of being seen as self-promoting, then, actually stifled her literary ambition as a dramatist by making her unavailable to her readers' visual imaginations. However, it did allow her to write serious dramas instead of the comic fluff pieces expected of women dramatists. Moreover, the texts of her plays show that she was as deeply concerned with the problem of subjectivity and of vision turned inward as was Smith. Moreover, her knowledge of dramaturgy led her to attempt to move the theater beyond spectacle just as Wordsworth attempted to move poetry beyond unmeaning visuality.

The London theater, though more inspiring for women artists than the Edinburgh milieu in which Baillie was raised, was unfortunately not yet ready to be moved away from the very spectacle that defined and gendered it. Although most of her plays were therefore rejected, one early exception was her tragedy, *De Monfort* (1800), a play that owed its popularity to Hannah More's highly successful sentimental drama *Percy* (1777). Anna Barbauld wrote that *Percy* is "Miss More's new play which fills the house very well and is pretty generally liked. Miss More is I assure you very much the ton, and moreover has got 600*l* or 700*l* by her play ... I cannot say however that I cried so much at 'Percy'" (Le Breton, 1874: 54–5). By the time Baillie was writing, 15 years later, the audience had been better schooled in the kind of visual sentimentality More depended on, and *De Monfort* was successful precisely because Baillie allowed it to be reworked for the stage along the lines of *Percy*. *De Monfort* is thus less in line with Baillie's more general purpose of displacing spectacle with complex and thoughtful heroines who demand the audience's intelligent sympathy. But for this exception, Baillie moves away from sentimentalism toward internalized subjective emotion, emotion that stems from sensibility and the experience of passion rather than sentimentality and the viewing of it. Her purpose was more acceptable and more practicable in textual than visual form, a point she realizes and defends at length in the 1812 preface to the third volume of her published plays. Her strategy of making the characters so clearly imaginable through their words instead of their acts or appearance opposes the more popular visual sentimentality, melodrama and pantomime. Baillie thus allows the reader to easily play out the drama in her or his own head as in the closet dramas of Byron and Shelley.

Melodrama, the spectacular form that swept audiences off their feet, and which provided competition during the latter part of Baillie's career, is even further from her revisionary intentions than the other theatrical forms. Indeed, it so reduces the female characters' action and rational intercourse that they are victims of the irrational and the supernatural rather than tragic or comic heroines, as her strong female leads are. In one of her last plays, *Orra* (1812), from the third volume of her work on the passions, Baillie attacks melodrama by taking on its subject through a female protagonist victimized by the effects of supernatural fear (Baillie, 1821: III, pp. i–xxxi). The ruler Orra is confined in a supposedly haunted castle; forcing this plot into the foreground is a larger plotting between three men, one who wants Orra to marry his son in order to gain her fortune, one who loves her, and one who lusts after her. Her attractions for them, that is, her value on the marriage market, pressure her emotionally until she is psychologically affected by physical confinement as well. Part of the pressure she feels is that none of the suitors measures up to her expectations, nor could they share her utopian vision of her kingdom ruled in peace and communal economic well-being. In the interplay between a political utopian vision and its underside, the spying necessary to intrigue and political plotting, *Orra* dramatizes the uses and abuses of social visuality. The overriding passion of supernatural fear telescopes this sightedness, exaggerating its proportions and displacing them with the irrational and unknown. Wordsworth's strange leech-gatherer, and Smith's indistinct ghost are mere actors on a realistic scene, but to Orra's terrified imagination the scene itself is supernatural: "Mysterious night! / What things unutterable thy dark hours / May lap! – What from thy teeming darkness burst / Of horrid visitations." Sight itself is illusory in any case, as Orra exclaims

> Look there; behold that strange gigantic form
> Which yon grim cloud assumes . . .
> Nay, look how perfect now the form becomes:
> Dost thou not see?
> (Act IV, scene 1)

The horror of putting spectacle in place of reality exceeds the viewer's tolerance for theatrics; the natural outcome is that Orra goes mad and can no longer tell the difference between what she sees and what she is looking at. The line between specularity and interiority is too fine to play with, Baillie suggests – an argument against all melodrama and visual exploitation.

In her preface to the third volume, Baillie spells out the more spectacular nature of the new, larger London theaters, and the reasons why she thinks this new stage is an estranging format for her style of drama. Actors cannot use subtle facial expressions or vocal nuances anymore since the audience is physically further away and more extensive. Only spectacles can provide the necessary pleasure in such an arrangement of space and light:

> The Public have now to chuse between what we shall suppose are well-written and well-acted Plays, the words of which are not heard . . . while the finer and more pleasing traits of the acting are by a still greater proportion [of the audience] lost altogether; and splendid pantomime, or pieces whose chief object is to produce striking scenic effect, which can be seen and comprehended by the whole. (Baillie, 1821: III, p. xvi)

The very structure of the new theater, built much larger to make more profit, forces audiences to choose between traditional tragedies and comedies such as she writes and the new melodramas, pantomimes, and other forms of spectacle. The alternative to this choice, which Baillie has already provided the reader with in the same volume, is the completely literary and non-visual closet drama.

Closet drama is a genre we associate particularly with Romanticism, perhaps because the Romantics were always attacking the dominance of the visual in their culture. Byron's *Manfred* (1817) and *Cain* (1821), Percy Shelley's *Prometheus Unbound* (1819), Goethe's *Faust II* (1832) are famous examples. Charles Lamb even argued that Shakespeare is best appreciated as closet drama in his essay, "On the Tragedies of Shakespeare." Closet drama is usually highly literary (a criticism often leveled at Baillie's plays), with lengthy speeches, and action that is minimal or difficult to stage. More a poem than a play, its most important feature is its use of the play's assignment of lines to different characters to produce a thick stratum of interweaving voices and personalities that is difficult to achieve in other poetic genres. When Wordsworth eventually decided to publish *The Borderers*, the blank verse drama he had unsuccessfully submitted to Covent Garden in 1797, he first revised it back into its original closet drama form, and, as he comments in an appended note, "without any view to its exhibition upon the stage." Which leads us to ask how important the physical nature of the theater is to the production of drama. Byron called closet drama "mental theater" and Mary Robinson subtitled her closet drama *The Sicilian Lover* "A Dramatic Poem"; others played on this imaginative aspect of the drama that nevertheless incorporates voices, character, and revelation in less elevated form. Imaginary "conversations," for instance, were a creative way to subdue the visual element and replace it with interlaced voices, personae of known or fictional characters for dramatic effect; the best known of these is John Wilson's *Noctes Ambrosianae* (1822–35). Still others used a posture of sincerity to present their extra-theatrical literary drama.

The most flamboyant of these others was Robert Merry (1755–98), a self-appointed ladies' poet. He was responsible for a brief craze that swept London in 1790 in the form of a public exchange of love poems written by the "Della Cruscans." While we know about the importance of the Della Cruscan phenomenon to the development of sensibility, scholars rarely discuss how it was possible for Merry's self-promoting group to be so successful. But the very attraction of Della Cruscanism was its promotion of theatrical drama to the social level, where it provided a reverse of the closet drama. Instead of making the theater an imaginary and internal space, it turned the world outside the theater into a stage itself. The result was that both the world of Drury Lane and "mental theater" became street theater, fully externalizing what should have been a private and introspective drama.

Merry certainly did not originally intend such a development, but he knew the value of visual drama and how to exploit it. In the early 1780s Merry had settled in the British colony in Florence, and immersed himself in the Renaissance culture of Florence's past. He was particularly enthused about the poetry academies from that period which still existed. With the aid of salon hostess for the British colony Hester Piozzi (previously Hester Thrale), Merry and several other young male poets began composing coterie verse which they privately printed as *The Florence Miscellany* (1785). When Merry returned to England he continued writing while on shipboard, sending a long self-dramatizing poem in the same style off to the London magazine ironically named *The World*, and signing it "Della Crusca" after the Florence poetry academy he particularly admired.

Without realizing it, Merry had begun a periodical "theater." Hannah Cowley (1743–1809), a successful playwright and poet (author of *The Runaway*, 1776, *A Bold Stroke for a Husband*, 1783, and *The Belle's Stratagem*, 1780) who was 12 years older than Merry, answered his poem with one of her own in the same magazine. She attached an equally Old World sounding name, "Anna Matilda," to her poem. Merry and Cowley exchanged numerous poems of sensibility and love-making without knowing each other's real names or meeting, and although Merry was disgusted to find he had been publicly seducing an older woman, the Della Cruscan "theater" had become high fashion. It attracted a small circle of pseudonymous poets writing highly personal poems. Later Mary Robinson, a member of the real theater world, added her role and character's name to this print theater; clearly the Della Cruscans had delineated a new stage for public consumption. For the older Cowley, stage emotions and a deeply moving sensibility were what allowed her to advance her role in the Della Cruscan phenomenon, but she couldn't have done it without the "stage machinery" of *The World*, a sensationalist magazine that more elite periodicals disparaged. As in the smaller, more intimate and simplistic theater of Cowley's youth, her verse exchanges in *The World* with Robert Merry provided staged dialogue between strange players and overheard by an intimate audience. Their print theater played extensively on the paradox available in both poetry and drama between the roles or personae we see and believe in and the illusion actors and writers must create to seem to become that character. At first the Della Cruscans attempted to elide this paradox by preserving their anonymity so that readers would be forced to accept the poems as sincere declarations even though the poets had never met. When this device became impossible – indeed, the whole city engaged in guessing who were the real poets behind the masking aliases – it turned into a theatrical game that continued with those who added their "names" to the circle.

Not everyone found the new poetry to their taste. Anna Seward wrote to Helen Maria Williams that "Charming Mrs Piozzi recommends Della Crusca's Diversity to me, as an extremely fine poem," but that she would be glad *not* to be sent something "strutting in such inflated defiance of every thing like common sense, as the compositions of Della Crusca!" (March 3, 1789; Seward, 1811: III, p. 249). The poems were indeed highly ornamental, but more important, and what was perhaps offensive to Seward's lyrical sensibility, was that they were also theatrically self-promoting while pretending to sincerity.

But prior to the advent of Della Cruscanism, Cowley's poetry was already theatrically inclined, revealing an imagination that worked in terms of the stage, although without the kind of role-playing that Merry promoted to make himself more socially visible. Cowley's use of landscape scenery and images of the "sublime" in her verse are clearly derived from stage screen paintings, as in the lines from "Invocation to Horror" published in *The World*, July 10, 1787:

> Far be remov'd each painted scene!
> What is to *me* the sapphire sky? . . .
> Those velvet hills? yes, there I see . . .
> (McGann, 1993b: 37–8)

However, although she retains some aspect of this in her poems to Merry, there the stage-effects are reconciled to the internalized theatrics of love-making. Merry's poems, by contrast, are more resonant of nature appreciation than stage backdrops, but they also involve a theatricality having to do with his own self-projection as heroic lover. In his "The Adieu and Recall to Love" (*The World*, June 29, 1787), Merry begins with an unequivocal imperative ("Go, idle Boy!"), and the reader quickly realizes the boy as Cupid and the speaker as love-forlorn. As the reference to Cupid indicates, the poem's despair takes place in the pastoral, so that the speaker's return to the possibility of love is couched in landscape terms:

> No more with devious step I choose
> To brush the mountain's morning dews;

> To drink the spirit of the breeze,
> Or wander midst o'er-arching trees . . .
> (McGann, 1993: 36–7)

A wanderer in nature, Merry's hero battles valiantly with his rejected love for an unknown beloved. Cowley's "To Della Crusca. The Pen," responds closely following Merry's lead, but she replaces his rejecting beloved with her own passionate presence, her passion a creation of that same Cupid whose arrow is Apollo's golden pen. As a new beloved, she insists the lover of Merry's poem exchange wandering in isolation for communication with her. Her ploy, to flatter and manipulate "Della Crusca" into a poetic response, is restricted to setting the stage for this communication, but in "Ode to Della Crusca" (*The World*, May 17, 1788) she resumes her earlier theatrical rhetoric. Here she returns to her illuminated backdrops as their public correspondence becomes even more self-dramatizing. His song

> . . . leaps through Night's scarce pervious gloom
> Attracted by the Rose's bloom,
> Th' illumin'd shrub then quiv'ring round,
> It seems each scented bud to wound . . .
> (McGann, 1993: 40–1)

The World became a stage for them, one in which the players' theatrics take place in the space between the public (the social world of known and seen entities whose behavior and manners can be judged) and the private (the personal world one creates in the act of reading which is not diminished when the material read is later discussed with others). It may be just this quality of performance, more outrageous than private flirtation but less self-promoting than stage performance, that attracted Mary Robinson's attention and caused her to add her own purposely Petrarchan pseudonym, "Laura Maria," to the circle. The significance of the female Della Cruscans' pseudonyms was that they provided the key to staging the characters. Robinson's deliberate choice to recall Petrarch's beloved "Laura" provides her character with more glamour than the less obviously named Cowley ("Anna Matilda") or the Gothic novelist Charlotte Dacre ("Rosa Matilda"). But both Cowley's and Dacre's choice of "Matilda" as part of their closet stage name recalls the delicate Matilda of Walpole's Gothic *Castle of Otranto* (1765). As members of the stage community, they could not be blind to the intrinsic value of a name that conjures up the hidden or closet heroine who is nevertheless the truly beloved and whose qualities far exceed those of the overtly recognizable heroine of the plot. For Cowley, it was a chance to be the heroine rather than merely her creator, but for Robinson it was the chance to play out a kind of vindication of her early life when she was valued for her sexuality and physical beauty rather than for her intellectual and artistic merits.

Cowley's Della Cruscan poetry reveals a theatrical view of the world, and her manipulation of the Della Cruscan phenomenon shows a sure hand in theatrical matters. Some critics perceived this authority in her even before she began publishing her poetry; in a farce satirizing Sheridan's *The Critic*, entitled *The Critic upon Critic* (1788), Leonard MacNally presents Sheridan as a character who must face a rioting audience that includes two women playwrights: Mrs Bulley (representing Hannah Cowley) and Miss Plausible (Hannah More). The two playwrights complain about the manager's ill treatment of their work by postponing play dates until no profit could be made, or by inattention to their work, faults Sheridan was often guilty of. Cowley appears to have been as much of a strategist in her plays as in her periodical poems. She in fact discovered the theater by accident, and her first play, *The Runaway* (1776), was supposed to have been written impromptu on a bet with her husband. But this first attempt shows Cowley's understanding of popular sentiment by ridiculing the "free-thinking Philosophy of a Female Student," Lady Dinah. Cowley herself wanted no part of bluestockingism, insisting on writing under inspiration and without any appearance of study, and putting her pen and paper away as soon as she was finished. Cowley's Della Cruscan poems also capitalize on a popular form, the private love poem, and she emphasizes their natural effect as if they are not, like her plays, being publicly staged and displayed.

Mary Robinson, like Cowley, also discovered the stage by accident, meeting David Garrick while at finishing school. Her mother believed she should marry before attempting the stage, however, and she did not reapply to Garrick until after she and her baby had accompanied her husband through debtor's prison, where she had published her first volume of poems. She was 18 by the time she finally played her first role at Drury Lane, and had a highly successful career for four years. These are the years that her life revolved on: Robinson again and again returns to her experiences on the stage as an imaginative field against which to comprehend her later experiences, as she does in her own Della Cruscan poems. The turning point in her career occurred in her last season when she played Perdita in Shakespeare's *The Winter's Tale*; it was as Perdita that she attracted the Prince of Wales, five years her junior, who enjoyed pretending to be her Florizel, and who asked her to end her career so that she could become his mistress (see Wu, 1998: 124). This event in itself was public theater: the couple appeared at Vauxhall and other public entertainments, the press and caricaturists rushed to satirize the two in their Shakespearean roles, and news of the Prince's reneging on his bond of £20,000 and her subsequent embarrassment was widely known. But perhaps its theatricality was predetermined. In David Garrick's adaptation of *The Winter's Tale*, titled *Florizel and Perdita, A Dramatic Pastoral in Three Acts* (1758), Garrick in his own person opens the play with a monologue that projects just such an expansive interpretation of "staging":

> To various Things the Stage has been compar'd,
> As apt Ideas strike each humorous Bard:
> This Night, for want of better Simile,
> Let this our Theater a Tavern be:
> The Poets Vintners, and the Waiters we.
> So . . . You're welcome Gem'min, Kindly welcome Ladies.
> To draw in Customers, our Bills are spread;
> You cannot miss the Sign, 'tis Shakespear's Head . . .

The extension not just of theater to any dramatic space, but of theatricality to participatory pleasure, provides a model for viewing the play as extendable not just to the Della Cruscan periodical theater or the public spectacle of Vauxhall, but in other directions as well. In playing Perdita within such a model of extension, Robinson is positioned to be interpreted as quite literally a princess in disguise, brought up among shepherds but certifiably fit to don the "novel garment of gentility,"

> And yield a patch'd behaviour, between
> My country-level, and my present fortunes,
> That ill becomes this presence. I shall learn,
> I trust I shall with meekness – but I feel,
> (Ah happy that I do) a love, an heart
> Unalter'd to my prince, my *Florizel*.

Perdita's confession and Florizel's response ("Be still my queen of *May*, my shepherdess, / Rule in my heart . . ."), except for a small speech from Leontes, conclude the play, so that those members of the audience identifying with Prince Florizel, such as the young Prince of Wales, find Robinson already dramatically in place for being the discovered beloved. Robinson did not need to actively promote this role for herself as Cowley did in her first Della Cruscan poem, it was already there to be taken up.

What is significant about the Prince's and Robinson's affair is that, at least according to her own accounts, it was entirely and asexually theatrical. As if to conjure up the deliciousness of the subterfuge used by Florizel to circumvent his father's anger at discovering his love for a shepherdess, the Prince of Wales delighted in midnight assignations and disguise. He also repeatedly asked Robinson to come costumed for her men's roles (known as "breeches parts" when performed by actresses) even though being seen in breeches off stage would have ruined her reputation.

> A proposal was now made that I should meet his Royal Highness at his apartments, in the disguise of male attire. I was accustomed to perform in that dress, and the Prince had seen me, I believe, in the character of the Irish Widow . . . The indelicacy of such a step, as well as the danger of detection, made me shrink from the proposal. My refusal threw his Royal Highness into the most distressing agitation . . . . (Robinson, 1895: 165; also see Pollock, 1988: 20, on a petition to the House of Commons which states that a woman who wears pants " 'drowns all sense of decency betwixt men and women, they resemble each other so much.' ")

Although she herself delighted in dressing in different women's costumes to ride through the park during the day, Robinson's theatrical play with identity had not the psychological quality nor the danger that the Prince associated with gender play, masked identities, and princesses in disguise. Unwilling to do more than play princess, Robinson was too conservative for the Prince's taste, and after a short time he unfeelingly threw her off for another mistress. In short, without sexual relations, Robinson served as a costume or a role only, a specter of the theatrical imagination that could be easily discarded.

For Robinson, this pattern of mutual attraction, dramatized interplay, and unforeseen desertion became a figuration for love relations, and a way to translate her theatrical thinking into the internalizing processes of poetry. It was this same aspect of Della Cruscanism that drew her there as well. By turning the matter of her life into verse, Robinson moves from displaying her stage talents that were fully exteriorized – her best assets were her elocution, her extreme beauty, and her good figure – to an internalized view. When the pattern established by her husband and continued by the Prince was then repeated with Colonel Banastre Tarleton, a dashing army officer, Robinson turned her story in on herself by imagining herself into the role of the Greek poet Sappho, disappointed in love. Although she was already well established as a poet and novelist by the time of their rupture, Tarleton's disloyalty replayed the Prince's and her own husband's humiliation of her and forced Robinson to re-imagine the face and poetic voice she presented to the public. Her sonnet sequence *Sappho and Phaon* (1796) recast her from the "Laura Maria" of the Della Cruscans to a fully interiorized Romantic poet whose allegiance is to the English Milton, poet of depth and "legitimacy." To emphasize this new self-portrayal, she prefaced the work with a discussion of the legitimate sonnet form and of the de-legitimizing of the poet's power in Britain: "I will venture to believe that there are both poets and philosophers, now living in Britain, who, had they been born in any *other* clime, would have been honoured with the proudest distinctions, and immortalized to the latest posterity" (Wu, 1997: 187). To this defense she appends a separate "Account of Sappho," a discussion that serves to authorize her new self-legitimizing voice as one already prefaced by classical brilliance and ancient tragedy.

Robinson still plays with visuality by portraying herself as Sappho, and Tarleton as the mythic lover Phaon (an invented figure used by Ovid to heterosexualize the great lesbian poet and then to humiliate her through rejection). But her method of using reality and illusion as ways to understand the complexities and disappointments of love and desertion are provocative and disturbing. In drawing such a Miltonic allegory, she pulls the theatrical imaginary inward and creates a visual space as intimate and enclosed as Merry's and Cowley's "theater" was public and displaced. This is not closet drama, however, but something closer to an internalizing of Smith's melancholic sonnets and a critique of the Della Cruscans' insincere love and public display in their periodical theater. Robinson creates a visual space that forcefully previews the writings of the male High Romantics soon to come, not just stylistically but in the use of complex emotional patterns (love, compulsion, rejection) to structure a poetics of nature. Similarly, so does her preference for the intensity of the Miltonic sonnet over the Petrarchan or the Shakespearean sonnet form precede a similar choice by most of the High Romantics, especially Wordsworth.

Sonnet XXVI of *Sappho and Phaon* (Wu, 1997: 201) exemplifies Robinson's revised visual strategy and her new concern with depth and intensities:

> Where antique woods o'er-hang the mountain's crest
>   And midday glooms in solemn silence lour,
>   Philosophy, go seek a lonely bow'r,
> And waste life's fervid noon in fancied rest.
> Go where the bird of sorrow weaves her nest,

Cooing, in sadness sweet, through night's dim hour;
Go cull the dewdrops from each potent flow'r
That med'cines to the cold and reas'ning breast!
Go where the brook in liquid lapse steals by,
Scarce heard amidst the mingling echoes round,
What time the moon fades slowly down the sky,
And slumb'ring zephyrs moan in caverns bound:
Be these thy pleasures, dull Philosophy,
Nor vaunt the balm to heal a lover's wound.

As in numerous sonnets in this sequence, sounds are used here to project internal emotions outward on nature, making images unimportant and the landscape imaginary and indistinct. Robinson thus inverts the method of the Della Cruscans, turning their self-dramatizing style of theater into a private space where emotions are the guide to meaning. Her focus here on culled sounds – a bird cooing, a brook "Scarce heard amidst the mingling echoes round," and moaning winds – are ones we associate with being alone in nature in a melancholic or meditative state. It is not the sounds themselves but what they conjure up in terms of the poetic imagination we can all experience that constitute the essence of this landscape. In this sense it is more literally an "inscape" than a landscape, precisely in the same sense as Keats's later "Ode to a Nightingale" (Wu, 1998: 1058–60). Both poems reject the picturesque approach or the stage sets of Cowley in order to fabricate an interiorized use of figures for nature that double as metaphors for poethood: birdsong, liquid, breezes, daytime gloom ("And midday glooms in solemn silence lour"; for Keats, "Through verdurous glooms and winding mossy ways"), and "dull Philosophy."

Keats's ode provides a good comparison for how these two poets thought about the internalized view. The complex structure of Keats's ode, with its formal and thematic progression through the sensory imagination, is also to be found in Robinson's sonnet. For instance, instead of a clear octave and sestet, she makes use of a Miltonic integration of the two parts to form a greater whole. She does so in order to draw attention to the emotional patterning of attraction and repulsion (the same dynamic Keats applies to the will to live). With the second quatrain, a series of imperatives begins that takes over the rest of the sonnet body, reconfiguring it into paired lines that break up and yet integrate the next six lines to create an internal or embodied sestet: "Go," "Go," "Go." Each imperative is associated with a figure Keats will pick up in his Nightingale ode: "the bird of sorrow," "the dewdrops from each potent flow'r / That med'cines," "the brook in liquid lapse." In just his first stanza Keats includes the "light-winged dryad of the trees," "Or emptied some dull opiate to the drains," "and Lethe-wards had sunk"; and for Robinson's bird "Cooing, in sadness sweet, " Keats has "Singest of summer in full-throated ease." The comparison of these two poems shows that Keats's poem is about *not being able* to see, a physical darkness that increases his inward poetic vision; Robinson's poem is about what happens when poetic vision has fled, and emotional response and literal vision are all that are left.

After the embodied sestet in Robinson's sonnet, what remains is a final quatrain that is both formally disembodied from the sonnet structure and bound to the poem's aesthetic integrity. "Scarce heard amidst the mingling echoes round," it begins, reminding the reader of the paradox created by the echo of the heard and the not-heard, and thus recalling the visual problem as well. Such a paradox reduces the importance of the standard play for love poetry on seen and not-seen, a paradox Keats also uses to redirect the significance of not-seeing into a poetic vision that is more true than mere sight. Robinson does not care to go so far, and she restrains herself to dealing with "Philosophy" rather than Keats's "viewless wings of Poesy," telling philosophy that it must "go seek a lonely bow'r" and integrate itself with the natural scene. In the end, however, she reaches the same conclusion as Keats does for the fancy: however natural and poetic philosophy's "pleasures" are, they cannot be "the balm to heal a lover's wound." Keats builds on and complicates a tradition in Romantic poetry that Robinson helps give voice to. It is important to his perception of the world that she does so through her peculiar and complex relations to the heroic quality of specularity, to theatricality, and to the privacy of the imagination.

In comparing this sonnet from *Sappho and Phaon* to Keats's ode, we can see that for Robinson, unlike Keats, the heroism of specularity is related to the Gothic through its connection between visuality and victimization. Although women writers struggle with ways to combat this connection in the social critique and radical critique Gothics, when the Gothic became highly popular as a dramatic form through melodrama and pantomime, women's visuality and victimization under Gothic conditions became a commonplace of the theatrical imagination. Cowley recognizes only women's visuality but Robinson understands how fully women's victimization is implicated in their staged appearance. Walpole himself set the terms in his early Gothic works for this connection eventually to become the dominant structure in visuality.

Display and the Specular Heroine

In his preface to *Marino Faliero* (1821), a play concerning Venetian political history, Byron comments that: "I have had no view to the stage; in its present state it is, perhaps, not a very exalted object of ambition," but then he refers to a playwright he does admire:

> It is the fashion to underrate Horace Walpole; firstly, because he was a nobleman, and secondly, because he was a gentleman; but, to say nothing of the composition of his incomparable letters, and of the "Castle of Otranto," he is the "Ultimus Romanorum," the author of the "Mysterious Mother," a tragedy of the highest order, and not of puling love-play. He is the father of the first romance and of the last tragedy in our language, and surely worthy of a higher place than any living writer, be he who he may. (Byron, 1970: 408)

Having, in his London years, been a member of the selection committee for Drury Lane, Byron's repudiation of the stage is based on first-hand knowledge, but so is the seductive appeal he feels for drama while living in exile. Using the Continent as his theater, Byron stages his own dramatic life-narrative for his reading public, but it is notable that when he thinks critically about plays his thoughts concern the value of rank and ambition, and the literary valuation of genre and style. Audiences and critics, actors or stage managers, even readers are beyond thinking about. Byron's attention is on the literary forefather, that father's rank and talent, and the desire to pit his own work about patriarchal rage and ambition against works that he considers "the first romance" and "the last tragedy in our language." What he does not say is that by the time of the publication of this play, he has left three daughters by three different women behind him. In all three cases he has forfeited or repudiated his paternal responsibilities in a manner he does not recognize as a semblance of the patriarch's treatment of the daughter-heroine Matilda in Walpole's *Castle of Otranto*. Byron's theatricality, like Merry's, lacks an internalized view; he can engage visuality only as a superficial phenomenon when writing through the masks of his poetic characters and personas. Theatrics and literary drama are dissociated phenomena for him. But women, both in fiction and in real life, cannot afford such dissociation. They must either recognize the connection of their appearance, the roles they are asked to play, and their own experience of themselves, or they must pay a price for dissociating these things, and Walpole's Matilda is a valuable resource for exploring that price.

216

Matilda, the name of the rejected daughter of Walpole's admired Gothic novel, links together Elizabeth Inchbald's novel *A Simple Story* (1791) and Mary Shelley's novella *Mathilda* (composed 1819; publication suppressed by Godwin). All three Matildas are magnets for illicit and tragic themes such as incestuous longings, self-sacrifice, and mental obsessions. But while Romantics chose to explore the transgressive desires of Faust figures such as Byron's Manfred, women writers seemed drawn to exploring the self-representations of Matilda. Matilda is not the figure who breaks laws, as Faust is, but she who is bound by law, the hapless daughter who by law has no possession, not even self-possession, except through her father. To women writers the figure of Matilda represents the double-bind of external appearance and internal experience, visuality and vision, the specular heroine. Although Walpole's Matilda is rejected by her father, she will substantiate through death at her father's hand the loss of all his ambitions and desires. Thus the daughter serves more to illustrate paternal abuse than to act as heroine, as is clear from the first sentence, "*Manfred*, Prince of *Otranto*, had one son and one daughter; the latter, a most beautiful virgin, aged eighteen, was called *Matilda*." Such a beginning to such a novel tradition makes clear the importance of the virgin's possession to the genre; makes it clear that the Gothic's dominant theme will be domestic abuse, the right of the patriarch over his chattel. The spectacle of the dramatically unimportant Matilda in Walpole's first sentence, aligned thus with her father and no one else, reveals the lonely nature of her legal standing and her need to take care how she presents herself to him.

The historical precedent for Walpole's defenseless Matilda was the medieval Queen Matilda, daughter of Henry I and rival of Stephen of Blois for the English throne after her father's death. She was described by an ecclesiastic as having "little of the woman in her," but she is transformed by Walpole into the ultimate mythic female, passive, loving, and punished, just as Ovid transformed the lesbian Sappho into a humiliated and rejected beloved. Both female figures have been revised from powerful actors to passive images of women. This figure of the passive and victimized Matilda is important to Walpole's notion of the Gothic, but also to his sense of the dramatic. That he understood the theatricality of his novel can be seen in his self-denying preface: "with all its faults, I have no doubt but the *English* reader will be pleased with a sight of this performance . . . It is a pity that [this author] did not apply his talents to what they were evidently proper for, the theater" (Walpole, 1924: 7–8; emphasis in original). Walpole's habit of italicizing characters' names adds to the sense that one is reading a play script rather than a novel;

indeed, he may have felt that his novel was a more theatrical work than his actual play, *The Mysterious Mother* (1768), which also and more forcefully deals with incest and sacrifice. Even Robert Jephson's 1781 adaptation of *The Mysterious Mother* as *The Count of Narbonne* uses elements of *The Castle of Otranto* as well, all with Walpole's approval and aid in the production. Jephson's combination of Walpole's play and novel indicates that he agreed with the supposition that the two stories had a common spectacular element. Both thematically and textually, the element Walpole's texts most dwell on is revelation. Revelation is a key element of the Gothic, but it is also highly important to stage productions because it draws the audience in through the unfolding of the plot. This can be best exploited visually, but it also works well in novels and in plays written in the style of the closet drama, such as Walpole's *Mysterious Mother* which he performed in private readings. Revelation is deeply necessary to a theatrical imagination as it pertains to the actors on the stage or characters in the scene revealing their persons and passions. But what women writers collectively took from Walpole's connection of the Matilda figure with revelation is how negative a bond this is for the female imagination. To counteract it, a number of women authors centered their texts around Matilda but use her to show how revelation becomes for women something fundamentally evil, "display."

Display is the negative effect of the internalized view, the desire of a woman to promote herself through dress and role-playing in order to attract attention. Austen's Mrs Elton in *Emma* is a perfect example of display; Austen and other women authors often use this behavior as an indication of superficiality and conceit to show how dangerous this kind of externalizing or theatrical attitude can be for the individual. Display takes theatricality or self-drama to a more conscious level, a more melodramatic self-promoting behavior in which a character purposefully adopts another role for herself, hiding or transforming rather than revealing her true personality, as Fanny Burney's character Elinor does in *The Wanderer*. Display as a negative act allows women writers to show the dangers of the internalized view, and the importance of a heroine's ability to acknowledge both how others perceive her and how she should remain true to her own identity. Self-perception becomes the author's weapon for fighting off the evils of revelation as display while retaining a proper self-knowledge.

As the one-word title of Jane Taylor's 1815 novella, *Display*, the term evokes a matrix of connected associations that include the consumerist, social, and domestic, as well as the theatrical and Gothic. For real-life patriarchs, Taylor reminds us, wives are for the display of wealth, they are metonyms who stand in for their husband's power. Self-possession and self-perception are replaced by a suppression of the self, and a masking of one's true identity. In being on display, in seeing oneself as the object of a "real" or male subject's gaze, a woman begins to watch herself dispassionately and objectively. Clearly, for Taylor, it is then that the female child begins to act a role, begins to be separated from a self in a way that already begins to make self-perception difficult and that later can make it impossible. The young woman begins to be less sincere, she suggests, and therefore less modest, even though this falseness has been demanded of her by the requirements of the marriage market. The problem of every heroine faced with the difficulties of self-perception is to hold on to a sincerity that others do not believe of her. Her sincerity allows her to hold on to herself, to know herself, and in the novels of this last part of the Romantic period such self-knowledge can be attained only through a vigilance that is a constant self-regard. Yet the problem women writers faced was that this ideal of sincerity as a female virtue provides a dull contrast to characters indulging in display.

Two other writers who understood the complexities of this issue, and who found *Display*'s treatment of it interesting were Anna Barbauld and Maria Edgeworth. Both were, like Taylor, writers marginalized from the dominant group of Romantic writers either by their religion (Barbauld was a Dissenter) or community (Edgeworth lived with her father in their utopian Edgeworthstown in Ireland). But because of their middle-class status, each felt Taylor to be too radical in her critique of display and the marriage market. Edgeworth, in particular, found a certain discomfort with Taylor's lower-class perspective, writing in an 1816 letter to Barbauld, "We have just got a little book called "Display,' a tale for young people, which we like much . . . The *good* people in this book, are more to my taste . . . because they are not so meddling. I only wish they had not objected to young people going to balls . . ." (Le Breton, 1874: 171). Barbauld responds,

> "Display" we sent for on your recommendation, and are much pleased with a good deal of it, but we are so entirely of your opinion with regard to balls, and indeed there is a great deal in her system that I should object to, particularly the doctrine . . . that all, the innocent and good a well as the bad, must undergo a mysterious change before they are in a safe state. Emily was very good for aught that I could see before her conversion. (Le Breton, 1874: 177)

This mistaking of Taylor's point, by a writer already invested in giving young people models for how to think for and about themselves, provides an index for how disturbing Taylor's text was to the dominant culture, with its emphasis on women's appearance and their selflessness. What Barbauld and Edgeworth do value in Taylor's critique, however disquieting it is to the middle-class obsession with the marriage market and social status, is her focus on female psychology. She is particularly interested in how young women are pressured to meet specific social criteria no matter how harmful to their own sense of self.

Taylor wrote *Display* to teach young women that displaying themselves for the regard of others, especially in differently privileged classes, diseases a woman's ability to regard herself accurately. Although Taylor does not name her self-perceptive heroine "Matilda," Emily is clearly the Matilda figure, while the displaying Elizabeth is the young woman consumed by a desire to act any role but that of herself. Elizabeth wants to be seen as the desirable object, and Emily wants to see, to be the feeling subject. "Emily was a *Realist*," we are told in the first page, "Whatever she did, said, or *looked* was in earnest: she possessed the grace of SIMPLICITY" as well as modesty, and her realism precludes her from the domestic romance as well as the Gothic realms. But Elizabeth rewards our desire for romance, and we are told that she has a "disposition to *display*," and that

> To speak, to move, to weep, or to smile, were with her but so many manoeuvres, which she was practising for *effect*, and to attract attention. The prospect, the picture, or the poem, which Emily admired with all her *heart*, Elizabeth admired with all her *eloquence*, – too intent upon exhibiting her taste or sensibility, to be truly the subject of either. (Taylor, 1815: 2; emphasis in original)

Elizabeth's desire to always "make an impression" leads the narrator to remark that, "They who are intent upon being heard and seen, are not often observers; nor can they believe how easily they are detected by those who know how to hear and see [whether their talents] are used as articles of display" (Taylor, 1815: 19). What I have been calling self-perception is, according to Taylor's description of Emily, a kind of sincerity because it is the ability to see correctly and to judge well. In her depiction of Elizabeth, Taylor shows that theatricality is the antithesis, the desire to perform, an externalized vision that does not depend on introspection. Yet the fact that Taylor's sincere heroine bears the same name as Radcliffe's Gothic heroine Emily in *The Mysteries of Udolpho* alerts us to the ambivalent relation between women's necessary ways of seeing and how they chose to write about it.

Elizabeth Inchbald (1753–1821), who does invoke the name of Matilda in her novel *A Simple Story* (1791) and whose play *Lovers' Vows* (1798) was used by Austen to dramatic effect in her *Mansfield Park*, is a key figure in this discussion because she was an actress, playwright, and novelist. As such, she was highly aware of the relation between visuality and subjectivity. Although her novel was written in the early radical years of the Romantic period, it foresees the effects of theatricality and visuality on women's sense of identity and so provides an important predecessor text to *Display*. Inchbald was born to a provincial farming family who delighted in the local theater and in acting plays in their home. Her brother ran away to join a small theater and Elizabeth attempted to do the same repeatedly, finally escaping to London, and, when that failed, marrying an actor and joining him in his small troupe appearances. Although her success as an actress never equaled her success as an author, her daring and theatrical experiences inform the psychological composition of her characters. This fact helps explain why two of her plays are the first of the period to fully implement a social thesis, from Blue-Book facts and prison reform (*Such Things Are*, 1788) to the French Revolution (*The Massacre*, never produced). The realism that underlies these plays never overwhelms them (the prison is displaced to the East; the massacre includes toddlers killing each other), but it certainly arises from an awareness of the impact the psychological has on the social dimension.

Her stunning novel, *A Simple Story*, begins as a pseudo-autobiography but as she revised and lengthened it she developed a more complex relation to the theatrics of the home and that same psychological–social space. To this end she turns her heroine into a doubled one of mother and daughter, the two women linked and bound by the patriarch husband-father. *A Simple Story* is actually two short novels interfaced through common characters, with the second narrative spelling out the denouement of the first. The first part is a domestic romance with Inchbald parlaying her own character into that of the beautiful heiress, Miss Milner, who becomes fixated on the unobtainable Mr Dorriforth, modeled on Inchbald's stage colleague, John Philip Kemble. This half of the novel is thus highly theatrical, with characters based on actors choosing roles to play, and complete with a thematically important masquerade ball. In the second half, Miss Milner's daughter by Dorriforth, Matilda, is obsessed like a lover over how to regain her father's love, and his rejection of her strongly reminds us of Manfred's rejection of his Matilda in *Otranto*. This second part of the novel is a translation of the theatricality of the first part into a Gothic world of melodrama and victimization. Matilda's real difference from her mother is that Miss Milner insisted on being seen, on being dramatically visible, while Matilda must learn to live invisibly, to live her life imprisoned and even dead to Dorriforth's rejecting gaze. Matilda is even brought to the castle by clandestine means, "steal[ing] into the house privately, [rather] than by any appearance of parade" so that Dorriforth would not "be reminded of it by the public prints" (Inchbald, 1967: 219). In refuting here the theatricality that dominated the first part of the novel, Inchbald emphasizes the passive daughter's loss of self-awareness, the selflessness that society demands of her, and self-sacrifice, and thus of her victimization by the visual. Because the father will not see her, she cannot see herself either, and the loss of her self-perception is a loss of identity, a disaffection of the self. Inchbald's warning could not be more clear; Miss Milner's self-dramatizing faults lead to misery and a Gothic home, where her daughter is forced into the antithesis of drama in not being seen by anyone. Matilda becomes a living ghost, as much alienated by her mother's lack of self-perception as by her father's suppression of her identity. Because both the Gothic novel and the real dictates of the marriage market concern the exchange or appropriation of property from women to men, this becomes an important aspect of Matilda's loss of self. In the second half of the novel, the heiress Miss Milner dies after having lost the respect of her husband, but refuses to leave a will for Matilda: "She had no will, she said, but what she would wholly submit to [her husband]; and, if it were even his will, [that] her child should live in poverty, as well as banishment, it should be so" (Inchbald, 1967: 203). The double meaning of "will" here equates money and selfhood. Without an inheritance, Matilda is a nobody on the marriage market, a nobody in her own self-perception. Matilda's inheritance is not her mother's money but her mother's humiliation, which she as the daughter must translate into a living death. Inchbald's achievement, at least before the last-minute reprieve of the novel's conclusion, is to condense her doubled heroine into nothing at all, an invisible woman who, like Frankenstein's creature, embodies a terrible truth and therefore draws the reader's eye irresistibly.

Mary Shelley's *Mathilda* depicts an even more disaffected heroine, first through the father's rejection of her, and then through his subsequent and incestuous love for her. The lesson here is that no matter how defensively a heroine may present herself, her desire to be a real self in the eyes of another can at any time be misinterpreted as self-display, and this causes her downfall. In her semi-autobiographical novella, Mary Shelley synthesizes and critiques the disparity between spectacle and specularity, between father's right and father's love. It was a critique so intense that her own father William Godwin suppressed it, revealing how literally the suppression of female identity could be achieved. As Mary Shelley had already represented in her text, and as Inchbald implies in hers, repression comes from an unlawful love that appears too much like lawful unlove (spouse abuse or child abuse). It is difficult to tell the difference, or to tell reality from play-acting and romance. As Mathilda narrates,

> Sometimes I said to myself, this is an enchantment, and I must strive against it. My father is blinded by some malignant vision which I must remove ... once while singing I lifted my eyes towards him and saw his fixed on me and filled with tears ... but he pushed me roughly from him ... And even from this slight incident he contracted fresh gloom and an additional severity of manner. (Shelley, 1990: 192)

The daughter's self-perception provokes the patriarch's gaze, which reads her actions as display. The father's speculation of her is a diseased version of her own self-regard; he thus destroys her mental health, making her a victim in and of his own eyesight.

Inchbald and Shelley look at Walpole's Matilda and realize her as the Gothic heroine, a romance figure unfit for real life, fleshing out her instability as an object of spectacle and speculation. But Taylor looks at the Gothic heroine and sees nothing but a woman watching herself in the mirror of her self-produced audience. A heroine must be warned away from such spectacle-making, such theatrics, and learn to see for herself – not at herself. But if neither the conservative Inchbald nor the progressive Shelley offers useful alternatives to Taylor's critique of the theater of domestic life in *Display*, Taylor's reader is also left less than satisfied. Without display, without patriarchal defilement, without tragic consequences, there is little left to tell. Elizabeth's poor marriage, the result of her theatricality, leaves her unseen by the narrative. The pain of her new marital life is therefore uninteresting: without a witness, pain is hardly romantic and her story loses its interest and its edge. That pain and victimization is uninteresting is a new idea, however. Gothic novels tend to romanticize pain, making its spectacle of pain self-legitimating and a valid substitution for the self. But in teaching her readers to see properly, to question spectacle and display, Taylor goes beyond her peers to dispel the Gothic's dreadful and improper pleasure, and its compellingly fantastic vision. Real life, she implies, makes no such compensation.

Fanny Burney, however, takes a different path from all these authors, by elevating above Gothic drama a more resolutely eighteenth-century conception of character. In this interpretation of the heroine's character, innate qualities must struggle with society's continuous misreadings of the body's appearance and of one's deeds, until she can vindicate herself. In Burney's view, the missing ingredient in the interchange between visuality and display taken on by Inchbald, Shelley, and Taylor, is "taste." Burney uses the ideal of "taste," as it was developed from Shaftesbury's philosophic treatise on manners, as the relation between the outward show of "social passion" and the heart's immediate sympathetic response that Shaftesbury called "moral sense." Here, taste is programmatically assimilated to beliefs about social behavior, including the affective solution to the discrepancies in class between the bourgeois and the very poor through "sympathy," and sympathy's aesthetic counterparts, sentimentalism and sensibility. For Burney, the heroine is always able to prove her superiority through her taste, and taste is a particularly useful weapon against the dangers of spectacle and display:

> [Cox's] Museum is very astonishing, and very superb; yet, it afforded me but little pleasure, for it is a mere show, though a wonderful one. Sir Clement Willoughby, in our walk round the room, asked me what my opinion was of this brilliant *spectacle*? "It is very fine, and very ingenious," answered I, "and yet – I don't know how it is, – but I seem to miss something." (*Evelina*, I, letter xix; emphasis in original)

In this example from Burney's first novel (1778), her heroine's response to the museum of mechanical toys was to see it as sheer display with little meaning behind it; she can see what is missing because her natural taste – a dislike of display in and of itself – has detected it.

Perhaps because she believes in the natural heroine, Burney has no philosophical response adequate to Taylor's educative view; her heroines are superior because they come already imbued with taste. This perspective provides an interesting difficulty for Burney's last novel, *The Wanderer* (1814). Her heroine, whose character does not change or grow, but rather shifts in the reader's perception as more and more is revealed about her, recuperates the theatrical perspective of revelation to the novel with full intensity and moves us away again from Romantic interiority and individuality. Curiously, this is a shift that Austen also follows in *Persuasion*, her last published novel, by beginning the novel's action after the heroine has already learned from her mistakes and changed. Again, the reader is given increasing insights into Anne Elliot's character, but in a manner more closely related to the revelations of dramatic presentation than of psychological treatments of the narrative.

For instance, Anne is often simply sitting or is otherwise still within a scene setting: when Captain Wentworth visits Mary and she is there as well, when she sits with her younger sister Mary while overhearing Louisa Musgrove flirting with Wentworth, when she must endure her relatives' unfeeling remarks about herself and others. Even when she is heroically active, her movements are limited to the domestic. She nurses, with maternal care, both her nephew and later Louisa, each suffering from a bad fall brought on by childish behavior. She acts as companion to the spoiled Mary and comforts her brother-in-law's family when they complain of her. She corrects Captain Harville when she disagrees with his analysis of women's faithfulness. But Wentworth does not value Anne's stilled behavior, when she must simply endure, and he certainly disdains the self-display of Anne's sisters Elizabeth and Mary. He does not care for any behavior that is not active or heroic, and he can even be attracted by theatrical behavior such as Louisa's if it appears to be active or based on heroic principles. Austen uses Wentworth's viewpoint in the novel to assess the dangers of stilled visuality in Anne, while showing through plot outcome the dangers of the other Elliot sisters' self-conscious display. It is self-actualizing behavior only that can be valued in Anne; the visual can only detract from women's individuality and worth, and resisting the internalized view is not sufficient to ward off the threat that visuality brings to women's identity.

Both Burney and Austen reflect a recognition that the end of the Romantic period begins a theatrical or speculative constraint of women that is more difficult to fend off than the earlier manner-oriented behaviors. Burney, however, finds she cannot so easily dismiss the visual, and so, for our discussion, her novel *The Wanderer* more helpfully illuminates the cultural importance of women's appearance than does Austen's.

Tableaux Vivants, Theatrics and Burney's *The Wanderer*

An important aspect of the intrusion of theater into the home that we need to recognize before turning to Burney's important novel is the tableau vivant. Closely linked to the parlor game of charades, but more dramatically imposing and spectacular, the tableau vivant represents for women writers the dangers imposed by the theatrical imaginary on the domestic haven. The tableau vivant was a parlor game women particularly enjoyed, in which they could costume for a role, and then strike a pose on a prepared "stage" for an audience of family and friends. This reduction of a theatrical scene into a single pose provides a true domestic staging of the female object. The woman artfully, playfully, and voluntarily poses in such a way as to compress her objectivity and her subjectivity into a space that at once seems internal and external, as a kind of dramatized projection. The woman herself becomes a complex and overwritten Romantic poem, a sonnet or ode of visual power within a limited field.

The tableau vivant as a genre is most vividly associated, at least during the Romantic period, with Emma Hart, the woman whose Grecian profile and ability to adopt Grecian-style poses in a tableau won the admiration of Sir William Hamilton, who eventually married her. Goethe and other luminaries visited the couple to witness her talents: dressed in Grecian costume, she would assume the positions depicted on ancient urns for her husband and his friends. Hamilton, we should note, did not marry her for wealth but for her performances – her ability to become something else. This and her facial profile appear to have been her only real assets, but she was able to translate them into something that was not counted as self-promotion or even imposture, but as revivifying the Grecian aesthetic, making the ancient aura walk again. Her dramatized projection rather than herself was what drew men to her. In itself this is a remarkable intensification of the impulse behind theatricality, where performance replaces individual identity in real life.

The actress Sarah Siddons performed similarly. When she transformed the very style of theater acting by entering into her characters as fully as did her brother John Philip Kemble, she did so by using gesture and facial expression to convey more than heightened emotion but the very possibility of being a heroine. For Siddons, elocution was no longer the mark of acting talent in a woman as it had been for Inchbald and Robinson, and her achievement was to make the drama real, a display of the self dredged in introspection and inner beauty. Joanna Baillie (1821: xix) called her "Our greatest tragic actress, Mrs Siddons, whose matchless powers of expression have so long been the pride of our stage," and many fell in love with her after seeing her perform. Tableaux vivants work on the fantasy of this complex relation by substituting a set piece in still form for an enacted play or charade. In elevating one pose or one aspect of the self for viewing, the woman turns herself into a metaphor

226

for fantasy. The difficulty, of course, is that however she intends her performance, the viewer is always free to speculate differently. This is the lesson of Burney's self-dramatizing Elinor, whose tableaux vivants and staged scenes, such as that in our opening epigraph, were so fatally misdirected that they always robbed her of love when she meant to contract for it.

But what Siddons shows is that in controlling the production of the self as art from conception to final criticism, the theatrical woman allows no space for the gaze to define her. Instead, she exploits it in order to create a fantastic space in which she is the truth at the moment that she turns herself into a fiction. The only way for the male spectator to know her is to passively appreciate her, to love her as the role she presents to him. How does the male artist make art when the woman has already objectified herself as art, and in doing so has already performed the artwork and defined the terms of the resulting critical interpretation?

This version of the woman's ability to control her own interpretation is not borne out in women's literary texts, however. Women writers feared that ordinary women viewed in their own homes cannot have the power or control of a Siddons, and would therefore necessarily be at risk when displaying themselves in a tableau vivant. The tableau's recurrence as a fictional and poetic theme in works by women writers usually provides a warning about the visual misappropriation of a woman's inner being. Such writers suggest that the tableau structure is too stilled to benefit the woman on view or to direct her interpretation beyond the private moment. By inviting the audience's gaze (whether in a text or in the parlor), the self-dramatizing woman also invites the theatrical mode of speculative spying; at the same time, this stilling can exert pressure on the psyche, threatening psychotic derangement, as it does for Baillie's Orra. Both these dangers are fully played out in the plots of late Romantic texts by women, as well as by Victorian women novelists. Such plots are always attended by the message that this compression is a terrible threat to female subjectivity, even when the woman believes herself to be in control of both herself and the situation.

Fanny Burney's *The Wanderer* is one of the best late Romantic interrogations of these dangers. It is an epic-length work that literally redresses her first novel, *Evelina*. When *Evelina* appeared anonymously in 1778, Burney was at the start of her career and the novel's immediate popularity allowed her to slowly unmask her identity as its author in a kind of private theatrical among friends. Her diary details encounters with friends anxious to discuss or read aloud from the new novel, and her embarrassment and pleasure at finding herself playing the part of a "not-author" in order to deny her authority without denying her social self. She herself becomes the spectacle as her diary records how she had acted or been seen to respond; in watching herself *not* play author of the text, she creates a self-reflexive role for the privacy of the parlor that reinterprets and privatizes the self-reflexivity of the theater-goer. The novel casts London as a theater replete with a cast of sentimental comedy stage characters. The city-theater contains side acts just as spectacular such as huge "private" balls, museums, pleasure gardens, opera, an Italian puppet show, and two plays by Samuel Foote. The heroine scrutinizes her behavior at each carefully in her diaristic letters home, since her quest is to learn how to behave properly within a spectacular world.

By the time Burney writes her last novel, she is well known but as Mme d'Arblay, and she is 62 rather than 26 (the age at which she published *Evelina*). *The Wanderer, or Female Difficulties* announces in its very title, a specific reference to Mary Hay's *Victim of Prejudice*, that it will differ from Burney's earlier works, and it does so most specifically in its relation to the theater and to the visual. The heroine is again away from home and dependent on friends, and is again pursued by suitors, but this time it is she who is the unknown and the self-reflexive agent. And this time it is not London that provides the theater setting and the spectacle, but the enclosed settings of each home the wandering heroine stays in. The domestic space is now the stage for the actress-heroine, yet nowhere is she at home and nowhere is she safe; how carefully she plays her part in order to keep her identity a secret will determine how safe both she and her friends remain. "Ellis," as she is mysteriously called for most of the novel, is English but has been raised in France, from which she has just escaped during the worst excesses of the French Revolution, and if her identity becomes known she will have endangered the lives of those left behind. Spectacle, however, is not treated in the Gothic terms of melodrama, but in theatrical terms. Elinor, Ellis's friend and rival, insists first on staging a play, and then on staging her own tragedy in several "acts" or tableaux. She forces Ellis against her will to pose in them so as to reveal whether the hero Harleigh prefers Ellis to herself. For Ellis, who is in hiding from spies for the French authorities, and who has an aversion to display in any case, it is a deadly serious version of Burney's early playful role as author. In its seriousness, the play-acting scenes provide just one of several such metaphors for the masking and revelation that threatens Ellis and excites Elinor. These repeated metaphors – a play, a concert, staged suicide attempts by Elinor, tableaux – create layers of visual moments that add up to an allegory about seeing and being seen, masking and unveiling as the most fervent pitch of existence. Countering the network of theatrical figurations is Ellis's own attempts to create a new inward identity for her new homeland. Her own defense is self-perception, to provide a defensively masking appearance that invites no speculation, and avoids display. But she experiences only the frustration of her attempts at a new, passive identity as social inhibitors again and again propel her attention and her participation outward into the network of displays and tableaux. Caught in these cross movements, both Ellis and Elinor attempt to determine their own plots and both fail sublimely. What Elinor continuously seeks and Ellis does indeed experience is the inability to get off the stage.

In creating a novel in which female characters are the directors and actors, whether spurred by their belief in women's nobility and women's rights as Elinor is, or by a well-schooled self-perception as Ellis is, Burney releases the sentimental heroine from her passivity. But in doing so, she dismisses an idealized female passivity for an informed taste that shows the ideal woman's Romantic identity. Although readers recognize Ellis's superiority through her inner taste, other characters always misconstrue it as mere play-acting and self-promotion. This is in part because they constantly speculate as to her identity without being able to truly see her. Burney uses the discrimination of taste to aid the heroine in sustaining her self-perception. She concentrates visuality down to such a pressure point that Ellis attempts always to contain the political danger to her friends within her, and to do so by secrecy and a vigilant stillness. This is a dynamic internalization of her perceptiveness that emphasizes the social and political dangers to women who are caught between internal and external expectations. Ellis's struggle is both active and heroic. She is no mere victim; her trials produce a heightened state of awareness and self-awareness meant to parallel the imaginable fear of those persecuted under the Reign of Terror in Paris. By contrast, Elinor is incapable of self-perception and can produce only an external show; she acts out her passion extravagantly and with ill-judged effect, and she can only in the end be a foil for the real heroine. And because Ellis is forced to be passive for the sake of political secrecy, and her natural abilities suppressed to repel all speculation, her rights are continually violated. The rights for women that Mary Wollstonecraft argued for are here depicted as an abuse of women's natural abilities. Elinor calls on the "Rights of Woman" only to free herself to act out her fantasies without any sense of the harm she inflicts on others. The stage director of Ellis's story, Elinor employs rights discourse to dispel feminine constraints at the same time that she insists even more heavily on the privileges that her rank and sex give her. Her self-casting as a sublimely tragic heroine is itself a tragedy because she invokes the "Rights of Woman" in order to escape engagement to one brother so that she may attempt to win the other. Viewing the "system" of women's intellectual and political equality with the general leveling system of France's revolution, Elinor's character allows Burney to criticize how women's self-display makes them misinterpret the potential of their true abilities and true selves. Burney's narrative also demonstrates that women of the bluestocking and sensibility mold, like Elinor, are the ones who misread Wollstonecraft, taking the "Rights of Woman" to mean even further self-delusion and indulgence in theatrical display. Burney is closest to Wollstonecraft's political project when Ellis, the victim of Elinor's display, meditates on her version of "the wrongs of woman," "Female Difficulties." Ellis muses

> how insufficient . . . is a FEMALE to herself! How utterly dependent upon situation – connexions – circumstance! how nameless, how for ever fresh-springing are her DIFFICULTIES, when she would owe her existence to her own exertions! Her conduct is criticised, not scrutinized; her character is censured, not examined; her labours are unhonoured, and her qualifications are but lures to ill will! Calumny hovers over her head, and slander follows her footsteps! (Burney, 1991: 275)

Into the concept of "female difficulties" Burney weaves an understanding of how society's inability to see into the heart of things, to judge someone on anything but appearance, is as much to blame for the French Terror as for women's willingness to display themselves, and so divide themselves from their true potential.

In a central segment of the novel, Burney illustrates this political interpretation of visuality through a "play" that Elinor stages involving a love triangle: herself, Ellis, and the love interest Harleigh (see chapter opening epigraph). She superintends the action so as to frame her several suicide attempts by arranging a tableau vivant in which, once the players are in place, none is able to rearrange or redirect the scene that Elinor produces. Harleigh, at whom the tableau is directed, is frustrated at every attempt he makes to change her "plot." Furthermore, because Elinor believes that the only reason Harleigh could not love her is because he must secretly love Ellis, her staging deliberately and repeatedly blames and defames Ellis as a love object, and as a woman without rights. Insisting on Ellis's help in such a way that she cannot refuse, Elinor plans her play:

I am fixed to cast wholly aside the dainty common barriers, which shut out from female practice all that is elevated, or even natural . . . My operations are to commence thus: Act I. Scene I. Enter Ellis, seeking Albert [Harleigh]. Don't stare so; I know perfectly well what I am about. Scene II. Albert and Ellis meet . . . The rest of my plot is not yet quite ripe for disclosure. But all is arranged. (Burney, 1991: 157; see chapter opening epigraph)

Elinor's contrivance so artificially calls attention to her love, that it is clearly her own passion and her own posturing that she is in love with. Indeed, her admission to Ellis that she believed she loved Harleigh's lawyer brother because she loved to argue with him on fashionable subjects reveals that her own performance determines the extent of her love for another. Harleigh, we realize, is destined for the same fate if he gives in to her drama and proposes to her. But this is a lesser danger than the unnatural love of self-dramatization which is Elinor's tragic flaw, her absorption in her inflated passion demonstrating the instability of her mind and future.

Elinor's unstable temperament creates an uncomfortable play between social convention, women's rights, women's identity, and the future implied by the new "leveling system" in France. The use of the term "play" imparts subtle nuances to Burney's unsubtle plot. Used to mean both theater and gaming, the word "play" shows how close Elinor's drastic measures are to gambling, and how high the stakes are for her as well as Ellis. Psychological game-playing, the manipulation of others through words and actions that designedly keeps the others always in defensive and reactive positions, is a particularly dangerous aspect of the theatrical mentality. This most damaging of games is, as Gothic novelists repeatedly illustrate, natural to tyrannical situations and abusive private domains. Burney depicts each home in which Ellis finds herself as a kind of gaming field where she is bombarded by social demands that conflict with her need to develop a strong inner identity.

Through all of this, Ellis appears to be the one actually acting a role since she is still the unknown and mysterious stranger who will tell no one her name, her family, her social position, or her place of origin. Called "Ellis" because her letters are directed to an "L.S.," itself a cipher for *letters*, the form of writing identified with the feminine, she herself remains unsigned. The "Incognita" as the narrator earlier calls her, or the "Wanderer" as she calls herself, is more than unnamed, she is multiplied, guilty of seeming to have several roles at once, and of having only a stage name that emphasizes the secrecy of her real identity. She believes her role-playing to be a necessary evil, but in contrast

231

to Elinor she uses it to protect and defend: "must she quarrel with her benefactors, because they gave not implicit credit to the word of a lonely Wanderer for her own character?" (Burney, 1991: 73). But her "benefactors" understand only the roles of display and theatricality, and cannot understand this unfeminine style of role. They therefore believe her to be playing a mere part for immoral reasons, either in order to enact a swindle on them, or to seduce one of the visiting bachelors into a marriage. Even Elinor accuses Harleigh of "fall[ing] so in love with mystery, as to lose your nobler nature, in a blind, infatuated admiration of the marvellous and obscure [i.e. Ellis]?" The very refusal to name her origins, either of family or county or estate, marks Ellis in this small world as an unstable entity who could belong to the very lowest order, as they first believed, or one of the highest, as Harleigh and Lady Aurora believe. Against the insistence that, without origin, Ellis is a mere cipher, both unimportant and contaminating, she does sustain an internal identity for herself of one who carries her wholeness inside her as a kind of portable origin. Burney ironically displays her heroine as an allegory of women in marriage who trade their own family origin for the identity of their husband's family. Losing their father's name, they wed and so lose both their given and family name in order to become the wife of another man and the mother of more. Even money cannot remedy this loss, since the dowry usually becomes the property of the husband, a fact Burney symbolizes by recycling any money given to Ellis by a man, while money from a woman never even reaches her hands. Ellis's uneasy relation to money (she loses her own purse in the crossing from France, and is completely dependent on those who offer her shelter) alienates her from the marketplace to such an extent that her only recourse is her own person.

Burney's complex novel structure anticipates Thackeray's Victorian novel of the London-as-stage theme, *Vanity Fair* (1848), but she does not allow the simplistic division of heroines into good and evil that his Becky Sharpe and Amelia Sedley represent. Repeatedly, Burney's characters and narrator call attention to Elinor's nobility of spirit; the implication of her dangerous enactments and play-making is that her greatness was led astray by the theatrical imagination which deterred her from what her talents could have accomplished. This message is supported by the fact that the hugely talented Ellis can only perform well when she believes she is not being watched, when she is not forced onto stage.

The direction of women's critiques of visual culture are clear: the connection of women with material consumption, consumerism, and fashion provides a more terrible threat than that to art that Wordsworth calls the "tyranny of the eye"; it makes terrible inroads on women's social and personal identity. This, combined with culture's increasing preoccupation with the theatrical, makes it difficult for women to discover themselves as individuals, since they are required to hide their self-knowledge under an attractive performance of the feminine ideal. Women writers attack this emphasis on the visual because it undermines women's individuality and their psychological health. As Fanny Burney implies, such identity and health are the real "Rights of Woman." Such social criticism, falling as it does in the aftermath of the Napoleonic Wars, responds to the social and political conservatism of these years before the Victorian period, but does so in order to fend off the threat of such conservatism to individual liberty. This attention to individualism, to the effects of the social on the imagination, and to social injustice is deeply Romantic, and a fitting end to the Romantic period.

Conclusion

The discussion followed throughout this book has been aimed not just at illustrating how one might produce a feminist reading of Romantic period literature, but at giving the reader enough of a feminist perspective that she or he may begin to recognize the kinds of issues needing to be highlighted. The underlying point of chapter 1 was to focus our thinking in such a way that we begin to see that Romantic period women writers and readers were not simple mirrors of their time, unconsciously reflecting cultural trends and social changes. Though we are familiar with the two main attitudes of Romanticism, sincerity and irony, there is a third, critique, and women writers primarily engaged this third attitude in order actively and purposefully to engage the main tenets and themes of Romantic thought and culture.

Subsequent chapters have been devoted to examining the different forms critique can take, and the kinds of subjects it can be applied to. Each chapter focused on a topic of importance to Romanticism to show how women writers engaging critique took on the same concerns as did their male counterparts: politics, the Gothic, intellectuality, and the visual. We could have likewise examined nature, colonialism, science, and lyric poetry with similar results; there are many ways to analyze and understand women's participation in Romanticism. What we discover throughout these chapters is that women were thinking just as hard about culture, society, and the individual as were men writers of the period. Reading from a critical feminist perspective, we can reassess the

233

role women played in Romanticism in the terms usually reserved for analyzing the role of male Romantics.

In chapter 2 we saw how women of the Romantic period interested in politics were led to critique the political situation as it involved women and women's concerns. In chapter 3 we saw how those women writers exploring the imaginative possibilities of the Gothic were led to use its various forms to critique society as it defined women's experience. This involved both an outward and an inward scrutiny, a social and a psychological universe, with the most powerful of these novels combining the two realms. These exploratory combinations involved either the individual's role in society or the individual pitted against society.

In chapter 4 we saw how women used their intellectual abilities to analyze more carefully the individual's place in the social world. In chapter 5 we have seen that women writers were equally concerned with understanding the individual's inner psychology, and how this internal awareness reflects critically unjust aspects of society. The significant discovery of this last chapter was that this interest in the female psychological experience derives from the Gothic, which provided the impetus for women's self-consciousness about their imaginative worlds. Such consciousness led to a critical awareness of the close relation between the nightmare aspect of imagination and its corollary in the real world of unjust social constraints. It thus exposed the very real potential for women's individual downfall and misery, but also posed ways for women to protect themselves against such a fate. Romantic period women were not romancers, providing escapist or fantasy solutions to very real problems; they examined their world with a critical eye and, whether or not they favored happy or tragic endings, their works always showed how much of their society they found in need of improvement.

Further Reading

Paula Backscheider, *Spectacular Politics: Theatrical Power and Mass Culture in Early Modern England* (1993). A highly sophisticated reading of the importance of the theater in shaping the cultural imagination.

Michael Booth, *Theater in the Victorian Age* (1991). A good resource for a more thorough familiarity with the technical details of theater production, and includes information about the theater prior to the Victorians as well.

Julie Carlson, *In the Theater of Romanticism* (1994). This book argues that

Romanticism in general is grounded in drama and the dramatic, and so offers a helpful place to begin understanding how women writers used this phenomenon to delve into their own experience within Romanticism.

Mary Poovey, *The Proper Lady and the Woman Writer: Ideology as Style in the Works of Mary Wollstonecraft, Mary Shelley, and Jane Austen* (1984). One of the most important works in Romantic studies on the difficulties women writers confronted in facing publicity and their own public identity.

Susan Wolstenholme, *Gothic (Re)Visions: Writing Women as Readers* (1993). Although more concerned with women writing after the Romantic period, Wolstenholme provides interesting readings of the use of visuality and particularly of the tableau vivant in women's novels.

Bibliography

Note: Primary sources are only included if the citation depends on a particular edition. The principal resource for textual citations where indicated is Duncan Wu (ed.), *Romanticism: An Anthology*, 2nd edn, Oxford: Blackwell, 1998.

Abrams, M. H. (1970) "Structure and style in the greater Romantic lyric," in Harold Bloom (ed.), *Romanticism and Consciousness: Essays in Criticism*, pp. 201–32. New York: W.W. Norton.

Abrams, M. H. (1971) *The Mirror and the Lamp: Romantic Theory and the Critical Tradition*, 2nd edn. New York: Oxford University Press.

Agulhon, Maurice (1981) *Marianne into Battle: Republican Imagery and Symbolism in France, 1789–1880*, trans. Janet Lloyd. Cambridge: Cambridge University Press.

Aikin, Lucy (1825) *The Works of Anna Laetitia Barbauld, with a Memoir*, 2 vols. London: Longman.

Andrews, Malcolm (1989) *The Search for the Picturesque: Landscape Aesthetics and Tourism in Britain, 1760–1800*. Stanford: Stanford University Press.

Ashmun, Margaret (1931) *The Singing Swan: an Account of Anna Seward and her Acquaintance with Dr Johnson, Boswell, and Others of their Time*. London: H. Milford.

Ashton, Helen (1951) *Letty Landon*. London: Collins.

Auerbach, Nina (1978) *Communities of Women: an Idea in Fiction*. Cambridge, Mass.: Harvard University Press.

Austen, Jane (1954) *The Novels of Jane Austen*, 6 vols, ed. R. W. Chapman. London: Oxford University Press.

Austen, Jane (1988) *Northanger Abbey, Lady Susan, The Watsons, and Sanditon*, ed. John Davie. Oxford: Oxford University Press.

Austen, Jane (1995) *Jane Austen's Letters*, ed. Deirdre Le Faye, 3rd edn. Oxford: Oxford University Press.

Backscheider, Paula R. (1993) *Spectacular Politics: Theatrical Power and Mass Culture in Early Modern England*. Baltimore: The Johns Hopkins University Press.

Baillie, Joanna (1812) *Orra: a Tragedy in Five Acts*. New York: Longworths.
Baillie, Joanna (1821) *A Series of Plays: In which it is Attempted to Delineate the Stronger Passions of the Mind*, 3 vols. London: Longman, Hurst, Rees, Orme, and Brown.
Baillie, Joanna (1836) *Dramas by Joanna Baillie . . .* , 3 vols. London, Longman.
Baillie, Joanna (1977) *A Series of Plays in Three Volumes*, ed. Donald H. Reiman. New York: Garland Publishing.
Baldick, Chris (1992) "Introduction," *The Oxford Book of Gothic Tales*, ed. C. Baldick. Oxford: Oxford University Press.
Barbauld, Anna Laetitia (1874) *Memoir, Letters and a Selection from the Poems and Prose Writings of Anna Laetitia Barbauld*. Boston: J. R. Osgood and Co.
Barker-Benfield, G. J. (1992) *The Culture of Sensibility: Sex and Society in Eighteenth-century Britain*. Chicago: University of Chicago Press.
de Beauvoir, Simone (1952) *The Second Sex*, trans. and ed. by H. M. Parshley. New York: Bantam Books.
Benhabib, Seyla and Cornell Drucilla (eds) (1987) *Feminism as Critique: On the Politics of Gender*. Minneapolis: University of Minnesota Press.
Bernbaum, Ernest (1958) *The Drama of Sensibility: a Sketch of the History of English Sentimental Comedy and Domestic Tragedy, 1696–1780*. Gloucester, Mass.: Peter Smith.
Bloom, Harold (1970) "The internalization of quest-romance," in Harold Bloom (ed.), *Romanticism and Consciousness: Essays in Criticism*, pp. 3–24. New York: W.W. Norton.
Booth, Michael R. (1991) *Theater in the Victorian Age*. Cambridge: Cambridge University Press.
Boumelha, Penny (1982) *Thomas Hardy and Women: Sexual Ideology and Narrative Form*. Sussex / Totowa, NJ: Harvester / Barnes and Noble.
Brown, Marshall (1991) *PreRomanticism*. Stanford: Stanford University Press.
Burney, Frances (d'Arblay) (1854) *Diary and Letters of Madame d'Arblay*, ed. Charlotte Barret. London: H. Colburn.
Burney, Frances (1982) *Evelina*, ed. Edward A. Bloom. Oxford: Oxford University Press.
Burney, Frances (1991) *The Wanderer, or Female Difficulties*, ed. Margaret Anne Doody, Robert L. Mack, and Peter Sabor. Oxford: Oxford University Press.
Butler, Marilyn (1975) *Jane Austen and the War of Ideas*. Oxford: Clarendon Press, 2nd edn 1987.
Butler, Marilyn (1981) *Romantics, Rebels and Reactionaries: English Literature and its Background 1760–1830*. Oxford: Oxford University Press.
Butler, Marilyn (1988) "Romanticism in England," in Roy Porter and Mikuláš Teich (eds), *Romanticism in National Context*, pp. 37–67. Oxford: Blackwell.
Buxton, John (1978) *The Greek Taste: Literature in the Age of Neo-Classicism, 1740–1820*. London: Macmillan.
Byron, Lord (1970) *Poetical Works*, ed. Frederick Page; rev. ed. John Jump. Oxford: Oxford University Press.

Calhoun, Craig (ed.) (1993) *Habermas and the Public Sphere*. Cambridge, Mass.: MIT Press.

Campbell, Colin (1990) *The Romantic Ethic and the Spirit of Modern Consumerism*. Oxford: Basil Blackwell.

Canfield, J. Douglas and Payne, Deborah C. (eds) (1995) *Cultural Readings of Restoration and Eighteenth-century English Theater*. Athens: The University of Georgia Press.

Carlson, Julie (1994) *In the Theater of Romanticism*. Cambridge: Cambridge University Press.

Carlson, Marvin (1993) *Theories of the Theater: a Historical and Critical Survey, from the Greeks to the Present*. Ithaca, NY: Cornell University Press.

Castle, Terry (1986) *Masquerade and Civilization: the Carnivalesque in Eighteenth-century English Culture and Fiction*. Stanford: Stanford University Press.

Clifford, James Lowry (1941) *Hester Lynch Piozzi (Mrs Thrale)*. Oxford: Clarendon Press.

Coleridge, Samuel Taylor (1956–71) *Collected Letters of Samuel Taylor Coleridge*, 6 vols, ed. Earl Leslie Griggs. Oxford: Clarendon Press.

Coleridge, Samuel Taylor (1957–73) *The Notebooks of Samuel Taylor Coleridge*, ed. Kathleen Coburn. Vols I and II (New York: Pantheon, 1957, 1961), Vol. III (Princeton, NJ: Princeton University Press, 1973).

Coleridge, Samuel Taylor (1983) *Biographia Literaria*, 2 vols, ed. James Engell and W. Jackson Bate. Princeton, NJ: Princeton University Press.

Copley, Stephen and Whale, John (eds) (1992) *Beyond Romanticism: New Approaches to Texts and Contexts, 1780–1832*. London: Routledge.

Cox, Jeffrey N. (ed.) (1992) *Seven Gothic Dramas, 1789–1825*. Athens: Ohio University Press.

Craciun, Adriana (1997) "Charlotte Dacre and the 'vivisection of virtue,'" Introduction to *Zofloya*, pp. 9–32. Ontario: Broadview Press.

Craft-Fairchild, Catherine (1993) *Masquerade and Gender: Disguise and Female Identity in Eighteenth-century Fictions by Women*. University Park: The Pennsylvania State University Press.

Cranston, Maurice (1994) *The Romantic Movement*. Oxford: Blackwell.

Curran, Stuart (1986) *Poetic Form and British Romanticism*. New York: Oxford University Press.

Curran, Stuart (1988) "Romantic poetry: the I altered," in Anne K. Mellor (ed.), *Romanticism and Feminism*, pp. 185–207. Bloomington, Ind.: Indiana University Press.

Dacre, Charlotte (1997) *Zofloya; or, The Moor: a Romance of the Fifteenth Century*, ed. and intro. Adriana Craciun. Ontario: Broadview Press.

Davidson, Cathy N. (1986) *Revolution and the Word: the Rise of the Novel in America*. New York: Oxford University Press.

DeJean, Joan (1989) *Fictions of Sappho, 1546–1937*. Chicago: University of Chicago Press.

Duncan, Ian (1992) *Modern Romance and Transformations of the Novel: the Gothic, Scott, Dickens*. Cambridge: Cambridge University Press.

Ecker, Gisela (ed.) (1986) *Feminist Aesthetics*, trans. Harriet Anderson. Boston: Beacon Press.

Ellis, Grace A. (1874) *A Memoir of Mrs Anna Laetitia Barbauld, with many of her letters*, 2 vols. Boston: James R. Osgood.

Ellis, Kate (1989) *The Contested Castle: Gothic Novels and the Subversion of Domestic Ideology*. Urbana: University of Illinois Press.

Favret, Mary A. (1993) *Romantic Correspondence: Women, Politics and the Fiction of Letters*. Cambridge: Cambridge University Press.

Favret, Mary A. and Watson, Nicola J. (1994) *At the Limits of Romanticism: Essays in Cultural, Feminist, and Materialist Criticism*. Bloomington, Ind.: Indiana University Press.

Fay, Elizabeth A. (1994) *Eminent Rhetoric: Language, Gender, and Cultural Tropes*. Westport: Bergin and Garvey.

Fay, Elizabeth A. (1995) *Becoming Wordsworthian: a Performative Aesthetic*. Amherst: University of Massachusetts Press.

Folsom, Marcia McClintock (ed.) (1993) *Approaches to Teaching Austen's "Pride and Prejudice."* New York: The MLA Association.

Fraisse, Genevieve (1994) *Reason's Muse: Sexual Difference and the Birth of Democracy*, trans. Jane Marie Todd. Chicago: University of Chicago Press.

Fried, Michael (1980) *Absorption and Theatricality: Painting and Beholder in the Age of Diderot*. Berkeley, CA: University of California Press.

Friedan, Betty (1963) *The Feminine Mystique*. New York: Norton.

Froula, Christine (1983) "When Eve reads Milton: undoing the canonical economy," *Critical Inquiry* 10: 321–47.

Furet, François (1981) *Interpreting the French Revolution*, trans. Elborg Forster. Cambridge: Cambridge University Press.

Gallagher, Catherine and Laqueur, Thomas (eds) (1987) *The Making of the Modern Body*. Berkeley, CA: University of California Press.

Garrick, David (1758) *Florizel and Perdita. A Dramatic Pastoral in Three Acts. Alter'd from The Winter's Tale of Shakespeare*. London: J. and R. Tonson.

Gay, Peter (1966) *The Enlightenment: an Interpretation / The Rise of Modern Paganism*. New York: W.W. Norton.

Gelpi, Barbara Charlesworth (1992) *Shelley's Goddess: Maternity, Language, Subjectivity*. New York: Oxford University Press.

Gilbert, Sandra M. and Susan Gubar (1979) *The Madwoman in the Attic: the Woman Writer and the Nineteenth-century Literary Imagination*. New Haven, Conn.: Yale University Press.

Gould, Evlyn (1989) *Virtual Theater from Diderot to Mallarmé*. Baltimore, MD: The Johns Hopkins University Press.

Greer, Germaine (1979) *The Obstacle Race: the Fortunes of Women Painters and their Work*. New York: Farrar, Straus, Giroux.

Grylls, R. Glynn (1938) *Mary Shelley*. Oxford: Oxford University Press.

Grylls, R. Glynn (1939) *Claire Claremont – Mother of Byron's Allegra*. Oxford: Oxford University Press.

Habermas, Jürgen (1992) *The Transformation of the Public Sphere: an Inquiry into a Category of Bourgeois Society*, trans. Thomas Burger and Frederick Lawrence. Cambridge, Mass.: MIT Press.

Hilbish, Florence May Anna (1941) *Charlotte Smith, Poet and Novelist (1749–1806)*. Philadelphia: The Mitre Press.

Hobsbawm, E. J. (1962) *The Age of Revolution, 1789–1848*. New York: New American Library.

Hoeveler, Diane Long (1997) "Charlotte Dacre's *Zofloya*: a case study in miscegenation as sexual and racial nausea," *European Romantic Review*. Special Issue "British Romanticism: global crossings,' eds Elizabeth Fay and Alan Richardson, 8: 185–99.

Homans, Margaret (1980) *Women Writers and Poetic Identity: Dorothy Wordsworth, Emily Brontë, and Emily Dickinson*. Princeton, NJ: Princeton University Press.

Howard, Jacqueline (1994) *Reading Gothic Fiction: a Bakhtinian Approach*. Oxford: Clarendon Press.

Howe, Elizabeth (1992) *The First English Actresses: Women and Drama, 1660–1700*. Cambridge: Cambridge University Press.

Hunt, Lynn (1992) *The Family Romance of the French Revolution*. Berkeley, CA: University of California Press.

Inchbald, Elizabeth (1967) *A Simple Story*, ed. J. M. S. Tompkins, Oxford: Oxford University Press.

Jacobus, Mary (1989) *Romanticism, Writing, and Sexual Difference: Essays on The Prelude*. Oxford: Clarendon Press.

Jacobus, Mary (1995) *First Things: the Maternal Imaginary in Literature, Art, and Psychoanalysis*. New York: Routledge.

Janes, Regina M. (1978) "On the reception of Mary Wollstonecraft's *A Vindication of the Rights of Woman*," *Journal of the History of Ideas*, 39: 293–302.

Jardine, Alice and Smith, Paul (eds) (1987) *Men in Feminism*. New York: Methuen.

Jewsbury, Maria Jane (1831) *The Three Histories. The History of an Enthusiast. The History of a Nonchalant. The History of a Realist*. Boston: Perkins and Marvin.

Johnson, Claudia (1988) *Jane Austen: Women, Politics, and the Novel*. Chicago: University of Chicago Press.

Jones, Chris (1993) *Radical Sensibility: Literature and Ideas in the 1790s*. London: Routledge.

Kaplan, Cora (1986) *Sea Changes: Essays on Culture and Feminism*. London: Verso Press.

Kaplan, Deborah (1992) *Jane Austen among Women*. Baltimore, MD: The Johns Hopkins University Press.

Keach, William (1994) "A Regency prophecy and the end of Anna Barbauld's career," *Studies in Romanticism*, 33: 569–78.

Kelly, Gary (1989) *English Fiction of the Romantic Period, 1789–1830*. London: Longman.

Kelly, Gary (1993) *Women, Writing, and Revolution, 1790–1827*. Oxford: Clarendon Press.

Kemp, Wolfgang (1994) "The theater of revolution: a new interpretation of Jacque-Louis David's *Tennis Court Oath*," in Norman Bryson, Michael Ann Holly, and Keith Moxey (eds), *Visual Culture: Images and Interpretations*, pp. 202–27. Hanover: Wesleyan University Press.

Kirkham, Margaret (1983) *Jane Austen, Feminism and Fiction*. Atlantic Highlands, NJ: Athlone Press, 2nd edn 1997.

Klancher, Jon (ed.) (1994) "Romanticism and its publics: a forum," *Studies in Romanticism*, 33: 523–88.

Kramnick, Miriam (ed.) (1975) *Vindication of the Rights of Woman by Mary Wollstonecraft*. Harmondsworth: Penguin.

Kristeva, Julia (1982) *Powers of Horror: an Essay on Abjection*, trans. Leon S. Roudiez. New York: Columbia University Press.

Labalme, Patricia (ed.) (1980) *Beyond their Sex: Learned Women of the European Past*. New York: New York University Press.

Landes, Joan B. (1988) *Women and the Public Sphere in the Age of the French Revolution*. Ithaca, NY: Cornell University Press.

Langbauer, Laurie (1990) *Women and Romance: the Consolations of Gender in the English Novel*. Ithaca, NY: Cornell University Press.

Lauter, Paul (1991) *Canons and Contexts*. New York: Oxford University Press.

Leavis, F. R. (1948) *The Great Tradition: George Eliot, Henry James, Joseph Conrad*. London: Chatto and Windus, 1979.

Le Breton, Anna Letitia (1874) *Memoir of Mrs Barbauld, including Letters and Notices of her Family and Friends*. London: George Bell.

Levin, Susan (1987) *Dorothy Wordsworth and Romanticism*. New Brunswick: Rutgers, The State University Press.

Littlewood, S. R. (1921) *Elizabeth Inchbald and her Circle*. London: Daniel O'Connor.

Lockhart, John Gibson (1871) *Life of Sir Walter Scott*, 2 vols. New York: Thomas V. Crowell.

Looser, Devoney (ed.) (1995) *Jane Austen and Discourses of Feminism*. New York: St Martin's Press.

de Maar, Harko G. (1970) *A History of Modern English Romanticism*. New York: Haskell House (originally published 1924).

McCarthy, William (1995) "'We hoped the *woman* was going to appear': repression, desire, and gender in Anna Letitia Barbauld's early poems," in Paula R. Feldman and Theresa M. Kelley (eds), *Romantic Women Writers: Voices and Countervoices*, pp. 113–37. Hanover: University of New England Press.

McGann, Jerome J. (1982) *The Romantic Ideology: a Critical Investigation*. Chicago: University of Chicago Press.

McGann, Jerome J. (1993a) "Literary history, romanticism, and Felicia Hemans," *Modern Language Quarterly*, 54(2): 215–35.

McGann, Jerome J. (ed.) (1993b) *Romantic Period Verse*. Oxford: Oxford University Press.

McGann, Jerome J. (1996) *Poetics of Sensibility: a Revolution in Literary Style*. Oxford: Oxford University Press.

Manvell, Roger (1971) *Sarah Siddons: Portrait of an Actress*. New York: Putnam and Sons.

Massé, Michelle A. (1992) *In the Name of Love: Women, Masochism, and the Gothic*. Ithaca, NY: Cornell University Press.

Maturin, Charles Robert (1968) *Melmoth the Wanderer: a Tale*, ed. Douglas Grant. London: Oxford University Press.

Mayne, Ethel Colburn (1929) *The Life of Lady Byron: the Life and Letters of Anne Isabella Lady Noel Byron*. New York: Charles Scribner.

Meisel, Martin (1983) *Realizations: Narrative, Pictorial, and Theatrical Arts in Nineteenth-century England*. Princeton, NJ: Princeton University Press.

Mellor, Anne K. (1980) *English Romantic Irony*. Cambridge, Mass.: Harvard University Press.

Mellor, Anne K. (ed.) (1988) *Romanticism and Feminism*. Bloomington, Ind.: Indiana University Press.

Mellor, Anne K. (1993) *Romanticism and Gender*. London: Routledge.

Millett, Kate (1970) *Sexual Politics*. Garden City, NY: Doubleday.

Mishra, Vijay (1994) *The Gothic Sublime*. Albany, NY: New York State University Press.

Moers, Ellen (1976) *Literary Women: the Great Writers*. Garden City, NY: Doubleday.

Moi, Toril (1985) *Sexual / Textual Politics: Feminist Literary Theory*. London: Methuen.

Monk, Samuel (1960) *The Sublime: a Study of Critical Theories in XVIII-century England*. Ann Arbor: University of Michigan Press.

Montagu, Elizabeth (1809–13) *The Letters of Mrs Elizabeth Montagu*, ed. Matthew Montagu. London.

Montagu, Elizabeth (1906) *Elizabeth Montagu, the Queen of the Bluestockings: her Correspondence from 1720 to 1761, by her Great-great-niece Emily J. Climenson*, 2 vols. London: John Murray.

Myers, Sylvia (1990) *The Bluestocking Circle*. Oxford: Clarendon Press.

Newton, Judith Lowder (1981) *Women, Power and Subversion: Social Strategies in British Fiction, 1778–1860*. Athens: University of Georgia Press.

Nochlin, Linda (1991) "Women, art, and power," in Norman Bryson, Michael Ann Holly, and Keith Moxey (eds), *Visual Theory: Painting and Interpretation*, pp. 13–46. New York: Polity Press / HarperCollins.

Ortner, Sherry (1974) "Is female to male as nature is to culture?," in Michelle Z. Rosaldo and Louise Lamphere (eds), *Woman, Culture, and Society*, pp. 76–87. Stanford: Stanford University Press.

Outram, Dorinda (1989) *The Body and the French Revolution: Sex, Class and Political Culture*. New Haven, Conn.: Yale University Press.

Paine, Thomas (1791–2) *Rights of Man; Common Sense; and Other Political Writings by Thomas Paine*, ed. Mark Philp. Oxford: Oxford University Press, 1995.

Pateman, Carole (1989) *The Disorder of Women: Democracy, Feminism and Political Theory*. Stanford: Stanford University Press.

Paulson, Ronald (1983) *Representations of Revolution (1789–1820)*. New Haven, Conn.: Yale University Press.

Pennington, Montagu (ed.) (1817) *Letters of Mrs Elizabeth Carter to Mrs Montagu, between the years 1755 and 1800*, 3 vols. London: F. C. and J. Rivington. Reprinted New York: AMS Press, 1973.

Pollock, Griselda (1988) *Vision and Difference: Femininity, Feminism, and the Histories of Art*. London: Routledge.

Poovey, Mary (1984) *The Proper Lady and the Woman Writer: Ideology as Style in the Works of Mary Wollstonecraft, Mary Shelley, and Jane Austen*. Chicago: University of Chicago Press.

Porter, Roy and Teich, Mikuláš (eds) (1988) *Romanticism in National Context*. Oxford: Blackwell.

Pratt, Mary Louise (1992) *Imperial Eyes: Travel Writing and Transculturation*. London: Routledge.

Radcliffe, Ann (1991) *The Romance of the Forest*, ed. Chloe Chard. Oxford: Oxford University Press.

Radford, Jean (ed.) (1986) *The Progress of Romance: the Politics of Popular Fiction*. London: Routledge and Kegan Paul.

Reeve, Clara (1930) *The Progress of Romance and The History of Charoba, Queen of Aegypt*, reproduced from the Colchester edition of 1785, with a bibliographical note by Esther M. McGill. New York: The Facsimile Text Society.

Rich, Adrienne (1980) *On Lies, Secrets and Silence: Selected Prose 1966–1978*. London: Virago.

Richardson, Alan (1994) *Literature, Education, and Romanticism: Reading as a Social Practice, 1780–1832*. Cambridge: Cambridge University Press.

Roberts, Warren (1979) *Jane Austen and the French Revolution*. London: Macmillan.

Robertson, Fiona (1991) "Introduction," *The Bride of Lammermoor*, ed. Fiona Robertson. Oxford: Oxford University Press.

Robinson, Mary (1895) *The Memoirs of Mary Robinson, "Perdita"*, ed. J. Fitzgerald Molloy. London: Gibbings and Co.

Ross, Marlon B. (1989) *The Contours of Masculine Desire: Romanticism and the Rise of Women's Poetry*. New York: Oxford University Press.

Roworth, Wendy Wassying (ed.) (1992) *Angelica Kauffmann: a Continental Artist in Georgian England*. London: Reaktion Books.

Sales, Roger (1994) *Jane Austen and Representations of Regency England*. London: Routledge.

Sapiro, Virginia (1992) *A Vindication of Political Virtue: the Political Theory of Mary Wollstonecraft*. Chicago: University of Chicago Press.

Schama, Simon (1989) *Citizens: a Chronicle of the French Revolution*. New York: Alfred A. Knopf.

Schor, Naomi (1987) *Reading in Detail: Aesthetics and the Feminine*. New York: Methuen.

Seward, Anna (1811) *Letters of Anna Seward: Written between the Years 1784 and 1807*, 6 vols. Edinburgh: A. Constable.

Scott, Sarah (1762) *A Description of Millenium Hall*, ed. Gary Kelly. Peterborough: Broadview Press, 1995.

Shelley, Mary (1990) *The Mary Shelley Reader: Containing Frankenstein, Mathilda, Tales and Stories, Essays and Reviews, and Letters*, ed. Betty T. Bennett and Charles E. Robinson. New York: Oxford University Press.

Showalter, Elaine (1977) *A Literature of their Own: British Women Novelists from Brontë to Lessing*. Princeton, NJ: Princeton University Press.

Smith, Charlotte (1993a) *Conversations Introducing Poetry* (poems only), in Stuart Curran (ed.), *The Poems of Charlotte Smith*. New York: Oxford University Press.

Smith, Charlotte (1993b) *The Poems of Charlotte Smith*, ed. Stuart Curran. New York: Oxford University Press.

Smith, Goldwin (1890) *Life of Jane Austen*. London: W. Scott.

Spacks, Patricia Meyer (1975) *The Female Imagination*. New York: Alfred A. Knopf.

Spacks, Patricia Meyer (1985) *Gossip*. New York: Alfred A. Knopf.

Summers, Montague (1964) *The Gothic Quest: a History of the Gothic*. New York: Russell and Russell (originally published 1938).

Sweet, Nanora (1994) "History, imperialism, and the aesthetics of the beautiful: Hemans and the post-Napoleonic moment," in Mary A. Favret and Nicola J. Watson (eds), *At the Limits of Romanticism*, pp. 170–84. Bloomington, Ind.: Indiana University Press.

Tave, Stuart M. (1973) *Some Words of Jane Austen*. Chicago: University of Chicago Press.

Taylor, Jane (1815) *Display: A Tale*. London: Printed for Taylor, Hessey and J. Conder.

Todd, Janet (1986) *Sensibility: an Introduction*. New York: Methuen.

Todd, Janet (1989) *The Sign of Angellica: Women, Writing and Fiction, 1660–1800*. New York: Columbia University Press.

Tomalin, Claire (1995) *Mrs Jordan's Profession: the Actress and the Prince*. New York: Alfred A. Knopf.

Tucker, George Holbert (1994) *Jane Austen, the Woman: Some Biographical Insights*. New York: St Martin's Press.

Ty, Eleanor (ed.) (1994) *The Victim of Prejudice by Mary Hays*. Peterborough, Ont.: Broadview Press.

Walpole, Horace (1924) *The Castle of Otranto, and The Mysterious Mother*, ed. Montague Summers. London: Constable.

Wasserman, Earl (1964) "The English Romantics: the grounds of knowledge," *Studies in Romanticism*, 4: 17–34. Reprinted in *Romanticism: Points of View*, eds Robert F. Gleckner and Gerald E. Enscoe. Detroit: Wayne State University Press, 1975, pp. 331–46.

Wellek, René (1986) *A History of Modern Criticism 1750–1950*. Vol. 2: *The Romantic Age*; Vol. 5: *English Criticism, 1900–1950*. New Haven, Conn.: Yale University Press.

Williams, Helen Maria (1790) *Letters Written in France in the Summer of 1790*, vol. I. London. The modern edition is *Letters from France*, ed. Janet Todd. Delmar, NY: Scholars' Facsimiles and Reprints, 1979.

Williams, Ioan (ed.) (1968) *Sir Walter Scott on Novelists and Fiction*. London: Routledge and Kegan Paul.

Wilt, Judith (1980) *Ghosts of the Gothic: Austen, Eliot, and Lawrence*. Princeton, NJ: Princeton University Press.

Wollheim, Richard (1991) "What the spectator sees," in Norman Bryson, Michael Ann Holly, and Keith Moxey (eds), *Visual Theory: Painting and Interpretation*, pp. 101–50. New York: Polity Press / HarperCollins.

Wollstonecraft, Mary (1975) *Vindication of the Rights of Woman*, ed. Miriam Kramnick. Harmondsworth: Penguin.

Wolstenholme, Susan (1993) *Gothic (Re)Visions: Writing Women as Readers*. Albany, NY: State University Press.

Wordsworth, William and Coleridge, S. T. (1981) *Lyrical Ballads*, eds R. L. Brett and A. R. Jones. New York: Methuen.

Wu, Duncan (ed.) (1994) *Romanticism: an Anthology*. Oxford: Blackwell.

Wu, Duncan (ed.) (1997) *Romantic Women Poets: an Anthology*. Oxford: Blackwell.

Wu, Duncan (ed.) (1998) *Romanticism: an Anthology*, 2nd edn. Oxford: Blackwell.

Index